LEGAL METHOD, REASONING AND RESEARCH METHODOLOGY

LEGAL METHOD, REASONING AND RESEARCH METHODOLOGY

Professor Dr. K.L. Bhatia
B.A. (Hons), LLM., Ph.D.
DAAD and Max-Planck Fellow and Alumni
(Former Head and Dean, Faculty of Law, and the Founder Director,
The Law School, University of Jammu; Director, Amity Law School;
Dean and Professor Emeritus, University of Petroleum and Energy Studies;
UNDP Professor Public Law)
Presently
Professor of Law, National Law University, Jodhpur

Professor Dr. S.C. Srivastava
LLM. (BHU), LL.D. (Calcutta)
(Former Chairman, Department of Laws and Dean Faculty of Law,
Kurukshetra University; Professor, Dean and Head, Calabar University
(Nigeria); UGC National Professor; Law Commission of India (1992-97);
Research Professor, Indian Law Institute)
Presently
Secretary General, Labour Law Assn., New Delhi

REGAL

REGAL PUBLICATIONS
New Delhi - 110 027

LEGAL METHOD, REASONING AND RESEARCH METHODOLOGY

ISBN 978-81-8484-287-6
First Published : 2014
Reprinted : 2019

Typeset by
THE LASER PRINTERS
8/15, 3rd Floor, Subhash Nagar, New Delhi-110027

Printed in India at
MAYUR ENTERPRISES,
WZ Plot No. 3, Gujjar Market, Tihar Village, New Delhi-110018

Published by
REGAL PUBLICATIONS
F-159, Rajouri Garden, New Delhi-110027 • Phone : 45546396
E-mail : regalbookspub@yahoo.com

Dedicated to the Cherished Memory
of our Grand Parents and Parents
who's Splendid Bliss nourish us to
Lead to Learning

CONTENTS

Preface

The subject "Legal Method, Reasoning and Research Methodology" has always fascinated us. It captivated us as students of law at our respective law schools where we have had the occasion to have legal training. It motivated us to be deeply associated with this subject as teachers of law in our respective law schools where we started our career. It encouraged us to have deep insights into it as researchers. We always wanted conscientiously to write on this interesting subject. There are some scholastic works from the perspectives of scholars' visions as per their own foreign legal system. We have, therefore, desired to write a book on this subject from the perspectives of our own legal system meant for niche Indian law students. This write up has been an endeavour from that perception and vision. As such, this is not a dry text. We hopefully believe that this book will help the niche law learners to have deep insights into the subject and give them a glimpse as well as an overview of the important field of law. We are grateful to our past and present students and scholars who encouraged us to write a textbook on this subject. We shall cherish the critique of our students and scholars. We express our sincere thanks to Mr. Sumeet Bhatia, Advocate, Mr. Sandeep Sharma, Advocate, Ms Manu Bhatia Sharma and Ms Komila Aggarwal Bhatia, Law Research Scholars for their academic and moral support in the successful completion of this book. We are also thankful to the angelic gifts of His Almighty, Madhav, Adhaya and Aanya, in time-stealing, which was otherwise theirs. Our warm thanks to Regal Publications, New Delhi for its neat and timely publication.

Professor Dr. K.L. Bhatia **Professor Dr. S.C. Srivastava**

TABLE OF CASES

Chapter I

INTRODUCTION TO LEGAL METHOD

A. CONCEPT, UTILITY AND SIGNIFICANCE

What is legal method? What are its utility, relevance and significance in legal studies? Why it should be a foundation course for the beginner in legal education? Legal method is a foundation course that provides an enliven foundation of legal knowledge, fundamental concepts of law, fundamentals of Indian legal system, fundamentals of Indian common law, and fundamentals of judicial process. Legal method aims at training law students with no knowledge of law to enabling them to have necessary conceptual framework/tools to deal with the modules of different laws operating in the Indian legal system requiring a minimum legal knowledge. Legal method aims at training niche law students to the rudiments of analyzing law as well as case (decision) law scientifically, systematically, methodologically, analytically, logically to arrive at logical conclusion with the aid of reasoning. Legal method aims at training new entrants in legal studies to the art of communication (oral and writing) skills, which shall help him in legal profession. Communication skills develop on the foundation of language skills, legal language learning (LLL), legal language writing (LLW) and legal language communication (LLC), study skills (both statutory law and decisional law), argument skills, and legal knowledge, and knowledge of these parameters is vital to every young (fresh) law student, professional lawyer, and academia. Legal method as such sharpens professional communication. The genesis of Legal method or professional communication relates/pertains to a basic question with which both the law Professors as well as law students wrestle: Why and what for do law students come to law schools? Do they come for only learning the basic principles of law or acquiring legal knowledge of the basics of laws or liking to develop legal writing skills? Seldom the students respond that they like to learn writing techniques to be a good lawyer, because to be a good lawyer, a law student must be a good legal writer, and to be a good legal writer, he must have both a good understanding of law and a good grasp of principles of writing.[1] As such, law learning and acquiring knowledge of law and knowledge about law primarily and predominantly require writing skills, writing habits, writing aptitude as well as attitude.

Legal method is a process of *study of law* and *thinking about law*. 'of law' and 'about law' is generic and genesis of knowing law methodologically, scientifically and systematically both analytically as well as logically to arrive at logical conclusion. In this sense, Law of any legal system including Indian legal system is a legal science, since it is the combination of mutually inclusive Law + Logic + Reasoning + Experience. Legal method does not intend to restrict its meaning and usage to 'legal method *per se*'. Legal method aims at describing 'Indian legal system' as a foundation tool to 'Introduction to Indian Law'. In the background of this, these are the methods that are employed by 'lawmen' [law Professor, lawyer, student, Judge, law-maker, law-enforcer] in analyzing legislative, decisional, and legal texts materials as a critique with an eagle eye.[2] It aims at introducing law students in the beginning to the traditional foundations of legal reasoning with the help of theoretical as well as socio-legal/empirical/heuristic scholarship including critical legal theories.[3] This shall indeed provide law students in the beginning of their legal studies with a firm grounding in traditional legal methods and ways of understanding Indian legal system including two major legal systems of the world—common law and civil law, which will encourage them to critique approaches.[4] Thus, legal method is an approach to law and legal reasoning and analysis.

1. See Helene S. Sharpo, Marilyn R. Walter and Elizabeth Fajans, Writing and Analysis in the Law, 2003, at p. 3.
2. See Carl F. Stychin and Linda Mulcahy, Legal Method, 2003.
3. *Ibid.*
4. *Ibid.*

B. WHAT IS LAW – "A LAW", "THE LAW" OR "LAWS"?

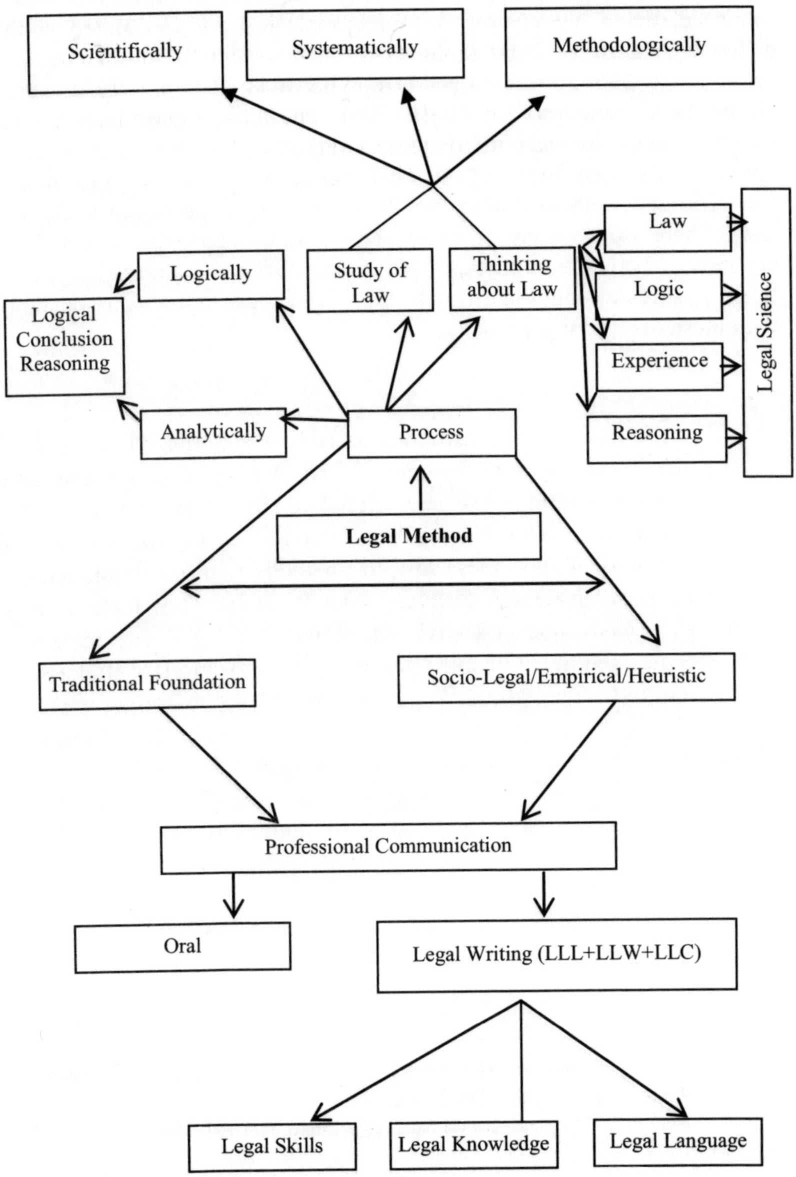

This helps the law students to think critically the basic question 'what is law'; is it 'a law', or 'the law', or 'laws'? The subject legal method exposes a beginner law student to a range of ideas about law espoused by a variety of scholars/jurists/authors associated with different schools of legal thoughts of their country's politico-socio-economic system as well as environ. What is law to one scholar may not be the same to another scholar. And, that is the precise reason that we try to know the meaning of law in a variety of scholastic approaches to law. We, therefore, try to understand the generic/philosophic/scientific approach to law in brevity inasmuch as 'an ocean within a tear'. There are a variety of approaches to understand what law is, but the most acceptable and acknowledged approach is 'natural law' and 'legal positivism' and the different schools of legal thoughts associated with these divergent approaches.

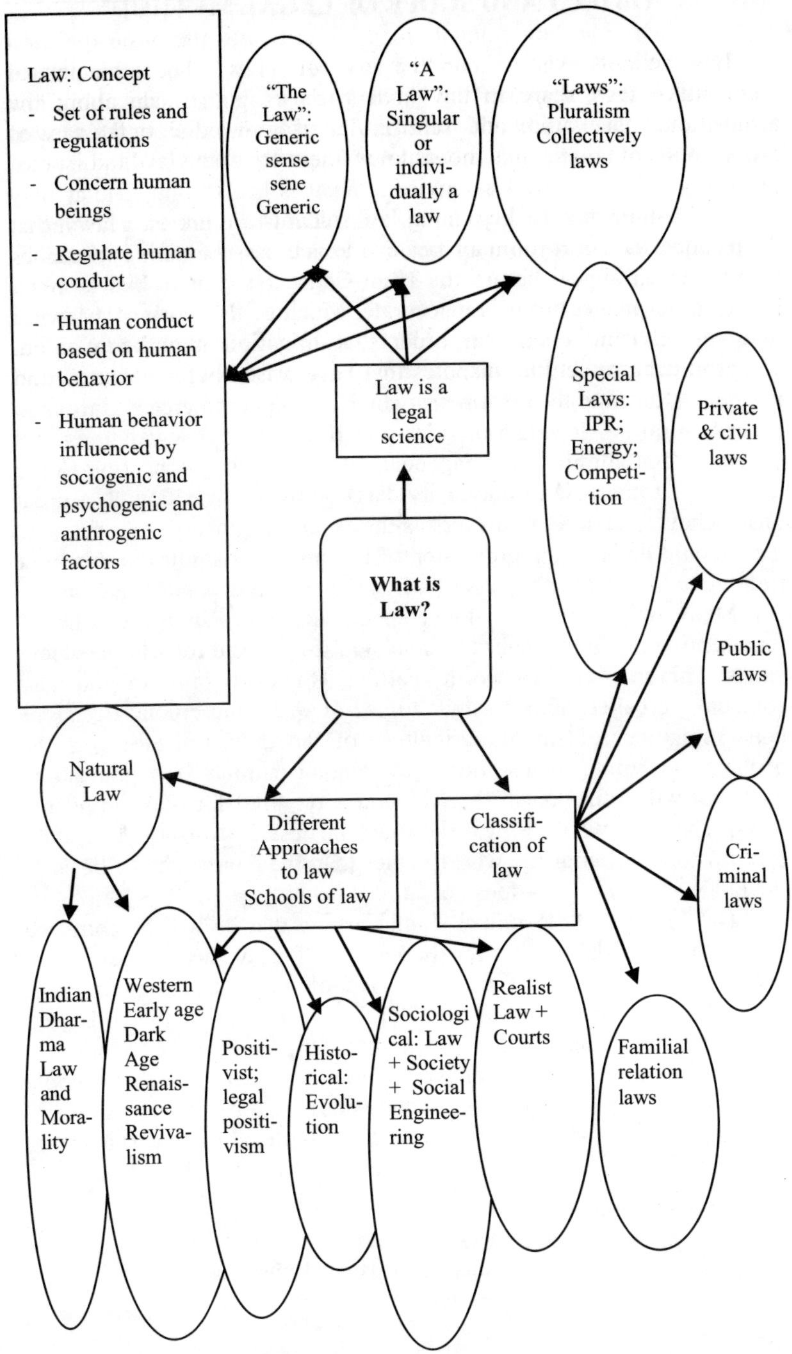

Law: Concept
- Set of rules and regulations
- Concern human beings
- Regulate human conduct
- Human conduct based on human behavior
- Human behavior influenced by sociogenic and psychogenic and anthrogenic factors
"The Law": Generic sense sene Generic
"A Law": Singular or individually a law
"Laws": Pluralism Collectively laws
Law is a legal science
What is Law?
Special Laws: IPR; Energy; Competition
Private & civil laws
Public Laws
Criminal laws
Natural Law
Different Approaches to law Schools of law
Classification of law
Indian Dharma Law and Morality
Western Early age Dark Age Renaissance Revivalism
Positivist; legal positivism
Historical: Evolution
Sociological: Law + Society + Social Engineering
Realist Law + Courts
Familial relation laws

C. OBJECT AND SCOPE OF LEGAL METHOD[5]

Law Schools exist to train lawyers. Most law schools are part of universities; they share in the three goals of higher education: the acquisition, conservation and transmission of knowledge. In the case of law schools, of course, this means knowledge about the law and its role in society.

It is natural for the beginning law student to think of a lawyer as the pleader, the court room advocate who is cross-examining witnesses or arguing an appeal before the High Court. Of course, this is not a totally false image, but it is inaccurate. Much of the work of a lawyer involves advising clients in order that litigation may be avoided, compromising or settling disputes that have arisen before court action has begun, drafting the documents which permit commerce and trade to flourish, drafting legislation, rules and orders in the legislatures and executive and administrative agencies, or transmitting a hearing to the lawyers of tomorrow in university classrooms. Roscoe Pound, a great legal scholar, referred to lawyers as the "social engineers" of a country. You should think of the profession of law and your studies in this light training to be social engineers of a free dynamic independent nation.

Many of you will no doubt spend your lives in the courtroom representing the individuals who make up society and for whom society exists. This in itself is a worthy calling. However, some of you may someday be called upon to give advice or make the crucial decisions concerning the reform of agriculture of the industrialization of the economy at home, or insuring peace among nations. It is your study here that will train you in the techniques required for these imposing tasks. The men who perform these are no less lawyers because their forum is the nation or the world, rather than the courtroom, or because the judge of their efforts does not sit on a bench.

The first year law student should expect that he will be confused during the early days of his legal education. Part of this confusion will result from the fact that the Law School aims at education for a profession. Part of the confusion will arise because of the methods used by law teachers when compared with those in other branches of studies.

There is a tendency to believe that the only goal of the law schools to teach you what the law is, in the sense of relating the rules and principles which form the various parts of the legal matrix. But this is wrong, and it is a misconception which must be expunged from your

5. This section is based on Prof. A.K. Pye, "Legal Method," a paper presented in the Law School, Banaras Hindu University

minds if you are to make the most of your legal education. The principal goal of the study of law is not informational.

Of course, you must acquire a working knowledge of basic principles of law, and to this extent the acquiring of information is an undoubted goal of legal education. There will be a good deal lecturing on "the rules" which belief any other than an informational goal. However, the principal goal of legal education is *formative* rather than *informative.* Consequently, you should not feel cheated when a teacher fails to lecture to you on what the law is, or when he asks more questions than he answers. Indeed, you should develop a healthy suspicion of dogmatic answers and of the feeling of comfort and security that the acquisition of new rules carried in its wake.

Phrased in positive terms, a basic objective of your legal education is to encourage you to "think like a lawyer". This is the object of the course in legal method. What does it mean "to think like a lawyer?" It can best be illustrated by a brief glimpse at the lawyer's professional life. The lawyer's life is problem-oriented. He must be prepared to analyze the complex grouping of facts and pierce to the very heart of the question presented. He then must determine, by analysis of cases and statutes, whether the question is one for which a solution has been formulated by the courts of legislature. In his position as an advocate he may seek to amplify subtle differences of fact as a means of removing his problem from the ambit of cases decided adversely to his position. Or, he may analogize his case to slightly dissimilar ones with favorable solutions. Law schools endeavor to develop the talents the lawyers rely upon in this process. The course in legal method is the beginning point in this process. To a very real extent all of your papers here will be courses in legal method. But this course is the introduction to how a lawyer solves problems. You will find your minds immersed in legal method. You will read and analyze cases, learn to select the importance from the unimportant facts and determine those upon which the case turns. You will ferret out the legal principles and identify the facts which gave rise to it. You will learn to make judgments as to whether previously extracted principles do or do not apply to the slightly dissimilar factual situations.

In sum, by the constant repetition of this process you acquire training in the inductive reasoning method and facility in the use of its component elements: analysis and synthesis. The concentrate study of individual cases will sharpen your powers of analysis. The study of case groupings and reflection upon the relationship of cases within the group will train you in the process of synthesizing, and thus complete the inductive reasoning cycle. And by synthesizing the individual cases you have read, you gradually accumulate a fund of legal rules or principles. In effect, you will be compiling your own textbook; and you can be secure in the knowledge that the rules it contains are based upon your own reasoning.

Ability in deductive reasoning is also vitally important. You must acquire skill in the use and application of the principles acquired by the inductive method. In concrete situations, you will be confronted with a novel set of facts containing a legal problem which you must resolve. In the course in legal method these problems may be presented by way of hypothetical fact patterns posed by the teacher. In the practice of law you will face the identical situation whenever a client seeks your advice. You must reflect upon your acquired fund of principles and select the one which arose from facts most closely similar to the facts of your client's case. If the appropriate rule is opposed to the just interests of your client you may seek to prevent its application by distinguishing the facts in your case from those which gave birth to the rule. Or, conversely, you may try to persuade that your problem is covered by a favorable ruling that appears to rest upon a different factual background. This deductive method must constantly be employed by the lawyer in his practice. It is the technique which you will be learning in the course on legal method.

By *inductive reasoning,* in this context, it is meant the process by which we infer the existence of certain principles from the study of the facts and results of a number of already decided cases. By *deductive reasoning* it is meant the process of applying principles derived by this method to new cases. The two work closely together in the lawyer's arsenal of problem-solving weapons. We infer that a principle exists by seeing the results which have been reached in a series of already decided cases. We then must apply this principle to a new case involving a set of facts, the legal implications of which are unclear.

Examples may prove more helpful than definitions. Assume A and B own farms adjacent to one another. A brings on his farm a tiger and does not confine it. It crosses onto the land of B and attacks him. I am sure that it does not shock you to learn that B may have a cause of action against A.

If A plants poisonous vegetation on his farm and it extends to B's farm, killing his crops, the same result again seems likely.

Likewise if A begins to use dangerous explosives to drill for gas and the effect of the explosions knocks down B's house, liability would seem appropriate.

Let us assume that a court has decided in all three cases that A is liable to B for the damages suffered by B. The function of inductive reasoning is to determine what principle we can infer from these cases which will help us in solving new cases which may arise in the future. To determine the principle we must use *analysis*—that is, determine what facts or policies are the real basis for the decision in each case, and *synthesis*, that is putting together the basis for each decision into a more general principle which will explain the reason for the result in all three cases and provide a guideline for the future. When we have accomplished this we have used *inductive reasoning*—the development of a general principle from specific instances.

What principle might we infer from the three cases? Perhaps, we would conclude that a landowner is liable to an adjoining landowner for any damage caused by the action of the first landowner in bringing something on the land which injures the property of the second landowner. However, we might decide that this principle is too broad—that is only when a landowner brings upon his land a substance which is *inherently dangerous* such as a tiger, poisonous plants, or explosives, that is he will be liable for injuries sustained by the adjoining property owner. Perhaps, we will decide that this principle is too narrow – that A would be liable to B for damage sustained by B even if the substance was not inherently dangerous, if it were a substance such as water—if he used it in an unnatural way—such as storing it behind dams. Upon reflections, we might conclude that this statement of the rule is too broad. Even if A stored water behind a dam and the dam broke and it flooded the property of B, A should not be liable if the dam broke because it was hit by lighting or was blown up by a saboteur.

The process can go on and on, but what is sought is a real understanding of the principle of law which was the basis for the decision in the three cases. We want to determine the principle so that we can use it in the future to decide new cases. When we use the principle to determine the result in new cases we are said to be using *deductive reasoning*—we are applying the general principle to specific instances.

Whatever principle we derive from our three cases will have to be applied to a myriad of new cases which may arise in the future—a few examples will suffice. A plants nothing on his land; wild thistles grow there naturally. The wind blows them to the land of B, damaging his property. A builds a two-storey house and leases the bottom floor to B. A installs a water system on the second floor of his house. A thief turns on the water in A's apartment. This results in an overflow which damages the property of B below. Does the principle derived from our first three cases require that A be found liable in these cases?

At the moment we are not interested in the result, only the method. The answer to how these cases will be decided will depend upon the use of the inductive reasoning which developed a principle of law from the previous decided cases and the use of deductive reasoning which applied that principle to the new cases.

These techniques involve the practice of an art, not a science. There will be inconsistencies. The same court may reach different results in very similar cases; it may even over rule a previous decision. Different courts or judges may disagree on the same case. But in most situations the process provides a method by which the outcome of future cases can be predicted without the loss of the capacity for growth which is essential to a sound legal system.

While the development of these skills in inductive and deductive reasoning is of first importance, it is not the only major goal. Other talents must be called into exercise and by their exercise be perfected. Most notable of these is the talent for critical and prudential judgment. A lawyer is not merely a technician who perfunctorily analyses problems, applied law to facts; and comes to logically dictated conclusions. By the exercise of his critical judgment he must constantly re-evaluate settled principles against a background of changing times. The positive law is, after all, but a network of principles serving to regulate relationships in society. And, as technological, scientific, and social upheaval changes the face of society, the law, if it is to fulfil its proper function, must adapt itself to the new order.

Lawyers, as guardians of the law, have a responsibility to assist in this change. Their participation may take different forms. They may seek to extend or narrow the application of an existing rule; in rarer instances they may call for repudiation of an old rule and the substitution of another; and, occasionally, they may have an opportunity to forge the solution for a new problem, and thus fill a vacuum in the existing legal fabric. Whatever form the lawyer's participation in the growth of law take, that participation requires the exercise of judgment. And, if the lawyer is to fulfil the responsibilities of his profession, that judgment cannot be rash. It must be made only after a thoroughgoing study of the bases for existing principles and the ramifications of a change in those principles. The responsible lawyer, before he makes his determination of the rightness of an existing or proposed solution, will open his mind to the entire spectrum of circumstances affected by the problem. Each factor, policy, or interest—social, economic, political, and philanthropically—to be affected must be weighed in connection with all others so that the ultimate decision takes account of the needs of society and the objective desirability of the solution espoused. On occasion he must borrow new concepts from other legal systems. On occasions he must insist that the customs, culture, and aspirations of his people be reflected in the law. Only by fulfilling the need for such preparatory study and reflection will the lawyer's act of judgment be an aptly prudential one. Only by accepting these responsibilities will the legal profession continues to merit the position of leadership in society which it deserves.

You should be proud to be a law student and producer to be a lawyer. Never forget that law was an ancient and honorable profession when medicine was being practiced by barbers and science was the province of magicians.

As law students you should early recognize the need for critical evaluation of the rules you study. The placing of emphasis on the facts from which a decision arises provides an excellent opportunity to do this. You will be asked to look beyond the mere rule derived from the case, to search out the bases upon which the rule rests, and to determine the interests and policies which its promulgation was designed to promote. Do this with a view to judging its present value as a societal norm. Yesterday's answer may be ill-suited to the problem and tempo of today and may properly be the subject of re-examination. Oliver Wendell Holmes, the great American jurist, made a point which we should never forget when he counseled that there must be a better reason for a rule than that it was the law in the reign of King Henry IV. You must learn to be critical of offered solution and to make your own judgments.

There are many other significant goals of your legal education to which you will be introduced in the course. You may begin to perceive the existence of an objective normal order which serves to limit the freedom of the law-maker. These limitations are broad and liberal and do not dictate specific norms in that wide area of legal activity where prudence is the only guide to "oughtness". But they are nevertheless vital and your education should promote a desire to probe their content.

Facility in speaking and writing is indispensible for the lawyer. You will be in classes small enough to develop these talents. You must also acquire skills in legal research and interpretation before your course in legal method is successfully completed. The school's responsibility to the legal profession likewise demands that you fully understand the ethical obligations of the lawyer before you assume the exercise of the prerogatives. You will be introduced to these problems as well.

You must never forget that you will be lawyers practicing in a democracy. Your obligation to the public far exceeds the requirements of technical competency in the cases which you undertake. You should remember that the practice of law is a monopoly—entrusted to the legal profession by the public in the interests of society. The legal profession must guard this trust placed in it and use its skills, techniques and knowledge to serve the society which has given it the opportunity and obligation for public service. There are many ways in which the public may be served—the assumption of leadership in community projects, initiative in reform of the institutions of society which impede social progress, creativity in finding solutions to new social problems within the framework of existing law—to mention but a few. The genius of the lawyer is his capacity for innovation, his flexibility, his ability to charge substance without altering form, his facility for separating the accidental from the essential. These and all we utilized to good advantage in seeking solution to social, economic, and political problems facing a nation, a village, or the world.

The law and lawyers can and should constitute dynamic forces for growth and change. The image of the lawyer as a relic of a bygone social order fails to appreciate that lawyers have been in the vanguard of almost very important reform in modern history. It is the lawyer's craft to devise ways by which needed change may be accomplished within the confines of the law. At the same time it may be his unpopular obligation to insist that even the Government is subject to the law if the rights of a citizen are jeopardized by unlawful action.

You will be acquainted with the broad outlines of the legal system —the relationship between Union and State Legislatures and the relationship between the courts and the legislatures. Then a discussion will centre round the sources of law in the sense of the materials which contain it, the constitution, statutes, and decisions, the textbooks, treatises and periodicals, and other sources. Then you will be told how and where to find the materials. When we end we hope and expect you will be able to apply these techniques to your other courses.

In addition, this course will lay the groundwork for more specific courses later in the curriculum—courses such as interpretation and drafting of statutes and research methodology.

D. OBJECTIVES OF LEGAL EDUCATION[6]

A competent lawyer must be trained as to how to tackle intricate issues relating to law. He must know a great deal of law—a very large number of legal "rules, principles, and standards"—but much more I involved than just learning a mass of legal doctrine. The lawyer must be able to *analyze* his client's problems, identifying the legally operative facts and elements. This is necessary to enable him to apply the legal rules to reach a conclusion, and more often than not it is a very complex task. Moreover, he can seldom find the pertinent law written explicitly for his client's affairs. He must be able to *derive* the applicable rules, often from a confusing welter (mass) of case law, statutes, and other legal materials. This involves knowledge and memory, and plenty of it, but it is more than just memory. Just what is involved?

The Objectives are:

1. *To acquire a working familiarity with the basic rules of the law*, consisting primarily of rules, principles, and standards derived from judicial decisions, statutes, and other legal sources applicable in the fundamental legal subjects such as Contracts, Torts, Property, Trusts, Constitutional Law, Criminal Law, Corporations, Civil Procedure, and Evidence;
2. *To obtain some understanding of the broad scope of the law* by making a reasonable selection from various elective "private law" and to get a view of the law as a broad means of social control such as may be obtained from Comparative Law, International Law, Law and Society, Legal Method, Legal Philosophy, and other jurisprudential subjects;
3. *To master the fundamental processes of the "common law" method*, i.e., the processes of analysis and of inductive, deductive, analogical reasoning so characteristic of the common law and necessary to enable the lawyer to derive the pertinent legal doctrines and apply them intelligently to human situations;
4. *To make a long start on the mastery of certain other important legal skills*, such as:
   (a) *Interpretative skill*, the process of interpreting and determining of words, phrases, clauses and provisions in

6. Extract from Law Students' Handbook, issued by Michigan Law School, 9-15.

statutes, constitutions, trusts, contracts, and other legal documents, a skill we develop wherever statutory or documentary language is met in our courses, for example, in Constitutional Law, Trusts and Estates, Legislation, Contracts, Taxation.

(b) *Skill in research*, the ability to "find the law" through the use of the authoritative legal materials and reference aids available in the law library, a skill we develop particularly in brief-writing for the Case Clubs (a most valuable part of the program) and Trials, Appeals and Practice Court and in the second year course in Problems and Research, but also in the preparation of require papers in such courses as Administrative Tribunals, Admiralty, International Law, and the various seminars. The lawyer must be able to assemble, organize and synthesize legal ideas and arguments.

(c) *Verbal skill*, the ability to express legal ideas in concise and accurate English, oral and written—a facility essential to competent advocacy as well to effective work in the preparation of briefs and the drafting of legal instruments of all kinds. Skill in this category is developed wherever the student participates in classroom discussion, but more especially is it developed in both oral and written aspects in Practice Court, Problems and Research I and II, the Case Clubs, and in courses requiring written papers.

(d) *Skill in draftsmanship*, the preparation in a competent manner of technical legal documents. This includes verbal skill, but it also requires professional craftsmanship. Students draft pleadings, corporate articles, wills, statutes, etc., and so doing they learn how to express precise legal content in a minimum of words with great accuracy. Furthermore, skill in draftsmanship calls for imagination, the ability to visualize what is sought to be accomplished and a consideration of the law and the economy in which it operates. The student must take care lest his necessary concentration upon controversies, which have arisen and been decided by the courts, shall prevent his consideration of how a wiser solution of the difficulty might have been achieved by use of imaginative foresight.

So it will be observed that our objectives really include three major matters, the substance of the law, the legal method of the common law, and specific legal skills. Notwithstanding occasional critical observations to the contrary, we do not overlook the imparting of the practical work-a-day skills, although we recognize that within the time available in three all too short years we cannot make finished practitioners.[7] Post-graduate self-education must take care of a large part of that.

E. EXPECTATIONS FROM LAW STUDENTS

1. Common Law Processes

A law student is expected to acquire somewhat more details as to what we mean by training in the "fundamental processes of the common law", i.e., training in analysis including inductive, deductive and analogical reasoning.

The student in the course of his legal study is expected to read and analyze the important judicial decisions, constitutional provisions, statutes and other legal materials. In the classroom, he must engage time and again in the following processes:

(a) *Analysis*: He will read cases, examining their statements of facts, identifying those which are legally operative—those which produce legal results. He will observe and record in his briefs how the courts apply existing principles of law to those operative facts. He will analyze, in classroom and without, numerous hypothetical situations to determine whether or not the same legal principles should be applied with like or different results. He will be given constant and intensive training in this kind of analysis, thus preparing his mind for what the lawyer does every day with his clients' affairs—a thoroughly practical operation.

(b) *Inductive reasoning*: Again and again, the student will study groups of related decisions, handed down by courts of last resort. They may be accompanied by pertinent statutory provisions, or law Review comments, or other legal materials. He will synthesize the legal materials thus assembled, to build up by inductive processes the mass of legal doctrine pertinent to each of his courses. As he outlines his courses he will in effect build his own textbook out of the raw materials of the

7. Besides three years LL.B. course, five years integrated Law Course is operative in almost all Law Schools in India leading to B.A. LL.B. (Hons.); B.B.A. LL.B. (Hons.); B.Com. LL.B. (Hons.); B.Sc. LL.B. (Hons.); B.Tech. LL.B. (Hons.). See in detail Bar Council of India Rules, 2008.

common law. The lawyer does this every time he goes into the law library.

(c) *Deductive reasoning*: Again, time after time, the student in classroom and particularly in examinations will take rules, principles, and standards which he had derived by inductive reasoning or otherwise and will apply them to a series of classroom hypothetical situations representing the varying facts of life—just as the lawyer does every time he advises a client.

(d) *Analogical reasoning*: Cases already decided seldom are "on all fours". Principles already evolved frequently fail to embrace new situations. It becomes necessary to determine the legal effect of such new situations, by reasoning from analogy. The student will engage in this analogical process again and again—just as the lawyer does in his office.

Accordingly, the law school system has as one of its principal objectives developing in the student, by constant repetition, skill in analysis and in inductive, deductive, and analogical reasoning. All along the way he is also acquiring vast knowledge of the details of the *Corpus Juris*, the substantive and procedural law that will determine the rights and duties of clients.

2. What the Student is Expected to do?

Individual study habits and efficiency vary, but law students in general find that an average of two or three hours of time outside the classroom is necessary for each classroom hour—probably more in the first few months. This includes the time required for reading and studying the cases assigned, briefing the cases, comparing the various cases contained in each assignment, going over notes after class, the preparation of outlines of each course, and discussion with other law students.

The first task is to read cases assigned, carefully and understandingly. If words are unfamiliar, use the law dictionary. Try to visualize the situation discussed in each case, to see what happened, what procedural steps were taken, what arguments were made, why the court decided as it did, and what the case means when considered against the background of other decisions. In reading any case you will want to make sure that you understand at least the following points: (1) what did the plaintiff seek in bringing the case to the trial court? (2) What did defendant want, and how did the case come to an issue? (3) What did the trial court do; what was the trial court's judgment? (4) What actions of the trial court were complained of by the party appealing to the court whose opinion you are reading? (5) Who won on appeal? (6) What were the facts of the case as assumed by the court, and what "issues" did they present? (7) What were the legal questions involved, and how did the court rule on each of them? (8) How did the court reason in arriving at the rulings? (9) What was the decision in the case? In studying the facts of the case, try to figure out what degree of generalization in expressing each fact is proper; often this can only be done after comparison with the other cases in the assignment.

Then it is desirable to think about each case, and the assignment as a whole, paying particular attention to what each case adds to what you have already learned and to the interrelationship of the cases in the assignment. Consider variations on the facts, and try to estimate the probable decisions which the court would render if those variations occurred. Only in this way are you able to see how broad or narrow the holding of the case may be. It is often useful in examining the facts of a case to try to determine from an advocate's standpoint the maximum value of the case as a precedent in your favor, and also the narrowest limits to which you could confine it as a case cited against you.

So as to have a convenient summary record of the case, you should digest or brief the important points of the case. This will be helpful for discussion in class and essential when it comes to review. Furthermore, it is the actual making of your own brief of each case that develops essential skill in use of judicial precedents, and aids you to master the common law techniques of handling decisions. Briefing your own cases will teach you far more than merely reading someone else's briefs—whether they are those of a classmate or "canned briefs" on which you have wasted good money. No champion swimmer ever developed his stroke and endurance by riding along in a motorboat and watching somebody else swim several miles a day.

Some students brief cases on gummed paper which is pasted into the appropriate place in their notes; others write the brief on part of a large page, leaving room to take class notes and to add to them when going over the class discussion afterwards. From the mechanical standpoint any system is satisfactory if it enables you to have conveniently at hand the brief you have made of each case and the notes concerning it. After you have mastered the fundamentals of briefing in your first year or two, you may feel that it is safe to leave some things out of your briefs, or to resort to understandings and marginal notes in your casebook. However, you should not try this until you are very sure that you have learned all you can by careful briefing, and that you can rely on such abbreviated notes and your memory to take the place of such briefing.

The content of the brief is suggested above in mentioning the points to be looked for in reading a case. Individual ideas will differ, but at the start you would do well to include:

1. The name and page of the case in your casebook for easy reference.
2. The court and the date, to orient the case in the law.
3. The facts of the case, stated briefly but including all those relevant to the decision.
4. What relief plaintiff asked for in the lower court?
5. What defendant asked the lower court to do?
6. What the lower court did?
7. What action of the lower court was complained of by the party appealing?
8. The specific disposition of the appeal.
9. The legal questions or issues involved.
10. The holding of the court, preferably phrased in substantially the court's own language.
11. Some indication of the line of reasoning and argument by which the court reached its conclusions, distinguishing between holding and dictum, and also observing dissenting opinions.

So much for preparation before the class. Instructors will differ in what is done during the classroom hour, but one of the main objectives in the first year will be to help you master the case system. To that end the instructor will quiz you concerning the principles derivable from the cases, ask you to apply the rules to hypothetical cases, or relate the cases one to another, to show how you would use the cases in advising a client or in argument before a court, and in various ways to show that you have mastered the small segment of the law represented by the days assignment taken both by itself and in relation to all that you have previously studied. Only if you have studied the cases before hand, have thought about them, and have asked yourself these questions, will you be ready and able to profit by the classroom discussion. Occasionally, the instructor will fill in the gaps by the lecture or will summarize the principles developed. During the classroom hour you have two principal tasks: (a) following the discussion, taking actual part in it when called upon or when you have something worthwhile to volunteer, and participating mentally regardless of whether you are talking at the moment; and (b) writing suitable notes. Don't try to prepare a longhand or shorthand transcript of everything that is said. Make your notes brief and thoughtful. Taking notes in this fashion is harder than just copying down everything that is said, but such notes represent thought on your part and they will have far more value, especially for reviewing purpose.

As soon as practicable after class, and in any event while the discussion is fresh in your mind, go over the class notes. Make sure that they represent what you think are the important points developed. Try to integrate your notes with the work you did before class, e.g. how far were you correct in the answers which you would have vent to the various hypothetical cases you thought about? Try continuously to apply what you are learning by discussion with your fellow students; group discussions are likely to raise many questions and problems which would never occur to any single student.

Most students, if not all, find it desirable to build up outlines of principles in each of the law courses. Don't just copy out your class notes and briefs of cases, but try to arrange the ideas systematically as if you were preparing your own textbook. The making of such an outline will help you see how the cases fit together, and will help reveal any points where you are uncertain as to the law. When you are working up your outline it may be desirable to go to the texts and law review articles in the library to see how well your conclusions coincide with those of the writers. "Canned outlines", whether prepared by other students or outsiders, will be of little, if any, value; it is the work of making your own that will be most helpful to you, and then if you want to check your outline against the ideas of another, use textbooks and law review articles.

You will find it useful from time to time to go over recent prior examination questions which you can obtain in the library. See if you can answer them intelligently. This is a splendid activity for informal discussion groups, and will develop your analysis skill and will test your outlines and help your review for the examinations. The preliminary examinations conducted in the first year are given to test what you are able to do with what you have learned, and to help you find out what is expected at examination time. If you are not doing as well as you believe you should on these preliminary examinations, try to find out how you can improve your study methods and your handling of law examination questions.

Finally, you will want to become familiar with the Law Library which in a very real sense is the lawyer's laboratory. Learn to use the law review and the index to legal periodicals, the encyclopedias, the Digest System for finding cases, the annotated cases, the statutes, and the other useful tools of the law student and lawyer. Case Club work in the first year will give you a chance to see what you can do along this line, but don't confine your use of the library to the minimum necessary to complete your Case Club assignments. Do a reasonable amount of collateral reading of law review and other items are suggested by the instructors in your courses and by the notes in your casebook. However, don't turn to the Law Library until you have worked with the casebook material yourself, doing what you can to put the cases together so that they "make sense". Then go to the Law Library to see what others make out of that area of the law. Trying to "tie in" such reading with the ideas you develop from your cases and class work and discussion with other students will make it much more valuable to you. Moreover, if you can possibly find the time, get into the habit of doing at least a little reading in legal fields not required in connection with your courses. Spend at least a little time on legal biography, on books or articles regarding the relationship of law to government, or politics, or history, or business and economic life, or psychology, or philosophy, or any of the other fields outside the strict law itself. Such semi-recreational reading in the Law Library's vast stock of materials will prove of interest and value, and help to correlate what you are learning in Law School with your prior studies in college and with the world outside the law.

3. The Task

Individual study habits and efficiency vary. However, law students, in general, may find that an average of two or three hours of time outside the classroom is necessary for each classroom hour. This includes the time required for reading and studying the cases assigned, briefing the cases, comparing the various cases contained in each assignment, going over notes after class, the preparation of outlines of each course, and discussion with other law students. This interaction shall help the niche law learners to emulate the art of communication, articulation, writing, briefs preparation, audit as well as critique of High Courts and Supreme Court judgements, which is a roadmap for advocacy. This interaction is a part of 'experiential learning' through legal materials. 'Experiential learning' at the law schools shall be a milestone in the court practice without initial turbulences. 'Experiential learning' should be through live cases as a compulsory part/component of legal education. 'Experiential learning' makes the 'legal education in action'. 'Experiential learning' shall also help to develop clinical legal education modules 'in class' and 'out of class' (teaching and learning in the field heuristically) law learning.

Chapter II

INTRODUCTION TO LEGAL SYSTEMS —COMMON LAW, EQUITY LAW, CIVIL LAW AND LEGAL PLURALISM

A. A BROAD FRAMEWORK

The four broad legal systems of the world, as comparative law scholars agree in their scholastic writings, referred to as families of law are the civil law, the common law, the socialist law and the Islamic law. Precisely, the civil law countries are known as civil code countries of the European continent whose legal systems have the roots in Roman law and derive either from the French or the German systems. The common law systems have their roots in the British law having the genesis of judge made law which was developed on the axiom of justice, equity and good conscience. The common law systems include all the members of colonial rules whose original legal systems were evaporated by the *jus receptum* of the common law.[1] The Socialist legal systems derived from the tenets of Marxism comprised the Soviet Union, China, and those countries of the Eastern Europe and Asia under the USSR domination seem to be a dying breed with the disintegration of the USSR and the decay of the Eastern Europe block.[2]

---

1. See M.C. Setalvad, *The Reception of Common Law in India*.
2. See William F. Fox, Jr., *International Commercial Agreements: A Primer on Drafting, Negotiating and Resolving Disputes*, 3rd Ed., 1998, pp.17-43.

The Islamic legal systems, mostly but not exclusively located in the Middle-East, obtain their doctrines from the teachings of Koran and other Islamic religious teachings. Besides, the legal pluralism, that is, indigenous or ethnic or aboriginal or religious tenets, also operates in the families of law. The contours of these legal systems are discussed as follows.

B. COMMON LAW

It is a system of law which has prevailed in England and United States of America and other former British colonies, namely, Australia, Canada, India and Ireland. The "common law" signifies the general law of England. However, Salmond defines the Common Law as "the total *Corpus Juris Angliae* with three exceptions, namely, (1) special law in its various forms, (2) statute law, and (3) equity."

Unlike the statue law common law consists of those principles, usages and rules of action applicable to the government and security of persons and of property, which do not rest for their authority upon any express or positive declaration of the will of the legislature. Thus, common law includes unwritten laws and usages which also change according to changing needs and conditions of each society. However, when common law becomes inconvenient, requires improvement, it is over ruled by legislation. For example, the doctrine of 'common employment' established in *Priestly v. Flower*[3] was abolished by the Law Reform (Personal Injuries) Act, 1948.

The origin of common law in England may be traced from the period of Norman Conquest in the 12th century. Prior to that, in Anglo-Saxon period there was no common law in England. Common Law developed as the royal power gradually increased and restricted the powers of the landlords. During 1154-89, when Glanville was the Chief Justice of King Henry II, the jurisdiction of the King's court had been enhanced by royal writs.

C. EQUITY LAW

The term 'equity' means 'right as founded on the law of nature', 'fairness', 'justice'. In jurisprudence, however, equity law is distinct from law. According to Sir Henry Maine, 'equity' means any body of rules existing by the side of the original civil law, founded on distinct

---

3. *Priestly v. Flower*, (1837) 3 M&W 1.

principles and claiming incidentally to supersede the civil law by virtue of superior sanctity inherent in those principles. All legal systems whether Roman or Anglo-Saxon had developed equity law as a corrective to the law of the land. In Rome the judicial administrator called *'praetor'* was to decide a case on the basis of natural justice whether the civil law was wanting or inadequate. In England the Chancellor administered this Law on the basis of fair play or equity.

Equity law developed due to deficiencies in common law. The major defects of English common law include: (i) absence of remedy, (ii) inadequacy of remedy, and (iii) excessive formalism which resulted in injustice. Thus, a need was felt to mitigate this hardship by supplementing it by the rules governed by the conscience of the Judge. The aggrieved party, not being in a position to get justice or obtain remedy, could approach the King for redress. The King referred the case to the Lord Chancellor who was supposed to be the keeper of the King's conscience. He considered those petitions and gave relief in suitable cases, particularly those relating to trust, specific relief, frauds, errors, unjust enrichment, etc.

Equity law, thus, developed out of necessity to supplement the deficiencies in the Common Law of that time. In course of time, the Lord Chancellor advised the Judges of the Court of Chancery to supplement the Common law with principles of justice, equity and good conscience. During the reign of Herry VI, the Lord Chancellor could grant the remedy of injunction which prohibited the execution of decrees passed by the Common Law Courts in appropriate cases. The remedy of injunction gave rise to constant clash and conflicts between Lord Chancellor Ellesmere of the Equity Court and Chief Justice Coke of the Common Law Court. These disputes were referred to Lord Bacon who was the Attorney General of England. He decided the matter in favor of Lord Chancellor of Equity Division. Thus, Equity Law in England developed to supplement the defects of Common Law and not to *persede* it. It was allowed to prevail over Common law in order to remedy the defects of the Common law. Though equity has now merged into Common law, but it is too often said that "the two streams, i.e., Common law and Equity flow side by side but their waters do not mingle". This, in other words means that even to this day, equity principles are as effective as the Common law principles in England.

Commenting on the development of equity law in England, Maitland said that the history, origin and growth of equity clearly shows that it grew up from the deficiencies or the deficiencies and inadequacy of remedies provided by Common law and it came to protect and promote the interest of justice against rigidity of the law. In Blackstone's view, equity and Common law are not two opposing systems, and there is little to distinguish them except their historical origin and modes of procedure.

Salmond attributes three meanings to the term 'equity'. Firstly, it connotes the embodiment of the principles of morality, honesty and righteousness. Secondly, it is synonymous with natural justice. Thirdly, in a narrow sense, it consists of set rule of equitable law as opposed to Common law.

Thus, equity has become a potential source of law in England. Some of the laws such as law of trusts, mortgages, quasi-contract, specific relief, etc., have emerged out of the equitable principles.

D. CIVIL LAW

Civil law means law of the land or municipal law. It is enforced by the Court of the State. The term 'civil law' is derived from the Roman word *jus civile*. While Salmond considers civil law as the law of the land, Austin and Holland prefer to call it as 'positive law'. It is territorial in nature because it applies within the territory of the State concerned. The force behind the law is the sanction of the State. The term Civil law has three meanings, namely:

(i) A secular law which is the part of a legal system of a theocratic government, which is uncommon as on today.

(ii) A private law which seeks to regulate relationships between private persons and organizations. In this sense, civil law consists of statues or customary rules which are enforced on the petition or claim by the parties. The court is entitled to award the damages, injunction or declarations in the case of violation of statutory or customary rights of the parties. This body of law includes the law of torts, family law, property law, etc. In continental system, it includes, Law of Obligations, Law of Persons, etc.

(iii) It is an alternative to 'common law system'. In this sense the civil law has its roots in continental system. It is generally found in most of European Countries. In most of the countries the civil law is codified in the form of civil codes, but in some like Scotland it remains un-codified. Most codes follow the Code Napoleon. The German code was developed from Roman law with reference to German legal tradition.

E. LEGAL PLURALISM

(1) Communist/Soviet Legal Theory

(a) Approaches and Significance of Soviet Legal Theory

Functional Approach: Soviet legal writers were mainly concerned not about nature of law but the functional aspects of law. This way it resembles with American legal realism because both are concerned with (1) social engineering, and (2) the functioning of the law and the factors that influence it.

Sociological Approach: Even though in the earlier writings it was predicted that law will wither away but subsequently it was realized that it is an effective instrument of the policy of Soviet Government, directed at the abolition of capitalism and the realization of socialism. In this respect it is akin to some sociological theories.

(b) Relationship of Law and Natural Law

Though Soviet jurists deny any connection between positive law and natural law, some of them appear to be indicating of norms superior to or even above positive law. Vyshinsky says:

> "A theory of law is a system of legal principles on the basis where of the entire science of law all branches of that science (irrespective of their definitive content) are built. Clearly the working out of these principles cannot have its inception in the norms of positive law: on the contrary, the norms of positive law-like all positive law as a whole must be built in conformity with the principles established by a legal theory."

Kelsen explaining the above stated:

> "What is most amazing in this theory of Bolshevic Vyshinksy is that it is exactly of the same type as that bourgeois theory which the Soviet writers have derided and ridiculed more than any another theory: the natural law doctrine, which, just as Vyshinsky, rejects a mere theory of positive law because of its 'sterlity and importance' and which, precisely in accordance with Vyshinksy's recipe, works out or pretends to work out, principles of law 'from life', that is, from nature in general and from the nature of society or, what amounts to the same, from the social relationships in particular; with the only difference that these principles are the ideal norms of capitalist law".

(c) Approaches of Karl Marx and Frederick Engles

Karl Marx and Frederick Engles have propounded the Communist

Theory of Law. Since it was originated in Soviet Union it is also known as Soviet Legal Theory. Even though Marx theory originated in Soviet Union it influenced some other countries of Eastern Europe, Latin America and China. Thus, it is not surprising that some juristic writings therein have been influenced by Marxian ideology. The key feature of the Soviet theory is that a legal system has been based on the political and economic philosophy of Karl Marx and his successors. Marxist legal theory has experienced many varieties and stages since inception especially since the revolution of 1917.

(i) Concept of Class struggle

The main thesis of Marx is that the history of all hitherto existing society is the history of class struggle. Class struggle forms the base of social conflict and social and economic development. Explaining his theory he highlighted the typical stages of community's development. He pointed out that in a very primitive stage of the exploitation of men by men there is slavery. He stated that slaves were regarded not more than chattels. Further, there was exploitation of slaves by the dominant class. The next stage in social development was the feudal system. It was based on land holding and property. Thus, there was domination and exploitation by serfs. The next stage dealt with the rise of a merchant middle class. It marked the beginning of the *Bourgeoisie*. At this stage the domination passes from feudal to capitalist. The final stage of development in Marx envisaged the socialization of society leading to the stage of perfect communism when all capitalist and *Bourgeoisie* elements have been eliminated. This stage may come either by evolution or revolution.

(ii) Concept of Law

Marx rejected Hegal idealist philosophy and substituted materialism. He said, "my dialectic method is not only different from Hegeliam, but it is direct opposite". Marx did not define law. However, he focuses his attention rather on how law is created. He was interested in ideology and law as a manifestation of the same. According to him, one of the main functions of law is to secure power relationships. He felt that law represents superstructure. It is used in *Bourgeoisie* capitalist systems of regulation in order to further the ends of the economically dominant and exploiting class at the expense of the proletariat, i.e., the suppressed class.

(iii) Legal Relations—Forms of State

Marx felt that legal relations as well as forms of State are rooted in the material conditions of life and the social production which men carry on independent of their will.

(iv) Concept of State

According to Marx the concept of State is a superstructure in a capitalist system.

(v) Withering away of State and Law

Marx felt that State and Law are temporary phenomena. It would break the power of the State. With the abolition of classes, the power of the State would disappear and governmental functions be transformed into simple one. He felt that in real communist society there will be no State, because there will be no need for it, and the existence of law and State shall "wither away". According to Engel, "Government over persons is replaced by the administration of things and the direction of process or production. The State is not abolished (as the anarchists demand) it withers away".

(vi) Future of Law

Since the communist manifesto was brought much before the revolution in Soviet Union, it was but natural that Marx and Engles were not able to provide a clear and definite picture of the future of the law in the period of the dictatorship of the proletariat. However, Marx felt that the period of transition prior to the achievement of socialism will not be perfect and the law of the socialist state will suffer from the evil of *Bourgeoisie* society.

(d) Lenin Theory and Practice

Lenin tried to resolve many ambiguities which remained unresolved and succeeded in providing a definite direction for the practical implementation of the doctrine. Indeed Lenin's writings fulfil this task. Quite apart from this Lenin tried to bridge the gap between the theory and the practical needs of the situation. He laid stress on the revolutionary character of Marxian doctrine. He restricted the possibility of the 'withering away' of law and of the state to the socialist state, and observed that during the transition period of the dictatorship of the proletariat there will be a definite need for the state and law in order to eliminate reactionary elements within the community. He stated:

> "the dictatorship of the proletariat produces a series of restrictions of liberty in the case of the oppressors, the exploiters, the capitalist. We must crush them in order to free

humanity from wage slavery, their resistance must be broken by force. It is clear that where there is suppression there is also violence, there is no liberty, no democracy".

After the complete abolition of the *Bourgeoisie* the coercive machinery of the state will disappear. He explains the difference between the capitalist state and the proletariat state as: "under capitalism, we have a state in the proper sense of the word, that is, special machinery for the suppression of one class by another. During the transition from capitalism to communism suppression is still necessary; but it is the suppression of the minority of exploiters by the majority of exploited. A special apparatus, special machinery for suppression, the 'State' is still necessary, but this is now a transitional state, no longer a State in the usual sense."

Lenin's approach has been summarized by Lloyd as under "Some of the more fervent prospects of the new order envisage the instantaneous accomplishment of the disappearance of the state and of the law with the successful outcome of the revolution. Lenin, however, adopted a more hard headed and realistic approach by recognizing that even a successful revolution could not result in the immediate elimination of all the apparatus of the state and the panoply of the law. It would take time for a totally classless society to emerge. Thus, even though Lenin did not abandon the Marxist conception of the ultimate withering away of the state, he still recognized the need, during an interim period when class conflict had still to be eliminated, and the surviving elements of the *Bourgeoisie* extruded for the apparatus of the state and coercive law to be retained.[4]

(e) Pashukanis's Approach of Law

Pashukanis, a Soviet jurist, emphasized that law like the State is an instrument of oppression in a capitalist society.

(f) Kelsen's Viewpoint of Pashukanis's Approach of Law

Dealing with Pashukanis's approach Kelsen observed that he imitates Marx's economic interpretation of political phenomena in the field of jurisprudence. He felt that legal phenomena and economic phenomena can exist only within a capitalist system of economy based on the principle of private property in the means of production. He rejects the definition of law as a system of norms as "ideological".[5]

4. Introduction to Jurisprudence (3rd Ed.), pp. 634-35
5. The Communist Theory of Law, pp. 89-90.

(g) Place of Administration

While dealing with State Kelsen observed that law would ultimately wither away to give place to administration. In a socialist community, the public sector becomes the ruling factor.

John D. French while dealing with recent approach to law, pointed on that "communism—the goal of socialist society, remains a distant vision..... The problems which still confront the socialist society are to be solved by careful approach to the improvement of social condition rather than with an eye to the rapid attainment of the end in the view. That end, communism, is now being sought by more pragmatic and less doctrinal methods than have been used in the development of the socialist semi-state". Be that as it may, there has been a gradual recognition of the authority of law. The most important is the sphere of economic and property relations between the agents of state enterprise, in industry and farming. The second sphere concerns the relation between the state and the citizens. Most of the relevant principles are embodied in the Constitution of 1936. They include such matters as the right and duty to work, the guarantee of a minimum standard of living, the right to social security and rest. These legal relations have not the character of protected civil rights and duties in the established sense of Western law. Unlike constitutions of the Western type, such as the America, the Australia, or new German Constitution, the Basic Law, provide no protection or method of enforcement through legal procedure. On the whole, these so-called rights and duties are a formal indication of the principles of which the state is built. They form the basis for law rather than law itself.

(h) Karl Renner's Approach to Legal Theory

Karl Renner of Austria has propounded his legal theory from Marxist premises. He attacked capitalistic system of law. In 'Institution of Private Law and their Social functions' Renner made an attempt to utilize the Marxist system of sociology for the construction of a theory of law. He also observed that capitalist, under the name of 'ownership' has assumed a power of command over men which is a public power. In this way the concept of private ownership has become transformed into an institution of public law. He, therefore, suggested that 'ownership', in modern times, must be recognized as a branch of public law and the state must intervene to protect the citizen. He pleaded for creating legal norms which may completely express the trend of social development. In order to understand a legal concept its economic base has to be penetrated. He also showed particular interest in the changing functions of the legal institution of private property and the need to explain the functions fulfilled by legal institutions at particular points in time.

(i) Quinney Approach: Quinney (U.S.)

Concentrates on the 'social reality' of crime. His ideas are similar of other Marxist authors. He states that in criminal law enforcement is a way in which the ruling classes preserve their interests. It is a way of protecting and promoting the continuation of the capital order. In his discussion, he made an attempt to apply the ideas of Marx to the contemporary problems of today.

Like Quinney, Bankowski and Mungham (U.K.) are other authors who described law in terms of Marxian ideas. They viewed law in capitalist society as oppression. They concentrated on 'poor man's law', welfare law, etc. They stated that socialization of production will eliminate the problems of capitalism. Society is envisaging by them as "System of Councils". Although law will wither away but the problem of running the complex society will remain. Socialist legal institution will be necessary to ease the problems of clashing diversities.

(j) Position in China[6]

Like Soviet Union political system in China is based on Marxian ideology. After the establishment of communist regime in the country, the Chinese society has passed through a number of phases and consequently law underwent a number of vicissitudes. In China, Party and Government exercised extensive control over law. Justice was dispensed by *adhoc* revolutionary People's Tribunals. However, when things started settling down, the importance of a regularized and effective judicial system was recognized. However, the judicial process suffered a setback by the Anti-Rightist Movement of 1957-58. Non-judicial agencies started handling cases. Again, the Cultural Revolution of the late 1960's felt the need of formal legal system. The Red Guards took over legal work. However, in late attempt to strengthen and rebuild the legal system started to be made. Llyod stated the present position in China in the following words:

> The present position of law and legal institutions in China cannot be ascertained with certainty. There are indications that law is being strengthened again; a new constitution is, for example, in the pipeline. But, nevertheless, non-judicial tribunals do adjudicate and impose sanctions. The Cultural

---

6. Soviet Legal Philosophy, p. 323.
Kelsen, The Communist Theory of Law, p. 124.

Revolution certainly has not strengthened legality; the injection of revolutionary fervor.

2. Indian Legal System—Hindu Law, Muslim Law, Christian Law and Parsi Law

(a) Hindu Law

The following are the main sources of Hindu law:

(i) The Sruti or the Vedas

The term "*Sruti*" is derived from the root '*srut'* which means 'revealed'. The *Vedas* are the repositories of all knowledge and anything beyond the *Vedas* is darkness or ignorance. Regarding the nature of the *Vedas*, there are certain basis dogmas: (1) the *Vedas* are self-existent or *Apavrusheva*, and (2) the *Vedas* are self-evident or *Swataha pramanya*. The *Vedas* are four in number: the *Rig*, the *Yejus*, the *Saman* and the *Atharva*.

Though the authors of the *Smriti*s and the commentaries accept the fiction that all knowledge has to be drawn from the *Vedic* reservoir, there cannot be two opinions about the scantiness of legal material in the *Vedic* literature; there are passages few and far between having remote relevance to law. In spite of it, the *Vedic* literature throws some light on certain aspects of social life of those times which in its turn assists us in formulating certain theories, such as *Dharma* (law) and immutable relationship between law and morality.

(ii) The Smritis

Though the *Smritis* are next to the *Vedas* in importance, they are, in fact, the primary source of Hindu Law. The term '*Smriti*' is derived from the root '*Samart'* which means 'remembered' or 'recollected'. The term *Smriti* is used in a general sense and a narrower technical sense. In its general connotation the term includes not only the *Smritis* in the technical narrower sense but also a class of literature designated as *Sutras*

Manu Smriti has occupied a pre-eminent position in the Hindu legal history. Its paramount authority has been conceded by every later writer. There is great diversity of opinion regarding the age of this work. Some writers are of the view that though the work professes to belong to the *primeval* times it is a product of post-*Mauryan* period and consequently reflects the political and sacerdotal prejudices of that age.

Yajnavalkya Smriti is later to *Manu Smriti* showing a distinct improvement in the treatment of the subject matter. The fact that the

Smriti belongs to *Satavahana* times when *Buddisim* was in its ascendancy accounts for the tolerance (unlike the fanatical zeal of *Manu*) reflected in the work. *Yajnavalkya* exhibits progressive ideas in a conservative garb. Unlike *Manu*, he has divided his work into three parts; *Achara, Vyavahara* and *Prayaschitta*.

Narada, Brihaspati and *Katyavana* form the great triumvirate of the Hindu legal literature. They have given highly developed legal rules and are successful in dissociating law from religion. *Narada's* treatment of judicial procedure and *Katyayana's* treatment of *Stridhan* have been classical.

(iii) Commentaries and Digests

The creative period of the *Smriti*s continued up to the 6th century and afterwards we find a galaxy of commentators who undertook the task of consolidating the laws promulgated by the *Smritikaras*. On account of the numerousness of the *Smriti*s and because of their having been composed at different times in different regions, they generated a welter of controversies. Of course, sometimes the conflicts were more apparent than real. So, an ascertainment of the authoritativeness of a text when it conflicted with another text was an imperative necessity in the administration of law. Therefore, it was left to the commentators, who were profound scholars of *Dharmasastra* and who at times occupied high political positions in their respective areas, to pronounce upon the authoritative character of *Smriti* texts. The commentators interpreted the law in terms of the needs of their times giving their own gloss to the *Smriti* which suited them most.

Medhatithi, Govindaraja, Dhareswara and *Kulluka* have written commentaries on *Manu Smritim* while *Viswarupa, Vijaeswara Aparaka, Sulapani* and others have commented on *Yajnavalkya Smriti*. Asahaya has written a commentary on *Narada Smriti*.

Vijnaneswara and *Jimithavahana*, are the celebrated authors of *Mitakshara* and *Dayabhaga* respectively have established their supremacy over other commentators and their works; in fact, their works have been the subject-matter of many later commentaries. The two authors have differed basically on many issues and thus have founded two schools of thought. Attempts, however, have been made by some writers to ascertain the "*raisodetre*" of this basic divergence, but their reasons are far from convincing.

Mitakshara reigns supreme in the whole of India except Bengal where *Dayabhaga* is the authority. Even in Bengal where *Dayabhaga* is silent on any issue or does not come in conflict with *Mitakshara*, the latter is considered to be an authority. *Mitakshara* has been modified to some extent to suit the local requirements of different regions and consequently it has given rise to various "sub-schools" (though there is no rational basis for designating them as sub-schools). When a Hindu family governed by one school of Hindu Law migrates to another region governed by a different school, the migrating family retains its original school—*Balwant Rao v. Baj Rao, 47 I.A. 213.*

(iv) Sadachara or Custom

'*Lex non Scripts*' must have necessarily preceded '*Lex Scripta*'. Every community evolves certain rules which are in consonance with its conscience, for observance among its constituents. The term *Sadachara* is of wider import than custom. It is resolvable into, the components *Sadhunam + Acharah* or *Sat + Acharah*, that is to say, the practices of the pious or virtuous men who are well versed in sacred lore.

The authoritative character of *Sadachara* is based on the fiction that the usage is founded on a forgotten *Smriti*. This fiction has, often times, landed the commentators in difficulties when a custom directly conflicts with an express text of a *Smriti* and in such cases we find the ingenuity of the commentators in resolving the conflict. Inspite of opposition from the orthodox section of the community, the later commentators have ungrudgingly conceded supremacy to *Sadachara*. (*Collector of Madura v. Mootoo Ramalinga,* 12 Moo, I.A. 397: The clear proof of usage outweighs the written text of law).

Classification of custom: Family customs, class customs, and local customs.

Requisites of valid custom: Antiquity, certainty, continuity; not unreasonable; not immoral; and not opposed to public policy.

(v) Legislation

Legislation is the most potent agency to alter law to suit the exigencies of the changing times. Though legislation in the modern sense of the term is incompatible with the dogmas of Hindu Law, it cannot be asserted that it was wholly unknown to the Hindu system. The Royal edicts professing to regulate the conduct of people within the framework of *Dharma*, served the object of legislation. In modern times Hindu Law has been altered beyond recognition by several enactments. The following are some of the statutes which have affected Hindu Law:

The Caste Disabilities Removal Act, 1850: It is a general statute applicable to all communities. Traditional Hindu Law imposed grave penalties on an apostate. Not only the apostate lost his '*locus standi*' in the family but also his rights in the family property were forfeited. The above act removes such disabilities and restores the property rights of an apostate.

Hindu Widow's Remarriage Act, 1856: Though there are certain texts of doubtful import in the traditional Hindu Law which might have provided for the remarriage of Hindu widows, the widow remarriage was eschewed completely by the orthodox section of the Hindu community. Even the legal position of a remarried widow and her issues was far from clear. The above Act is an enabling statute which not only legalizes widow remarriages but also declares the issues of such marriages to be legitimate.

Native Converts Marriage Dissolution Act, 1866 is a general statute enabling the convert to Christianity to get the former marriage dissolved.

Hindu Inheritance (Removal of Disabilities) Act, 1928: According to the traditional Hindu Law persons suffering from certain diseases and infirmities were excluded from taking a share at the time of partition as well as in the inheritance. They are entitled to the bare right of maintenance. The Act has ameliorated the position of such disabled persons by removing the disqualifications.

Hindu Gains of Learning Act, 1930: Though a Hindu coparcener was permitted to make self-acquisitions, not in all cases had he the absolute control over his acquisitions. The Act has freed the self-acquisitions of a coparcener from all liabilities of the family.

Hindu Women's Rights to Property Act, 1937: Prior to 1937, the widow of a Hindu *Mitakshara* coparcener had no right to succeed to the coparcenary property in which her deceased husband had an interest; and she was entitled to maintenance only. This Act conferred on her the right to succeed *to the interest of her deceased husband* in the coparcenary property. Even as regards the separate property, the Act brought about a departure by permitting her to succeed concurrently with the son.

Hindu Marriage Act, 1955
Hindu Succession Act, 1956
Hindu Adoption and Maintenance Act, 1956
Hindu Minority and Guardianship Act, 1956

These enactments have brought about sweeping reforms in the respective branches of Hindu law to which they pertain.

(vi) Judicial Decisions

Judicial decisions have unprofessedly altered the rules of law. However, laudable the sentiment that judicial discretion should be unhampered by any other consideration may be, the public policy of maintaining a certain degree of consistency in the judicial administration, demands that the judicial decisions ought to conform to certain legal principles, the doctrine of precedent being one such principle. When the judicial decisions have withstood the passage of time, the principles of "*stare decisis*" requires that the later decisions should abide by the earlier ones, even if they have departed from the traditional systems.

(vii) Justice, equity and good conscience

In the absence of express provisions in the other sources the principles of justice, equity and good conscience are to be applied in arriving at decisions. Even the traditional Hindu Law recognized this principle by emphasizing the importance of *yukti* or *nyaya.*

(b) Muslim Law

Before examining the sources of Islamic Law, it has to be borne in mind that law proper or positive law is only a part of the *Shariat* which regulates all human actions. "*Shariat* as a technical term means the cannon law of Islam, the totality of *Allah's* commandment. It is fundamentally a Doctrine of duties, a code of obligations". The law proper or the Science of Jurisprudence is known as *fiqh* and a person well versed in the Science of *fiqh* is a *faqih*. "*Fiqh or the Science of law may be defined as the knowledge of one's rights and obligatons derived from the Quran or Sunna or deduced there from or about which the learned have agreed*".

(i) The Quran

The Quran is the principal source of Islamic law. It is the sum total of the revelation made by God to the Prophet through the agency of the angel Gabriel. It was revealed piecemeal during a period of twenty three years. Quran is divided into 114 Chapters of unequal length, the largest being one twelfth of the entire book while the smallest contains only three verses. The compilation of Quran was undertaken during the period of *Abu Bakr*, but the present edition of Quran is the one that was edited by *Zaid Ibn Thavit* (who was constantly associated with the Prophet and acted as his amanuensis) during the period of *Usman* who caused the destruction of all other unauthentic editions. It is remarkable indeed that despite the differences between the two schools the *Sunis* and the *Shia*, so far as the contents of Quran are concerned there is complete concordance.

(ii) Traditions

Quran with Traditions (*hadith*) constitutes the primary source of Muslim Law. Quran is the direct revelation of God whereas Tradition is the indirect revelation, since all actions of the Prophet were inspired by God. Although the words *Hadith* and *Sunna* have been used indiscriminately by many writers, there is still a subtle difference between the two; "*Hadith is a story of a particular occurrence: Sunna the practice deduced from it, is the rule of law*". Tradition is authoritative only so far as its contents go, whereas the Quran has its legal force in itself and its very words constitute the law. The authoritative character of the *Hadith* has been laid down in the tradition. "*That which the Prophet of God hath made unlawful is like what god hath made so*".

On account of the fact that Traditions were most important regarding their contents than their form and because no authoritative collection was attempted at an earlier date, forging of tradition became a common practice among political parties to suit their political designs. This spurious manipulation of Traditions could have been prevented if only cared had been taken to collect the authoritative texts immediately after the death of the Prophet. But it was not done. It was, however, by the publication of "*Muwatta*" of *Malik Ibn Anas*, the founder of the *Maliki* school which contained about 700 traditions, that their systematic collection and study received attention. Great care was then bestowed upon scrutinizing the authenticity of the traditions. It is noteworthy that *Abu Hanifa*, the founder of the *Hanafi* school accepted only eighteen traditions out of a vast number on account of the severity of tests applied by him. The classification of the Traditions was undertaken in two forms. In the first form all the traditions narrated by the earliest attester in the chain of narrators (for instance, *Ayesha, Ali Fatima*, *Umar* and others) were classified under one head and such a collection was known as "*Masnad*". In the second, the traditions were classified topically (such as prayers, fasting, pilgrimage, etc.) and designated as "*Musanaf*". *Iman Ahamad Ibn Hanbal* collected about 50,000 traditions of about 700 companions in the first form whereas Bukhari, Muslim and other undertook their work in the second form.

(iii) Ijma

It is one of the fundamental tenets of Islam, that the sovereignty vests in God and next to him in '*Jammat*' or the masses. The people are the best judges of their weal and the general concordance on an important matter pertaining to the community regarding which there is no mandate in the Quran or the tradition, is known as *Ijma*. In a narrower sense *Ijma has been defined as agreement of the jurists among the followers of Muhammad in a particular age on a question of law*. Though as regards the religious and secular matters the *Ulemas* could arrive at a consensus of opinion, so far as questions pertaining to law were concerned, it was insisted that the participants should be *mujtahids* or *faqihs* (i.e. jurists well versed in law).

The authority of *Ijma* is based on the well known traditions of the Prophet " *my people will not agree in error*". "*It is incumbent upon you to follow the most numerous body*". The Prophet not only advised his followers to take the guidance of '*consensus ecclesia*' but he himself used to consult the '*Sahaba*' or the companions giving considerable weight to their opinion.

(iv) The Qiyas

The application of private judgment in arriving at solutions regarding problems, gave rise to the fourth source of law, the *Qiyas*. "*Qiyas has been defined as an extension of law from the original text to which the process is applied to (in a particular case by means of common illat or effective cause which cannot be ascertained merely by interpretation of the language of the text*". In *Qiyas* a rule is deduced by analogy, the basis of which could be traced to a rule expounded in any of the three earlier sources although the language of the original text does not cover the new circumstances. All the four *Sunni* schools recognize *Qiyas* as a valid source of law and as a matter of fact must of the *Sunni* law has been evolved through the application of this agency.

In addition to the above principal sources of Muslim law, there are three other modes of reasoning allied to Aiyas which have not received the same importance as the latter. They are *Istihsan, Istislah, Istidlal* and, *Istihsan. Istihsan* is the doctrine by which a jurist is enabled to get over a deduction of analogy either because it is opposed to a text or consensus of opinion or is such that his better judgment does not approve of it. *Istihsan* has been rendered as juristic preference and it is meant to soften the rigors of analogy.

At times the rule deduced by analogy may cause individual hardship or inconvenience and in such a case the jurist has the discretion to reject the *Qiyas* and adopt his own reasoning.

Although Iman Malik objected to the principle of *Istihsan*, he adopted a similar doctrine to serve almost the same purpose. He based the doctrine on the purpose of "*Public Welfare or advantage*". According to Malik, a rule of law deduced by analogy cannot be set aside by an individual jurist merely to suit the circumstances of a specific cases it could be disregarded only if it is injurious to the public in general.

Istidlal is another form of reasoning which means the inferring of a thing from another thing, *Hanafi* Jurists use the word in this sense in connection with the rules of interpretation. But with *Malikis* and *Shafis* *istidlal* is the name for a distinct method of juristic ratiocination, not falling within the scope of interpretation of analogy.

(v) Custom

Custom as a source of law has the same sanctity as that of *Ijma*. It is based on the same texts that uphold the validity of the latter. In establishing the legality of partnership, it is remarked in *Hedaya* that "partnership is lawful because the Prophet found people practicing it and confirmed them therein". Custom does not command any spiritual authority like *Ijma* of the learned, but a transaction sanctioned by custom is legally operative; even if it be in violation of a rule of law derived by analogy; it must not, however, be opposed to a clear text of the Quran or an authentic tradition. A line of demarcation between customs and usages of pre-Islamic Arabia and those that have come into existence after the advent of Islam, has been carefully drawn by the Muslim jurists. They seldom make any reference to pre-Islamic Arabian customs and assiduously avoid inquiry into them while tracing the evolution of many rules of Islamic law. Inspite of this wilful commission on the part of the scholars to draw upon the usages of the period of "*Jahj liyya*" (period of ignorance), it is undeniable that many of the institutions of Muslim law were influenced by pre-Islamic customs and usages. As regards the Islamic period, the customs of Medina have received special *veneration*.

(c) Christians and Parsis Law

Christian and Parsis are governed primarily by Statutory Laws. The establishment of British rule led to the formation of another community, that of the Christians, in India. As the number of adherents to the new religion grew, it posed some difficult problems regarding the administration of law, because unlike Muslim invaders the Christians did not bring with them a traditional system of law. Consequently, the set of laws were partly local and partly English laws. In the last quarter of the nineteenth century enactments applicable to Christians were passed. As stated above, the Parsis are governed exclusively by enacted laws.

Law of Marriage

Christians

The position is similar to that of the Hindu system. Neither a Christian spouse nor a Parsi spouse could alter his or her marital status by the mere act of apostasy. If a Christian having a Christian wife becomes a convert to Islam and marries another women according to Muslim law, the second marriage is of doubtful validity.[7] Similarly, a Parsi wife renouncing *Zoroastrianism* and embracing Islam cannot sue her Parsi husband for the dissolution of her marriage even though the Parsi husband has refused to accept her offer of Islam.[8]

Parsis

Section 3, cl. (c) of the Parsi Act prescribed that the parties should have completed the age of 21 years; if they have not attained that age then the consent of the father or guardian has to be obtained. So, Parsi minors can be validly given away in marriage, the age limits being governed by the Child Marriage Restraint Act. A Parsi who has attained majority (age of 18) if he has not attained the age of 21 cannot enter into the contract of marriage without the consent of parent or guardian. Contravention of this rule renders the marriage void.[9]

Special Marriage Act, 1954

Under this Act the bridegroom must have completed the age of 21 years and the bride the age of 18 years [Sec. 4(c)]. It has to be noted that in the case of other enactments, contravention of the rule relating to age limits does not affect the validity of the marriage but in the case of the Special Marriage Act *contravention of this rule renders the marriage void.*[10]

Soundness of Mind

Christian System: Though the Christian Marriage Act, is silent in this regard it can be inferred from other provisions that soundness of mind is a prerequisite for a valid marriage. Under Section 19(3) of the Indian Divorce Act a decree of nullity can be obtained by the aggrieved party.

Parsi System: Section 3 of the Parsi Act which lays down the requirements of a valid marriage is silent regarding the soundness of mind. But under Section 32(b) unsoundness of mind is a ground for

---

7. See *Skinner v. Orde* (1871) 14 M.I.A. 309.
8. See *Robaba Khan-um v. Khodabad* (1946) 48 Bom. L.R. 864.
9. Section 3.
10. Section 24.

seeking divorce. By the implication of this provision the marriage of a person of unsound mind is valid.

Special Marriage Act, 1954

Under Section 4(b) of the Act soundness of mind of the parties is absolutely essential. If either of the parties to the marriage is of unsound mind then the marriage is void .

Prohibited Degree

Christian System: For a valid marriage under the Christian marriage Act there should not be impediment of kindred or affinity (Section 18 and Section 42 of the Act). Contravention of the rule entitles the parties to obtain a decree of nullity (Section 19(2) of the Indian Divorce Act).

Parsi System: Under the Parsi Marriage and Divorce Act the Parties should not be related within the degrees of consanguinity or affinity. (Sec. 3(a)). For the list of persons who are within the prohibited degrees of relationship see Schedule I.

Special Marriage Act

Section 4(d) of the Act lays down that the parties to the marriage should not be related within the prohibited degree of the list of persons related within the prohibited degrees under Schedule I.

Solemnization of Marriage: In every system of law the status of husband and wife is constituted by observing certain formalities which may vary from community to community. The mere cohabitation of a man and a woman without the observance of the formalities does not create the marital tie. The nature of the formalities differ as to whether the particular system lays stress on the contractual or sacramental character of the institution; a society which considers marriage as a contract may prescribe least formalities, while a community which considers marriage as a sacrament may insist on a plethora of religious ceremonies. Some of the modern enactments have prescribed formalities similar to those required for completing a civil transaction.

Christian System: Part III and Part V of the Indian Christian Marriage Act provides for the solemnization of marriages before the Ministers of Religion and Marriage Registrars. Part VI provides the simple procedure for the solemnization of marriages of Indian Christians.

Marriages Solemnized by Ministers of Religion: Sections 12 to 26.

One of the parties to the intending marriage to issue the notice of such marriage (Section 12).

Publication of such notice by the Minister of Religion (Sections 13-16).

Chapter III

Approaches to the Study of Law: Various Schools of Thought

I. SCHOOL OF LEGAL THOUGHT: AN OVERVIEW

A range of ideas about law have been espoused by a variety of scholars/jurists/authors through their scholastic writings associated with different schools of legal thoughts of their country's politico-socio-legal-economic system as well as environ. What is law to one scholar may not be the same to another scholar. And, that is the precise reason that we try to know the meaning of law in a variety of scholastic approaches to law. We, therefore, try to understand the generic/philosophical/scientific approach to law in brevity inasmuch as "an ocean within a tear". Be that as it may, "Law is a seamless system with its own autonomy. It provides one correct answer to any cases, difficult or not, by application of its rules, precedents, principles and spirit." In the backdrop of this, there are a variety of approaches to understand what law is, but the most acceptable and acknowledged approach is 'natural law', 'positivist' or 'legal positivism' and the different schools of legal thoughts associated with these divergent approaches, e.g. historical, sociological, realist, etc.

Analytical school of thought, by contrast to natural law, expounded by legal positivists like Bentham, Austin, Hans Kelsen, H.L.A. Hart, Joseph Raj, etc., holds that there is no inherent or necessary connection between the validity conditions of law and ethics and morality or there is no berth for morality in the domain of law and that the force of law comes from some basic social facts although legal positivists differ on what those facts are. In legal positivism, law is seen as being conceptually separate from moral and ethical values, and it simply sees the law as being posited by law-makers, who are humans. The positivist argument is solely about the nature of law as a human institution. Analytical or 'Clarificatory School of Thought' rejected natural law's fusing of what law is and what it ought to be. David Hume made the famous is-ought distinction in the famous words that by analysis and clarifying the way the world is must be treated as a strictly separate question to normative and evaluative *ought* questions.[1] The most fascinating as well as chilling questions of analytical jurisprudential thought are: What are laws?; What is the law?; What is the relationship between law and power/society?; and What is the relationship between law and morality? Legal positivists through their legal positivism perspectives assert that law is something that is posited. Law is determined by social facts or sources. Law is nothing more than a set of rules to provide order and governance of society. In the perception of legal positivists, morals have no place in the domain of law. Both are distinct from each other and having no correlations. Jeremy Bentham was one of the earliest legal positivists who were the staunch supporter and propagator of "utilitarian" concept of law. He advocated utilitarian concept of law through 'pleasure' and 'pain' perspectives that the chief purpose of law was the greatest happiness of the greatest number of people with least pain. John Austin, a student of Bentham, and a Professor of Jurisprudence at University of London, popularized Bentham's utilitarianism by asserting, law is "commands, backed by threat of sanctions, from a sovereign, to whom people have a habit of obedience".[2] His theory is also called 'imperative theory of law, because of the presence of an element of command.[3] However, the contemporary legal positivists have derecognized and denounced Austin's over-simplification utilitarian answer to 'what is law'? Hans Kelsen, a 20th century jurist of Civil Law systems of Europe and Latin America and less influenced by common law countries, contends, in his Pure Theory of Law, that the abidingness of legal norms to norms to Grundnorm (Constitution), their specifically legal character, can be understood without tracing ultimately to some superhuman source such

1. David Hune, A Treatise of Human Nature, 1739.
2. John Austin, The Province of Jurisprudence Determined, 1831.
3. C.K Allen, Law in the Making.

as God, personified Nature or of great importance in his time—a personified State of Nation. H.L.A. Hart, a pivotal writer and a Professor of Jurisprudence at Oxford University, argued by rejecting Kelsen's normative thesis that the law should be understood as a system of social rules.[4] Hart as a positivist insisted on the importance of the separation of law from morality. He rejected the "command theory" of Austin and asserted that law comprises rules. Hart said, rules are divided into primary rules (rules of conduct or duty-imposing rules) and secondary rules (rules addressed to officials to administer primary rules or power-imposing rules). Primary rules grant rights or impose legal obligations upon the citizens, e.g. criminal law consists of primary rules. Secondary rules stipulate how primary rules are formed and validated, e.g. the rules that stipulate how Parliament is composed and how it enacts legislation are secondary rules. Secondary rules are divided into rules of adjudication (to resolve legal disputes), rules of change (allowing laws to be varied) and the rules of recognition (allowing laws to be identified as valid). Mac Cormic refined Hart's penumbra. Other critiques are Ronald Dworkin, John Finnis, and Joseph Raj in this perspective.

Historical School of Jurisprudential Thought does not mean knowing the history of law; it means explaining the evolutionary process of law, i.e. how law evolves. The historical school of legal thought came to prominence during the German debate over the proposed codification of German law. Friedrich Carl von Savigny in his famous book "On the Vocation of Our Age for Legislation and Jurisprudence" (1831) argued that Germany did not have a legal language that would support codification, because the traditions, customs and beliefs of the German people did not include a belief in a code. The Historicists believe that law originates with society, i.e., *volk giest and volk richt*.

Legal Realism or Realist School of Legal Thought, with some Scandinavian and American scholars, espouses that law should be understood and determined by the actual practices of courts, law officers, and police stations—law in reality—rather than the abstract rules and doctrines set forth in statutes or learned/scholastic treatises—law in books. It has had some affinities with sociology of law. The genesis of legal realism is that all law is made by human beings, and, thus, is subject to human foibles, frailties and imperfections. Justice Oliver Wendell Holmes, Jr., is the chief precursor as well as architects of American Legal Realism inasmuch as that "What the courts say in

4. H.L.A. Hart, The Concept of Law, 1961.

reality, there is nothing pretentious about it, is the law in the real sense".[5] Dean Roscoe Pound, Karl Llewellyn and Justice Benjamin N. Cardozo are other precursors of legal realism movement. Dean Roscoe Pound's "Law is social engineering" is acknowledged and renowned legal language of legal realism. Benjamin N. Cardozo asserts that judicial process unfolds "judge-made law as one of the existing realities of life".[6] This philosophy is a method along the line of logical progression or rule of analogy or the method of philosophy; along the line of historical development or the method of evolution; along the line of the custom of the community or the method of tradition; along the lines of justice, morals, and social welfare, the mores of the day or the method of sociology.[7] This is an intellectual passion for *elegantia juris*.[8] Article 142 of the Constitution of India enjoins judicial legislation as inclusive in powers inherent in the Supreme Court of India and compatible with constitutional permissibility, viz., judicial legislation is a step forward to fill in the voids or gaps caused by legislative vacuum, since Article 142 works as "flashing the flaming sword of its inspiration".[9]

With Dean Roscoe Pound's perception that "law is social engineering", the discipline of the sociology of law and legal sociology or an interdisciplinary approach within legal studies or interaction of law and society, and law and sociology or law as a social science or "the systematic, theoretical grounded, empirical study of law or heuristic study of law as a set of social practices or as an aspect of or field of social experience" has gained prominence as well as eminence in the legal pedagogy. More precisely, the sociology of law consists of various sociological approaches to the study of law in society, which empirically examine and theorize the interaction between law and legal institutions, on the one hand, and other non-legal or social institutions and social factors, on the other hand. Areas of socio-legal inquiry include the social development of legal institutions, forms of social control, legal regulation, the interaction between legal cultures (legal pluralism), the social construction of legal issues, legal profession, the socio-legal issues of social disorganisation, deviant behaviour, criminality, criminal psychology, re-socialisation and social

5. Justice Oliver Wendell Holmes, Jr., The Path of Law, 10, *Har. Law Rev.*
6. Benjamin N. Cardozo, The Nature of the Judicial Process, 1921.
7. *Ibid.*
8. *Ibid.*
9. Justice Vivian Bose, *Ram Jawaya Kapoor v. State of Punjab*, AIR 1955 SC 549.

reorganisation of criminals as well as victims of crimes, and the relationship between law and economics and law and social change. This, in brevity, may be called the functional approach to law or functional jurisprudential thought.

Natural law shows imperishable or immutable or inseparable relationship between law and morality. A succinct analysis of Western approaches and the literature to law and morality shows that law and morality or natural law are the older, which live not yesterday nor yet today, but stand for ever that has protean concept with a compendium term. Natural law or law and morality have had a chequered history of periods of forzen turbulences either acceptance or rejection or neglect of law and morality. This appears to be the suspicion of the thinkers about the expression natural law that has changed from one age to the next presenting varying or different profiles of ideas about natural law thus confounding it with confusions of incongruent theorems making it a riddle wrapped in mystery inside an enigma. A succinct scanning of the literature shows that natural law has had been the scorn of bitter circumstances and has had several deaths. This has occurred in the hands of those who have worked against natural law in favor of positive law by declaring the death of natural law wishing that it would "never rise again from its (grave) ashes." Yet natural law survives and still calls for discussion, because the "funeral orations for the natural law have been premature". Thus, natural law could neither be defaced nor defiled irrespective of the endeavourers to perceive the complete divorce of law from morals. It survives and sustains because of new enlightenment in the perceptions of law and morals interdependence and co-operations, which is a seamless web. What is natural law? The simple way to answer this ticklish question seems to give vent to: Natural law, in the background of it, means a tradition in morals; natural law is a law that it provides a name for the point of intersection between law and morals.[10] Natural law in the late antiquity was conceived as a set of innate rules, which the God engraved upon the heart of the human beings when He created mankind. Greek stoic philosophers had the speculation that a man who lived naturally was a man who lived by reason. This was the natural order contrary to contrived order (artificial or man-made). There was obviously superiority of natural order over contrived/artificial/man-made order. Natural order was indeed inherent and actual or potential. This speculation was the conjecture of nature, moral and human reasoning. Cicero's formulation of natural law is enjoined in *De Re Publica*:

10. A. Passerin D' Entreves, Natural Law, p. 116.

True law is right reason in agreement with Nature; it is of universal application, unchanging and everlasting. ... It is not a sin to try to alter this law, nor is it allowable to attempt to repeal any part of it, and it is impossible to abolish it entirely. ... God is the author of this law, its promulgator, and its enforcing judge.[11]

It discerns that laws which failed to conform to morals and reasons might be regarded as invalid. It also discerns that in Stoic view 'natural law meant in accordance with reason'. Thus, laws which were incompatible with reasons were invalid. Plato and Aristotle conceded that nature manifests a law or design by designing reasons, viz., mankind is governed by two laws: the law of nature and custom. That is, law if contradicts natural law is void and of no effect.

St. Thomas Aquinas in his distinguished work *Summa Theologiae* gives four distinct as well as distinguishing features of natural law, which seem to be the most comprehensive exposition of natural law that in unequivocal terms states that human posited law draws its power to bind from natural law, viz., participation of eternal law in rational creatures:

1. *Lex aeterna* (eternal law): Divine reason—known only to God. God's plan for the Universe. Man needs this law without which he would totally lack direction.
2. *Lex naturalis* (natural law): Participation of the eternal law in rational creatures discoverable by reason.
3. *Lex divina* (divine law): Revealed in the scriptures, viz., God's positive law for mankind.
4. *Lex humana* (humanly posited law): Supported by reason; enacted for the common good of human beings; necessary because *lex naturalis* cannot solve many day-to-day problems; and, people are selfish by nature; compulsion is required to force them to act reasonably.[12]

The modern philosophers as Thomas Hobbes, John Locke, Immanuel Kant, Fuller, Finnis have strived to give a rational theoretical frame for the State or Nation-State in their respective works encapsulating a de novo recognition to natural law.

---

11. Book 3, Chapter 22, Section 33; see also Brian Brix, A Dictionary of Legal Theory, 2004, pp. 142-44.
12. Summa Theologia, Part 2, 1st Part, questions 94, 96, articles 2-4; see also Anthony J. Lissa, Aquinas's Theory of Natural Law: An Analytic Reconstruction, 1996.

II. INDIAN PERCEPTION: CONCEPT OF *DHARMA*—LAW AND MORALITY

A. Dharma: Vision and Concept

Dharma is the *corpus juris* of Indian perception and vision of natural law or law and morality. *Dharma* is ubiquitous in Indian *Vedic/Indic/Hindu* philosophy. *Dharma* is "law", or "moral law", or "law and morality", or "natural law" by acceptance—*jus receptum*—which is believed to have been ordained by Divine Author; it is not a law as we understand it today.[13] With such pedigree of law, yet the idea of law figures seldom or at the remotest margins of Indian studies as a field of law, law and morality, and law and nature. The reasons are not far to seek. A modest attempt has been made to present the immutable relationship between law and morality as engraved in the concept of *Dharma* as follows:

- *Dharma* as law and morality is the legal heritage of traditions in morals. How these traditions have evolved? Where from these traditions come? Who is the inventor of these traditions? For whom such traditions were evolved? Who says what to whom for what purpose and under what circumstances? These basic questions have grappled the minds of thinkers from antiquity to date. Thinkers have devised the transcendental of law and morality into nature and artificial and contrived paradigms. Thus, making law and morality a riddle wrapped in mystery inside an enigma, because minimal insights into Dharma as law and morality. This riddle seems to be inasmuch as riding while saddling the artificial horse. Maximalists' perception is that there is a seamless web between Dharma and law and morality.
- Be that as it may, Dharma and law and morality traditions should not be construed as mere museums of different tools, instruments and mechanisms. Tools, instruments and mechanisms of Dharma and law and morality are far from theoretical speculations, rather those have rational humane approach to human good, human happiness, social utility, national relevance, and international coexistence.
- To have broader Insights into the perceptions and visions of *Dharma* as law and morality, one must have humane vibrations, rather than an old tired machine.

---

13. K.L. Bhatia, Concept of Dharma—*Corpus Juris* of Law and Morality—A Comparative Study of Legal Cosomology, 2010.

- Ensuring the welfare of the people is the quintessence of *Dhama* as law and morality that encompasses *Vidhi* [positive command], *Nishedha* (negative command], No *himsayet* [don't injure living beings], *Satyam Vada* [tell the truth], *Satyam Shivam Sundram* [only in truth lay the beauty of the system), *Yato Dharmastato Jaya* [where there is righteousness there is the victory and that is the concept of justice).
- This modest write up on the legal cosmology of *Dharma* is not to exotic either India for the West or the West for India, because both have had their own perceptions, visions, conceptions, methodologies, and techniques—sociologically and psychologically. I encapsulate—

  The East as East and the West as West
  Cradle the mind as mere concepts
  Simply because:
  The human soul knows no compass
  No geographical encapsulations
  The present and the future
  Hold the key
  We know reality is the thought
  Discovery of the thought is a challenge
  Present and future becomes a probe
  Delving into the mind-brain linkage
  As, Law and Nature and Law and Morality
  It helps flow of thought and flow of information
  In the colloquy
  Who are well informed?
  Those whose actions are sound
  Then whose actions are sound?
  Of those who are well informed
  This leaves us where we were
  This leads us where we are
  This tells us where we ought to be

B. Dharma: Law and Morals by Acceptance—*Jus Receptum*

- *Dharma* is ubiquitous in Indian *Vedic/Indic* philosophy. *Dharma* is law and moral law by acceptance—*jus receptum*—which is believed to have been ordained by Divine Author; it is not "law" as we understand it today. It is corpus juris of scholastic moral and legal traditions as well as cultural ethos. Therefore, *Dharma* is magnum opus of *Vedas, Upanishads, Ritis, Nitis, Smritis, Dharmsastras, Mimansas*, *Ramayana,*

Mahabharata, Bhagavad Gita, and scholastic writings who devoutedly not only vouch for but describe the gigantic aspects of practical law in several periods of *Indic/Vedic* history.

Dharma is solicitous of noble birth origins Invented by the Great Creator—God—readied in three stages of *Vedic* philosophy:

Three manifestations—*Trimurti/Triumvirate—Satyam, Shivam, Sundram* of one God *[Ekam svadipra bahuda vadantij,* disseminated and assimilated by the great sages, saints, seers, and mystics through millennia after millennia. Therefore, *Dharma* as Law and Morals is entrenched and as such immutable since it is heritage stronger than governments and kings, and rulers and kings of modern elected democracy.

Succinctly, *Dharma* as law and morality has had been the scorn of bitter circumstances and has had several deaths. This has occurred in the hands of those who have worked against it by declaring its death wishing that it would never rise again from its ashes/grave. Yet *Dharma* law and morality survives and still calls for discussion, because the "funeral orations for *Dharma* law and morality have been premature".

- *Dharma* as legal science and moral science is not without reasoning as well as rationality; it is not without conscience and conscientious reasoning; it is not purely religious-cosmetic; it is not closed-minded system of legal reasoning leading the people to say that *Dharma* as legal and moral science is formalistic, pedantic or simply non-workable. Had it been so, how it could be possible that five utmost foolish sons of a king could be made intelligent in law, ethics, values, diplomacy, kingdom management and good governance, developing sustainability, promoting human dignity for human good as well as human happiness.
- *Dharma* relates to the relationship between law and human beings, human conduct and human behaviour.
- *Dharma* is the Legal Cosmology scientifically of legal and moral science. It may be termed as a guide to the law-conceivers as well as law-makers. It deals with all natural, legal, moral, and ethical duties and obligations, and rights.
- *Dharma* is theoretically beautiful and heuristically practical method of societal ordering through the sanction or threat or force of *Danda* [punishment, sanction, force], ruler's or justice dispenser's or *Nayaya Devta's* [Goddess of Justice], who is not blindfolded, punishing rod.

- *Dharmo rakhshati rakhshita:* If you respect or protect *Dharma* [law, morals, duty, obligation], *Dharma* [law] protects you; if you disrespect or disobey *Dharma* [law], *Dharma* [law] will not only scorn at you but destroy you, because its rod will not spare you.
- *Dharme Sarvam Prathishtam: Law is the foundation of the universe.*
- *Vasudev Kutumbkam and Sarva Dharma Sambhav:* The whole universe is one family.
- It aspires *Sarve Bhavantu Sukhina Sarve Santu Niramaya...:* Aspiring the human good, human happiness, human dignity and human flourishing as well as flourishing of all creatures universally equally; its aspiration is for the whole mankind universally. This is the inbuilt concept of the universality of *Dharma.*

C. *Dharma—Dhri*—Modules

- The expression *Dharma* has no parallel either in English vocabulary or any other vocabulary.
- *Dhorma* is *mtmoria technica* of Law+Morals+Ethlcs+ Actions+Justice and taken together constitute Natural Law or Law and Morality.

  This combines the knowledge and interpretation of different times and continued to flourish from millennia after millennia entrenched as Memory *[smriti* that follows to hold and support *Sruti* from extinction], *Shabad* [the script, the language, the expression, the pedagogy] that supports perceptual knowledge *[Praman and Anuman]* for posterity *[Parampara],* dissemination and assimilation of knowledge *[Vidyytr,* deriving from Memory that is a form of perception] in search of true knowledge [*Hetu*: sign: Aim: Goal: Inquisitiveness] to reserve and preserve it *[Sanskara].*
- *Dharma* is the essence of Law and Morals approach that is entrenched in *Vedic* knowledge, which is universal—*aarayya*—to all human beings to follow with continuity as a duty as well as obligation for the full development of a universal aspect of human nature to promote right action with a developed intellect, clear mind, balanced emotions, and full perceptions.
- *Dharma—Dhri*—Modules;
- The conceptual relationship between law and Morality may be presented as follows:

(i) Module I

- Etymologically, *Dharma* is derived from the root *Dhri: Dharma Dharayati Dhartam* and this infallible legal cosmology is indicated in Rigveda: *ato dharmani dharayam* that spells its value *Dharme, viz.*, to uphold, to hold together, to support: *Dharyate iti.*
- To sustain [sustainabllity]
- To conserve [soil conservation against erosion and protecting from environmental erosion, global warming]
- To retain [values]
- To preserve [cultural heritage and values]
- To observe and to promote [human good, well-being of human beings, human happiness, human dignity, human rights, human flourishing]
- To develop [relationship between Law and Nature, and Law and Morality]

  This, in brevity, is the *corpus juris.* of Law and Morality of *Dharma.*
- It is the creation of the world order [Cosmos] against chaotic disorder—insecure, unstable and shaky. This creative action is "law" both the "eternal law" of nature/Creator/God as also the "moral law" governing mankind.
- In the *Vedic lexicon* the term *Dharma* has been used 63 times in *Rigveda;* it occurs 13 times in *Atharvaveda;* it is found in 22 passages in *Yajurveda;* it invariably is used in 9 passages in *Upanishads.*

(ii) Module II

- *Dharma:* God The supreme Divine
- His Divinity
- His Nature and His Nature of Laws
- His Morals and His Moral Laws

  To regulate the Universe: Cosmos: the World Order against chaotic disorder
- His reasoning and Rationality

(iii) Module III

- *Dharma*
- Duty

  – Obligation

  – On His Creatures: People, Society, State, Nation State: Rules

  – *Karma*

- **Action *Prescribed for human beings to follow***

(iv) Module IV

- *Dharma*
- Law
- Divine Law
- Universality and rationality:
  Rajdharma
  Rajayadharma
  Rajsasana
  Rajayasastra
- True knowledge
- Memory: → External → Internal
- Perpetual knowledge: → Perceptions, Visions
- *Hetu:* → Object, aim goal, purpose → Reasoning, Retaining, and Preserving → *Sruti* in *Smriti*, Memory, *Shabad* → Script, language, expression, pedagogy
- *Vedas*, *Puranas*, *Upanishads*, *Ritis*, *Nitis*, *Smritis*, *Mimansas*, *Nimbadhas*, *Dharmsastras*, *Ramayana*, *Mahabharata*, *Bhagavad Gita.*

(v) Module V

- *Dharma:* Manifestations and Strategies
- Rule of Law to serve Rule of Life
- To eradicate/eliminate administrative deviance/recidivism for achieving sustainable governance

(vi) Module VI

- *Dharma:* Free flow of knowledge and Information: *aa no bhadhra kratvo yantu visvatah*
- Transparency and accountability
  Good/sustainable governance/management

D. *Dharma*: An Evolution of Law and Morality

The essence of *Dharma* as law and morality, is as follows:

"*Dharma as Law and Morality or Natural law is a law and a set of such rules that regulate human conduct and human conduct depends upon human behaviour, which is controlled by psychogenic and sociogenic influences*".

"*Dharma is the law conceptually the relationship of Law, Life and Morality [LLM]. The copyright of Dharma belongs to the Creator God*

Who Himself disseminated to the human beings to assimilate it for follow-up action with Nayaya [Justice] and Yukti [natural reason, logic, rationality and equity]".

E. Misunderstanding and Misconceptions about Dharma

Teaching and learning of *Dharma* as a study of law and morality has remained confined to philosophy and humanity disciplines, and has seldom been a part of legal studies in the Indian Universities. May be, due to the ubiquitous weigh the common law manifestations have in the Indian legal fraternity.

The British administrators did not accord recognition to *Vedic* concept of *Dharma* as law and morality, because they had intended to introduce their own common law in India to advance their own interests in India. British judges in India needed access to the original legal texts of India to implement the British policy of "administering native law/personal law to the natives, and also common law to the natives", and so were born a "well-intentioned as well as calculated misunderstanding".

Though there may have been its eclipse due to the stifling of time and tide, yet we have to strive extremely hard for its transformation for the present as well as future. Otherwise, we shall be wrestling with the proverbial phrase like perfect past, imperfect present, and indefinite future.

F. *Dharma* and *Danda*

Dharma has a broader connotation. It means the whole gamut of law, justice, morals, ethics, manners, and customs. It ordains an ordered social hierarchy with duties, obligations and responsibilities as first priority living harmoniously as well as happily with psychological and sociological state of affairs within the framework of *Dharma.*

Dharma is the treasure house of values+ethics+morals+law+ action+duties+obligations and together constitutes the "science of law", life and literature as well as the repository of civil society that man seeks to have civility.

- It refers to the underlying order in nature, and also signifies the way things are.
- Legally, morally, and ethically, *Dharma* means 'right way of living' and 'proper conduct'.
- *Dharme sattyam prathishitam:*
  Righteousness is paramount in the world and on righteousness is truth founded.

Ancient Indian literature unequivocally demonstrates the juristic-moral correlations of *Dharma,* and it shall be absurdity to supersede it by the vocabulary of rituals, cultic, communual, religious, and unscientific rhetoric.

* There is close affiliation between *Dharma* and law and morals, such as *Dharma* of rulers, *Dharma* of ruled, *Dharma* in familial as well as filial relationship, *Dharma* in society, and *Dharma* of others.
* *Dharma* as law is conceived to speak of justice and order with perpetual effects that produce results in both intermediate and ultimate goods for the performer and society.
* ***Vidhi Jnapakahetu:***

  Dharma as law expresses in the form of heuristically ascertainable rules that is the cause of knowing *Dharma* realistically, rather than confining to mere arm chair speculations.
* This view unfolds that just ends are reached by just means.

  This also unfolds that law is discerned through an investigation of empirical sources, and this is the most scientific way of comprehending *Dharma* as law.

■ ***Danda and Prayascitta:***

Dharma as law provides for correct or proper procedure to take into account inevitability of mistakes, intentional or unintentional, for effective mode of action both punishment and penances that ameliorate or rectify legal mistakes or transgressions.

■ ***Vyavahara, Samadehanir, Nayayahetu:***

Dharma as law is also concerned with legal procedure, the object of which is truth, how to eliminate doubts and adjudicate conflicts over differing claims to be right or just or the cause of making judgment in cases of doubts about *Dharma.*

■ ***Sastravirudhacara, dosa*:**

Transgression of *Dharma* as law is crime, violent crime, recidivism, delinquent, and legal transgression that produces sin/wrong.

It discerns that *Dharma* as law is conceived inasmuch as inquisitive as jurisprudence of the training and discipline of lawyers, judges, and thinkers in how to think legally reasonably as well as rationally,

Law goes with *Dharma* and similarly Influences other conceptions, and is a legal way or lawful manner to put it into practice or actions or to give actions meaning.

***Dharmo vishvasaya jagatah pratishtha, loke dharmishthampraja upsarpanti, dharme sarvam prathishtham*:**

Dharma constitutes the foundation of all affairs in the world; people respect one who adheres to *Dharma. Dharma* insulates man against sinful [wrongful] thoughts and actions. Law [*Dharma*] is the foundation of the universe.

Anger [*krodha*], passion [*moha*], greed [*lobha*). Infatuation [*mada*], and enmity [*matsarya*] are the natural impulses recognized enemies of man and if allowed to act like unruly horse may instigate him to entertain evil thoughts resulting in deviant as well as recidivist actions causing civil and criminal injuries to others.

Dharma is the king of kings. Kings/rulers, in/of any system, are subordinate to *Dharma* law, to the Rule of Law, and then alone Rule of Law becomes the Rule of Life.

Vyavahara: It is secular law and procedural law.

Caritra: It is customary law.

Rajasasana: It is a law for good/sustainable governance/ management, transparency as well as accountability.

Kuladharma: It has been conceived to governing family.

Deshdharma: It has been conceived to governing the State.

Arajaka: It is a code of law to restore conditions of order, law, justice, and security to prevent anarchy for the protection of all in the world.

This could be achieved by the State with its principles of statecraft as its protecting branches, with its four beautiful flowers of *Sama* [conciliation), *dana* [concession], *danda* [force, punishment, sanction], and *bheda* [dissension], and its three fruits of *Dharma, artha, and kama* [law, social, economic welfare], which encapsulate the entrenched concept of access to justice and distributive justice, *viz*., law, morals, justice—economic, social, political, human dignity, fraternity, and integrity.

"Namo'stu rajyarksaya sadgunyaya prasakhine, samadi charupuspaya trivarga phaldayine:

"Let us bow to the State for the sake of *dharma* and *artha*—social and economic well-being—which may be regarded as the aims of the State."

- It seems that *Dharma* as law and constitutional law constitutes constitutional functions of the State and secures social, economic, and political justice, welfare and well-being, as the objects/aims/ideals of the State.

Arajake hi lokesmin sarvo vidrute bhayat, raksarthamasya* sarvasya, *rajanamasrjat prabhu:

Good/sustainable governance alone prevents anarchy, and enables one to enjoy his/her life and property.

- It discerns that *Dharma* as law, justice, morals, legal and moral duties has been founded on the conceptual framework of "right" and "wrong", and, therefore, all laws being deemed to be grounded in *Dharma* or law and moral duties which is a law throughout ancient Indian literature and perceptions thereby.
- *Dharma* is known as *purushartha,* viz., fair approach to take righteous action.
- It is conceptually law, morals, duty *[kartavya],* actions and activity *karma and pravriti, Varna shramadharma* [nothing to do with castes because it is not included in *varna; varna* means laws of four patterns of life or four social orders], justice *[Nayaya],* rules of conduct, code of conduct, mores, customs, religio-legal-ethical code of rationality *[vayavahara],* logic and reasoning *[Yukati],* and as such *Dharma* surely serves the stabilisation of society.
- Justice has not been identified with blind justice as a blind guide to the solution of disputes because Indian Goddess of Justice is not blindfolded; rule-of-thumb decisions have been avoided, and mutual adjustments favoured as court practices [*Dharma vayavahara*], which in the modern legal language is called 'mediation', 'conciliation', and 'arbitration'.

Sarvo dandajito loko, duriabho hi sucimara, dandasya hi bhayat sarvain, jagad bhgaya kalpate:

Danda or punishment or sanction or force behind the State is the most valuable device for the benefit of mankind.

Law without the authority of *Dharma and Danda* is impotent that shall lead to *matsyanayaya* where big fish swallows the small fish. It may be submitted that the condition of law without *Dharma, Morals, and Danda* shall be the same as that of a person/ruler/king who is voluptuous, partial and deceitful.

Danda sashist praja sarva danda aivbhirakshati, danda supteshu jagriti danda dharmam vidurbudha:

Danda keeps awake when all are sleeping, *viz.*, it is ever vigilant.

With its all pervading force keeps thieves, criminals away and hence *Danda* is *Dharma.* It prevents lawlessness [*arajakata*].

Danda sanrakshate dharmam tathaivartham janadhtp, kamam sanrakshate dandistrivago dand ucayate:

Punishment or fear of punishment protects *Dharma, artha and kama* [the law, the lawful wealth and lawful desires of human beings].

Law and Morality: A Remaking for Rehabilitation:

The debate on *Dharma* and law and morality and its insights is illustrative of inconclusive discussion.

However, in the backdrop of the emergence of new constitutional and legal culture, it is in need of new approach.

The concepts enshrined in constitutional vocabulary like legality, reasonableness, equality before the law and equal protection of the laws, human dignity, the rule of law, the rule of law to serve the rule of life, the legal order, judicial activism, judicial creativity, judicial innovation, judicial craftsmanship, justice, access to justice, distributive justice, disadvantaged/marginalized/neglected/underserved segments of the society, aboriginals, minority, seem to be very near or like or actually assimilable to law and morality or *Dharma* expressions.

The above terms seem to be value expressions and rarely as well as insufficiently investigated by socio-legal eagles heuristically and empirically with social science research methodologies nevertheless do not lay far away from the eternal and internal morality, and in this area law and morality of *Dharma* can play its part.

It is submitted that *Dharma* is the epitome of whole legal matter entailing all aspects of law that sensitizes the relationship of law and morality which in legal cosmology is the conceptual relationship between law and morality.

Dharma is born of the belief that law and morality is ingrained in it and has its roots and its analog in traditional Language of Law, Life, Literature, Morals, Ethics, Actions, Justice, Right and Wrong, that is about the requisites of morality, viz., "the good life". Strip away these terms, plumb the inarticulate debates stating problems, clarifying questions, determining facts, interpreting language, formulating and analyzing concepts, perceptions, and visions, and indecisive conclusions concerning justice delivery system.

Thus, positive law, in fact, cannot survive without a "therapy" of *Dharma* Law and Morality.

III. WESTERN PERCEPTION

Analytical school of thought, by contrast to natural law, expounded by legal positivists like Bentham, Austin, Hans Kelsen, H.L.A. Hart, Joseph Raj, etc., holds that there is no inherent or necessary connection between the validity conditions of law and ethics and morality or there is no berth for morality in the domain of law and that the force of law comes from some basic social facts although legal positivists differ on what those facts are. In legal positivism, law is seen as being conceptually separate from moral and ethical values, and it simply sees the law as being posited by law-makers, who are humans. The positivist argument is solely about the nature of law as a human institution. Analytical or 'Clarificatory School of Thought' rejected natural law's fusing of what law is and what it ought to be. David Hume made the famous is-ought distinction in the famous words that by analysis and clarifying the way the world is must be treated as a strictly separate question to normative and evaluative ought questions. The most fascinating as well as chilling questions of analytical jurisprudential thoughts are: What are laws?; What is the law?; What is the relationship between law and power/society?; and What is the relationship between law and morality? Legal positivists through their legal positivism perspectives assert that law is something that is posited. Law is determined by social facts or sources. Law is nothing more than a set of rules to provide order and governance of society. In the perception of legal positivists, morals have no place in the domain of law. Both are distinct from each other and having no correlations. Jermy Bentham was one of the earliest legal positivists who were the staunch supporter and propagator of "utilitarian" concept of law. He advocated utilitarian concept of law through 'pleasure' and 'pain' perspectives that the chief purpose of law was the greatest happiness of the greatest number of people with least pain. John Austin, a student of Bentham, and a Professor of Jurisprudence at University of London, popularized Bentham's utilitarianism by asserting, law is "commands, backed by threat of sanctions, from a sovereign, to whom people have a habit of obedience". His theory is also called 'imperative theory of law' because of the presence of an element of command. However, the contemporary legal positivists have derecognized and denounced Austin's oversimplification utilitarian answer to 'what is law'? Hans Kelsen, a 20th century jurist of Civil Law systems of Europe and Latin America and less influenced by common law countries, contends, in his Pure Theory of Law, that the abidingness of legal norms to norms to Grundnorm (Constitution), their specifically legal character, can be understood without tracing ultimately to some superhuman source such as God, personified Nature or of great importance in his time—a personified State of Nation. H.L.A. Hart, a pivotal writer and a Professor of Jurisprudence at Oxford University, argued by rejecting Kelsen's normative thesis that the law should be understood as a system of social rules. Hart as a positivist insisted on the importance of the separation of law from morality. He rejected the "command theory" of Austin and asserted that law comprises rules. Hart said, rules are divided into primary rules (rules of conduct or duty-imposing rules) and secondary rules (rules addressed to officials to administer primary rules or power-imposing rules). Primary rules grant rights or impose legal obligations upon the citizens, e.g. criminal law consists of primary rules. Secondary rules stipulate how primary rules are fromed and validated, e.g. the rules that stipulate how Parliament is composed and how it enacts legislation are secondary rules. Secondary rules are divided into rules of adjudication (to resolve legal disputes), rules of change (allowing laws to be varied) and the rules of recognition (allowing laws to be identified as valid). Mac Cormic refined Hart's penumbra. Other critiques are Ronald Dworkin, John Finnis, and Joseph Raj in this perspective.

Historical School of Jurisprudential Thought does not mean knowing the history of law; it means explaining the evolutionary process of law, i.e. how law evolves. The historical school of legal thought came to prominence during the German debate over the proposed codification of German law. Friedrich Carl von Savigny in his famous book "On the Vocation of Our Age for Legislation and Jurisprudence" (1831) argued that Germany did not have a legal language that would support codification, because the traditions, customs and beliefs of the German people did not include a belief in a code. The Historicists believe that law originates with society, i.e., volk giest and volk richt.

Legal Realism or Realist School of Legal Thought, with some Scandinavian and American scholars, espouses that law should be understood and determined by the actual practices of courts, law officers, and police stations—law in reality—rather than the abstract rules and doctrines set forth in statutes or learned/scholastic treatises—law in books. It has had some affinities with sociology of law. The genesis of legal realism is that all law is made by human beings, and, thus, is subject to human foibles, frailties and imperfections. Justice Oliver Wendell Holmes, Jr., is the chief precursor as well as architects of American Legal Realism inasmuch as that "What the courts say in reality, there is nothing pretentious about it, is the law in the real sense". Dean Roscoe Pound, Karl Llewellyn and Justice Benjamin N. Cardozo are other precursors of legal realism movement. Dean Roscoe Pound's "Law is social engineering" is acknowledged and renowned legal language of legal realism. Benjamin N. Cardozo asserts that judicial process unfolds "judge-made law as one of the existing realities of life". This philosophy is a method along the line of logical progression or rule of analogy or the method of philosophy; along the line of historical development or the method of evolution; along the line of the custom of the community or the method of tradition; along the lines of justice, morals, and social welfare, the mores of the day or the method of sociology. This is an intellectual passion for elegantia juris. Article 142 of the Constitution of India enjoins judicial legislation as inclusive in powers inherent in the Supreme Court of India and compatible with constitutional permissibility, viz., judicial legislation is a step forward to fill in the voids or gaps caused by legislative vacuum, since Article 142 works as "flashing the flaming sword of its inspiration".

With Dean Roscoe Pound's perception that "law is social engineering", the discipline of the sociology of law and legal sociology or an interdisciplinary approach within legal studies or interaction of law society and law and sociology or law as a social science or "the systematic, theoretical grounded, empirical study of law or heuristic study of law as a set of social practices or as an aspect of or field of social experience" has gained prominence as well as eminence in the legal pedagogy. More precisely, the sociology of law consists of various sociological approaches to the study of law in society, which empirically examine and theorize the interaction between law and legal institutions, on the one hand, and other non-legal or social institutions and social factors, on the other hand. Areas of socio-legal inquiry include the social development of legal institutions, forms of social control, legal regulation, the interaction between legal cultures (legal pluralism), the social construction of legal issues, legal profession, the socio-legal issues of social disorganisation, deviant behaviour, criminality, criminal psychology, re-socialisation and social reorganisation of criminals as well as victims of crimes, and the relationship between law and economics and law and social change. This, in brevity, may be called the functional approach to law or functional jurisprudential thought.

Chapter IV

CLASSIFICATION OF LAW

Broadly speaking law may be classified as Public Law and Private Law, which includes Civil Law, Criminal Law, Familial Relation Laws, Special Laws such as Intellectual Property Law, Energy and Power Laws or POISE Laws, i.e., Power, Oil and Natural Gas, Infrastructure, Safety and Energy, Competition Law, Arbitration, Mediation and Conciliation (Law pertaining to Arbitral Process), etc. Public law involves relationship between State (sovereign) and State (sovereign), and State and Individual. It involves a conviviality between individual and State when State action affects rights and Fundamental/Basic Rights of individuals.

I. PRIVATE LAW

The Province of private law is the adjustment of relations between person and person whereas the public law deals with relationship between person and the State. In case of private law, the parties to a case may either be natural or artificial persons and the State only acts as an arbiter through its courts. The laws of property, contracts, corporations, torts, trusts, etc. are instances of private law. Private law or civil law as some scholars call it (not in the sense of civil law system) is that branch of law which deals relationship between private individuals, viz., *res* or subject matter is private law and *lis inter-partes* or dispute or conflict between parties to the litigation. *Lis inter-partes* may involve *res* under mercantile law, commercial law, corporate law—contract law, partnership law, sale of goods law, company law, transfer of property law, easement law, trust law, sale law, lease law, tenancy law, consumer protection law, estate law, real estate law, etc. These laws involve contractual relationship, ownership issues, and possession issues; these laws may also involve issues in the nature of compensation and compensatory costs. Civil procedure code and evidence law take care of procedural niceties and angularities.

II. PUBLIC LAW

Public law seeks to regulate the activities of the State. The important sub-divisions of Public law are: (1) Constitutional law, and (2) Administrative law. Broadly speaking, public law deals with the rights and obligations of the State towards its citizens and *vice versa.* The criminal justice system in India encapsulates the fundamentals of substantive criminal law and procedural criminal law. Criminal law is a law that culls out the conceptual as well as definitional aspects of offences having the elements of deviance, *mens rea*, guilty mind, guilty intention, malice, accomplice, conspiracy and criminality. Conspiracy thou art hatched in secrecy and executed in darkness. Secrecy and suspicion have no shore to reach except committing crimes of any magnitude. Because, crime is a crime may be heinous or non-heinous. Offences are crimes against the State. State is meant to maintain law and order in the society. It is the duty of the State to ensure peace in the environ of the system and peaceful life of the people so that they enjoy the life and liberty with dignity.

A. Constitution of India

Constitution of India is a branch of public law. It is our National heritage. Constitution of India is the Soul of our country India that is Bharat—Union of States. It is the Supreme Law of the land of India. The Constitution of India is not static law, because a static law is like a dead wood that makes the system and its structure rigid and inflexible inasmuch as dead wood. It is a living organism; it is dynamic and *receptum* of a living thought and may vary greatly, without losing its color, content and basic sacrosanct character, according to the circumstances and the felt necessities of time in which it is used. Our Supreme Court has not only been interpreting it, but expounding the constitution inasmuch as espounding keeping it out of legalese and legal archaisms. Our Constitution is based on two schools of thought: One, that it is a beautiful patchwork, an ably conceived and drafted document, showing creative, if not an original approach to the nation's constitutional needs, we cannot justly doubt.[1] And, second, that the Indian Constitution, though Euro-American in appearance, is native in its spirit.[2] Be that as it may, we know that our patchwork heritage is our strength, not a weakness, because, though being far from perfection, it has withstood unity in diversity, sustaining diversified democracy rooted in constitutional culture, constitutional morality, constitutional politics embedded in equality as well as rule of law. Therefore, to save the Constitution of India from being defaced and defiled, we need "a set of honest men who control it and operated it having the interest of the country before them".[3]

1. Preamble

Our Constitution's Spirit is the Preamble, which is the Backbone of our Constitution[4]. We the People of India have constituted India into Sovereign, Socialist, Secular, Democratic, Republic; to promote Justice—social, economic, political; Equality—status and opportunity; Freedom—thought, faith, belief, worship; Fraternity; assuring the Dignity of the individual and Unity and Integrity of Nation. We the People of India created India that is *Bharat*, which shall be the Union of States, thus a unique type of federalism, which evolves a synergetic comity of federalism that permeates rule of law and rule of life to flourish together with the least possibility of seceding any part of its territory.[5] State ensures the promotion, observance and development of the fundamental and human rights of the individual-citizens with human **dignity**.[6] State actions must be just, fair and reasonable, and must not be discriminatory, arbitrary, fanciful and whimsy. However, State's Affirmative Action is a permissible gesture of "Protective Discrimination" or "Compensatory Discrimination" or "Permissible

---

1. Graville Austin, The Indian Constitution, A Cornerstone of a Nation, 1996, pp. 327-28.
2. M.P. Singh, The Constitution of India: Symbol of Unity in Diversity, Year Book of Public Law (Max-Planck Institute, Germany), Vol. 53, 2005, pp. 649-86.
3. Dr. Rajendra Prasad, Chairman of the Constituent Assembly of India and the First President of India, Concluding Speech in the Constituent Assembly of India, CAD, Vol. VII, pp. 31-44; B. Shiva Rao, Framing of India's Constitution, Vol. IV, p. 436
4. See Justice R.C. Lahoti, Preamble The Spirit and Backbone of the Constitution of India, 2004.
5. Articles 1-4 of the Constitution of India.
6. Articles 5-11 and Articles 12-35 of the Constitution of India; Article 35-A in relation to J&K vide Constitutional (Application to J&K) Order, 1954.

Discrimination" in favour of disadvantaged or neglected or marginalized or poor or disabled or neglected or underserved segments of the Indian society, viz., SCs, STs, OBCs/SEBCs, women, children. We the People of India also promise to achieve social rights, which are in the nature of directives to the State to formulate its policies in such a way that these social rights are translated into reality.[7] Over the years, the Indian State's policies have strived to secure these social rights to the sustainability of common man. The Supreme Court of India has adopted a wider approach in the implementation of social rights in the progressive language that denial of social rights amounts to denial of right to life and personal liberty in terms of Article 21. Thus, the Apex Court of the country has successfully bridged the gap between Fundamental Rights and Social Rights. If Fundamental Rights come in the way of Social Rights, Fundamental Rights shall give way to Social Rights so that common man of India feels that courts are not ajar to have access to justice.

2. Fundamental Duties

Fundamental Duties are cast upon the citizens of India to propel their energies which protect and honor symbols of National heritage.[8]

3. Fundamental Rights

Fundamental Rights, Social Rights and Fundamental Duties together make the edifice of the Constitution culture, Constitution values, Constitution morality, and Constitution politics. Together, it is a well-knit edifice of perambulatory philosophy translated in other provisions of the constitution that speaks about jural and conceptual correlations of fundamentals of constitutional law of India.

4. Forms of the Constitution

For the form of the Constitution of India, form of the Government at the Centre and the States, distribution of powers, the Indian Judiciary, etc., the students are advised to see Chapter on Constitutional aspects of legal method, under the title: "Constitution of India —The Genesis", that shall provide deep insights into the making of the Constitution, its adoption, its enforcement, and its working with the constitutional democracy.

---

7. Articles 36-51 of the Constitution of India
8. Article 51-A of the Constitution of India.

B. Administrative Law

Administrative Law is another branch of public law. Administrative law precisely and concisely is the law of administration. But, this is an old concept of administrative law which was conceived in early twentieth century when the societies progressively moved from *laissez faire* to social welfare. Social welfare State continues in twenty-first century, too. But with the dawn of free economic market with the blending of privatization and globalization, and interdependence, the new concepts of regulatory authorities/commissions have, of course, brought in new perceptions of administrative process. A new power structure brings inroads of anew decision-making process culture. Several events in India and abroad such as militancy, terrorism, attack on the World Trade Centre of September 11, 2001, attack in Mumbai of November 26, 2008 have dramatically not only affected but diametrically changed the landscape of administrative law.[9] The passages of TADA, POTA, MCOCA, etc. have led to concomitant changes in the structure and nature of administrative branch of the government. In addition, economic liberalization as well as privatization and the events of Enron, Satyam and 2G spectrum like scams and scandals have led to financial irregularities, which have not only led to substantial changes in financial and securities regulation and enforcement, but also led to the establishment of (Ombudsman) Financial Regulatory Bodies in India through SEBI and Competition Law thus tremendously changing the nature of relationship between private company and the government thereby effectively overhauling the gamut of the nature and scope of administrative process in India.

Besides, India has a complex governmental framework of Regulatory Authorities such as Petroleum, Oil and Gas, Telecommunication, Electricity, Insurance, Pension, Airport, Reserve Bank, Shipping, Foreign Trade, Excise and Customs, Taxation, Information, Competition, etc. governed by a variety of ministries have replaced the concept of traditional authority of administrative agencies by the introduction of the perceptions of "Information, Investigation and Disclosure", and as such the dimensions of expanding horizons of administrative process in India. This unequivocally reflects the emergence of the concept of "Regulatory Management, i.e., Learning to live with the Regulatory State", viz., a new dimension in the Indian

---

9. See Bernard Schwartz, *et. al.*, Administrative Law A Case Book, 6th Ed., 2006; Aman, Jr., Democracy and the Need for a New Administrative Law, 49 UCLA, L. Rev., 1687 (2007); K.C. Davis, Administrative Law Treatise; Administrative Law A Text Book.

Administrative Law and its process.

New Legal Glossary and Vocabulary of Regulatory Authorities' Laws contain new items related to the changes in thinking about the distinction between legislative and non-legislative rules and as such developing afresh law language of administrative process which is a milestone in the dissemination of perceptions and assimilation of vision of New Administrative Order plus the evolution of new administrative process.

Thus, the purpose of administrative law with the birth of new power structure of the administration makes inroads to have deep insights in this interlock, which, of course, is a new dimension of administrative process in India. The primary purpose of administrative law is to regulate administrative deviance by control mechanism. This unequivocally shows the natural reflection of growing concern with the "procedural aspects of administrative action" which is the recent development of the nature of administrative process, and may be reflected as follows:

1. The powers vested in the Administrative Regulatory Authorities;
2. The requirement imposed by law upon the exercise of such powers;
3. The procedure followed by such Regulatory Authorities in their decision-making process or administrative action process; and
4. The remedies against unlawful administrative action by judicial process.

It clearly seems that regulatory authorities' action can include rule-making, adjudication/decision-making process, and the enforcement of a specific regulatory agenda. As a body of public law, administrative law, therefore, deals with the decision-making process of administrative wings of government, viz., administrative tribunals, administrative boards/bodies/commissions, regulatory authorities/ boards/commissions as a part of national regulatory policy in areas like police law, international trade law, international tax law regulated vide OECDMC (Organization for Economic Co-operation and Development Model Convention), UNMC (United Nations Model Convention), etc., manufacturing, environment protection, taxation, customs, broadcasting, telecommunication, competition, transport, infrastructure, etc. In this process, the horizons of law and legislatives have expanded, which have created more and more government/administrative authorities to regulate the increasingly complex social, economic and political spheres of human interactions, and as such the horizons of administrative law and administrative process have expanded. Taxation decisions are the decisions based on administrative law, which are mostly contested in courts challenging the incompatibility of administrative process. The administrative process involves administrative action and administrative decision-making process which is largely controlled by governmental bodies/agencies/regulatory authorities reviewed by a court under the principle of judicial review. Judicial review is different from an appeal. Judicial review is the basic feature of the Constitution, and is a Constitutional guaranteed power of the Apex Court of India or High Courts to pass appropriate writs. This power is fundamental to the power of judicial review and a significant aspect of the independent judiciary. Judicial review is based upon due process (USA)[10] or fundamental justice (Canada) or processual justice (India) or fairness in decision-making process, viz., justly, fairly, and reasonably (India), i.e. rules of natural justice aim at securing justice or to prevent miscarriage of justice (no one shall be a judge in his own cause—*nemo debet esse judex propria causa sua*; no decision shall be given against a party without affording him a reasonable hearing—*audi alteram partam*; and fair hearing must be held in good faith without bias, arbitrarily and unreasonably, viz., hearing must be held justly, fairly and reasonably)[11] or legitimate expectation and proportionality (India). [12]

C. Public International Law

Public International Law as a branch of public law governs the relations between Sovereign States/Countries/Nations, and determines their mutual rights and obligations. It is inter-nation relationship based on international agreements called treaties and general international law. Public international law is a body of law comprising the principles and rules of conduct of the sovereign States/Nations feel themselves bound to observe and, therefore, commonly observe in their inter-relationships. This is international synergetic comity. Besides Nation States, individuals to some extent may also be the subjects of the rights conferred and duties/obligations imposed by public international law.[13]

10. Now extended and applied in India under *Maneka Gandhi v. Union of India*, AIR 1978 SC 578 and aftermath.
11. *Ibid.*
12. See K.L. Bhatia, Judicial Activism and Judicial Review, 1997.
13. See Robert Jennings and Arthur Watts, Oppenheim's International Law, 9th Ed., 1992; J.G. Starke, Introduction to International Law, 10th Ed., 1989.

International conventions establishing rules expressly recognized by States, international custom, as evidence of a general practice accepted as law, the general principles of law recognized by civilized nations, and certain judicial decisions and legal teachings are the sources of public international law as per Article 38(1) of the Statute of the International Court of Justice. Customary international law refers to the international practice of States. Customary laws may or may not be codified through treaties. Customary international law is based on the common view of States on certain matters along with the belief that it is obligatory. However, "the practice of States in this context embraces not only their external conduct with each other, but it is also evidenced by such internal matters as their domestic legislation, judicial decisions, diplomatic dispatches, internal government memoranda, and ministerial statements in parliament and elsewhere.[14]

In international law arena, new and fascinating areas International Trade and International Economic Law, and International Tax Law and Negotiations have emerged. International Trade and International Economic Law are linked inasmuch as International Trade and International Peace are inextricably linked.[15] International tax law refers to the principles derived from public international law and deals with inter-nation transactions in trade, commerce and business and tax conflicts involving cross-border transactions. In an area which involves international transactions in the form of trade, commerce and business and capital investments, the unilateral efforts taken by one country to attract foreign investments can hardly be enough and satisfactory in an age of free economic market with the blend of privatization and globalization. This is due to international investment activities, which involve international measures and actions. Though the international efforts designed to promote foreign capital investment are diverse and consist of fiscal and non-fiscal incentives, the international tax treaties entered between countries constitute the international dimensions of fiscal incentives intended to promote foreign private capital investment. In 2000 alone, there were no less than 1800 tax treaties entered among developed countries themselves as well as among developed and developing countries which directly or indirectly affect international trade, commerce and business and foreign investments. Countries the globe over are increasingly entering into many economic, capital investment and contractual relationships owing to interdependence as

14. Jennings, *Ibid.*
15. US President Truman is quoted to have said in 1947, see WTO, Globalization and Trade, Annual Report, 1998.

well as economic co-operation and development in inter-nation transactions. To have deep insights into this law, students are advised to see the following PowerPoint lectures.

International Taxation Law and Tax Treaty Negotiations

- International Taxation Law
  - International Global Market;
  - Interdependence;
  - Free Economic Market;
  - Privatization;
  - Globalization;
  - Competitive Market: Shift from Caveat Emptor to Caveat Venditor;
  - Development of MNCs and Corporate Sector; and
  - Resulting in LPO, BPO, KPO.
- Combine of International Trade and International Taxation as a consequence of:
  - Trade, Commerce, Business and Intercourse, i.e., free flow of trade, commerce and business, and taxation proximities, because of:
  - Foreign capital;
  - Patents;
  - Trademark;
  - Licences;
  - Royalties;
  - Income;
  - VAT (Value added tax);
  - Investment; and
  - Movement of goods, persons, services and capital.
- Proximity of Taxation:
  - "No tax shall be levied and collected save in accordance with the law."
  - Now, question is which law?
  - Is it international tax law? Is there any international body/forum that makes international tax law?
  - Is it domestic tax law?

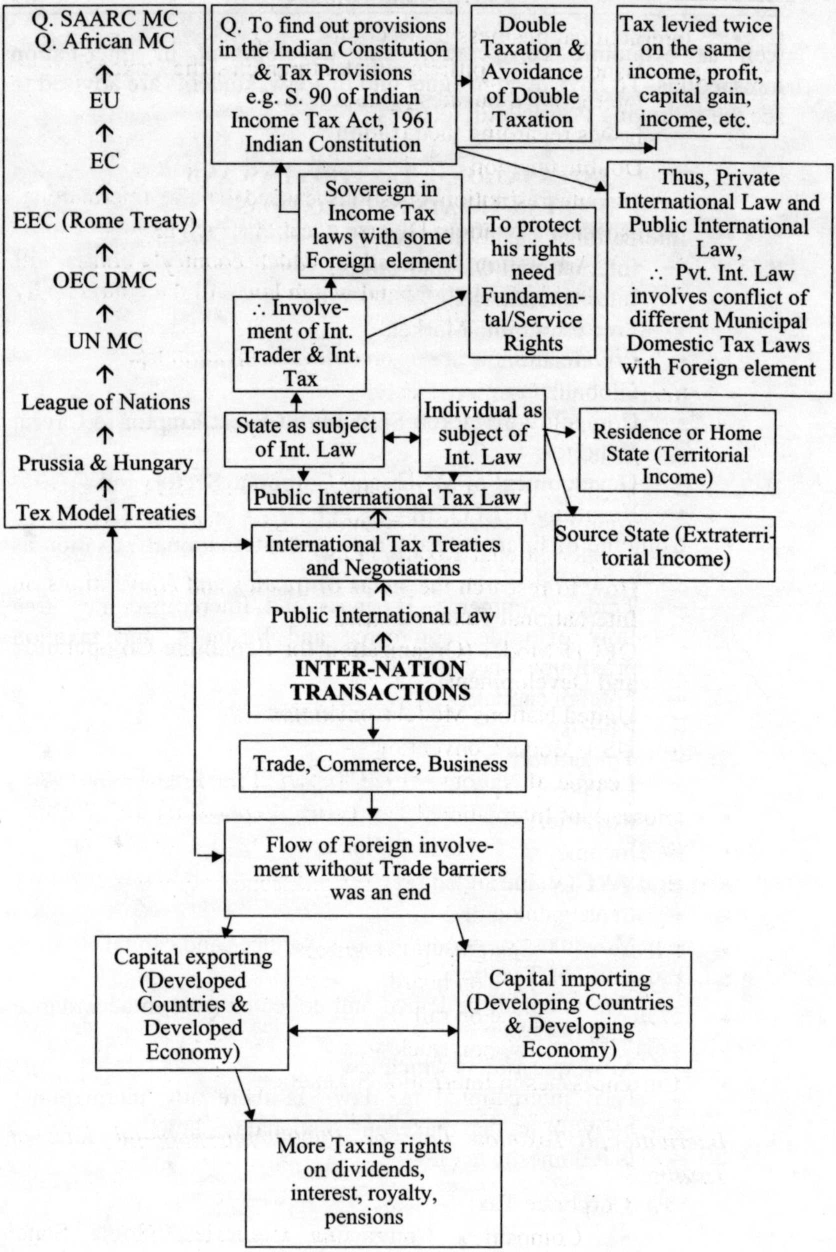
Q. SAARC MC
Q. African MC
EU
EC
EEC (Rome Treaty)
OEC DMC
UN MC
League of Nations
Prussia & Hungary
Tex Model Treaties
Q. To find out provisions in the Indian Constitution & Tax Provisions e.g. S. 90 of Indian Income Tax Act, 1961 Indian Constitution
Double Taxation & Avoidance of Double Taxation
Tax levied twice on the same income, profit, capital gain, income, etc.
Sovereign in Income Tax laws with some Foreign element
To protect his rights need Fundamental/Service Rights
Thus, Private International Law and Public International Law, ∴ Pvt. Int. Law involves conflict of different Municipal Domestic Tax Laws with Foreign element
∴ Involvement of Int. Trader & Int. Tax
State as subject of Int. Law
Individual as subject of Int. Law
Residence or Home State (Territorial Income)
Source State (Extraterritorial Income)
Public International Tax Law
International Tax Treaties and Negotiations
Public International Law
INTER-NATION TRANSACTIONS
Trade, Commerce, Business
Flow of Foreign involvement without Trade barriers was an end
Capital exporting (Developed Countries & Developed Economy)
Capital importing (Developing Countries & Developing Economy)
More Taxing rights on dividends, interest, royalty, pensions

- International business transactions:
  - Issues and pitfalls that threaten the success of international business transactions
  - Issues regarding the taxation
  - Double taxation
  - Dispute resolution questions caused by the international aspects of taxation: Diverse questions such as ------
    - Arbitration or litigation; which country's courts will have jurisdiction; and which law will the courts apply to the matter?
    - General questions on domestic taxation law
- International Taxation Treaty:
  - How to analyze, understand, comprehend and interpret treaty?
  - Vienna Convention on Law of Treaty (VCLT)
  - Sources of Public International Law shall be the sources of International Taxation Law
  - How to research the status of treaties and conventions on International Taxation Law?
  - OECD Model (Organization for Economic Co-operation and Development)
  - United Nations Model Convention
  - USA Model Convention
  - League of Nations—1923 Report of the Four Economists
- Glossary of International Tax Terms, Expressions and Words:
- BOL Bill of lading contract
- BOLERO Bill of lading electronic registration organization
- C&F Cost and freight
- CIF Cost, insurance, freight
- FOB Free on board
- FOR Free on rail
- FOT Free on truck
- Current Issues in International Taxation

International Taxation Law or Public International Law of Taxation!

1. Corporate Tax:
   - Companies: Contracting Countries: Home State/ Resident State and Host State/Source State.

- Tax on Income: By whom? Host State or Home State?
- Issue of Double Taxation.

2. Cross-border business transactions.
3. Personal tax payable by expatriate—personnel on overseas assignments—Who is to levy and collect tax?
   (a) Home State/Resident State (See Domestic Tax Law).
   (b) Host State/Source State (See Domestic Tax Law).

Principles of International Taxation

- What is international taxation? (Conceptual)
  (i) International taxation refers to the global tax rules that applies to transactions between two or more countries (called States and contracting States) in the world.
  (ii) It encompasses all tax issues arising under a country's income tax laws that include some foreign elements.
  (iii) Taxes are not international.
  (iv) There is no separate global tax law that governs cross-border transactions, e.g. India-Pak; India-Bangladesh; India-China; Ethiopia-China; Ethiopia-USA; Ethiopia-Germany, etc.
  (v) There is no international tax court or administrative body for international tax issues to resolve international tax issues. (Is arbitral process sufficient and expedient, such as Mediation, Conciliation and Arbitration?)
  (vi) All taxes are levied under the domestic law of the respective country/State by federal, national, or local governments. (Tax on income; trade and commerce tax; excise tax; municipal tax; entertainment tax, etc.) These taxes have an impact on cross-border transactions.
  (vii) International taxation governs these domestic tax rules under customary international law and treaties. (Brian Arnold and Michael McIntyre, International Tax Primer, 2002, pp. 2-7; Charles McLure, Globalization, Tax Rules and National Sovereignty, 2001, pp. 328-41).

Objectives of International Taxation

- International taxation supports objectives of domestic tax systems, such as measures to—
  1. promote fairness by imposing equal tax burdens on

domestic and foreign taxpayers with equal income and ability to pay, regardless of the source of the income;
2. enhance domestic competitiveness through fiscal measures and to promote economic growth;
3. obtain a fair share of the revenues from cross-border transactions; and
4. ensure an equitable balance between capital export and capital import neutrality.

- Principles of international taxation are influenced by:
  (a) tax equity, and
  (b) tax neutrality
  within the *national economic sovereignty of each nation.*
  (a) *Tax equity* requires that the tax revenues from international economic activities be shared equitably by nations. It also requires that taxpayers involved in cross-border activities be neither discriminated against nor given undue preference in their (contracting countries) tax burdens.
  (b) *Tax systems are neutral* when they do not influence the economic choices of taxpayers. They may be tax neutrals either on capital export or on capital import.
- *Developed countries* tend to favor capital export or domestic neutrality, under which the taxpayer's choices between investing at home or abroad remain unaffected (i.e. world efficiencies).

I. Any African Country

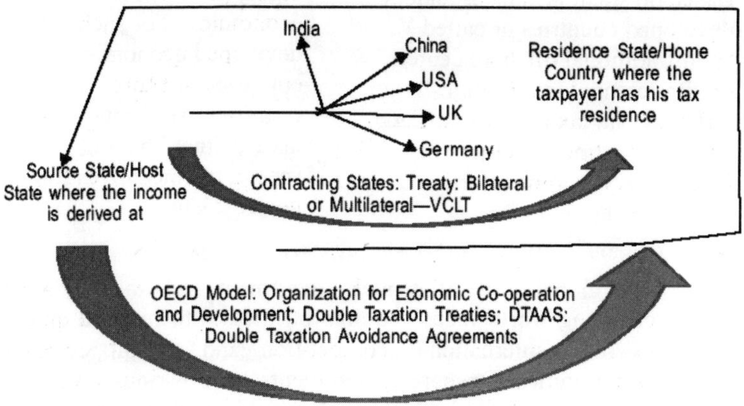

II. OECD: Committee on Fiscal Affairs of OECD

– Organization for Economic Co-operation and Development

UN Model: International Co-operation in Tax Matters

III. Domestic Tax Systems

Taxpayer (Tax subject) | Taxable event (Tax object)

Tax residence of the taxpayer

Double Tax Treaties generally override the domestic law. They are internationally binding obligations between sovereign States under Public International Law. (Not binding on taxpayer)

IV. International Financial Centers: The Genesis

Offshore : Tax Havens
Based on small islands or under developed countries or called "non-traditional offshore centers" or "Preferential tax Regimes". Offer special tax incentives: Land cheap; investment facilitation; labor; heavy income returns.

Onshore countries with highly developed economies . For such developed economies countries offshore countries are "Preferential tax Regimes" having special tax incentives for non-residents.

- The global flow of capital, investment and trade in a fast changing world today requires businesses to respond quickly to meet international competition and exploit emerging opportunities. Onshore governments have various limitations that restrict their ability to react quickly to these international market changes. The offshore industry fulfils this international business needs. Over half the world's financial transactions today take place offshore and this upward trend is likely to continue.

V. Anti-Avoidance Measures

- Anti-avoidance rules under domestic law or Judicial Practices.
- Anti-avoidance measures under the tax treaties between the contracting States.
- Doctrines:
- "Substance over form" doctrine to prevent sham transactions.
- "The commercial jurisdiction rule" under the business purpose test.

VI. International Tax Planning

- The primary objective of international planning is to minimise or defer global taxes lawfully to meet the desired business and other objectives of such transactions.
- Tax planning may be defensive or offensive. The *defensive tax planning attempts* to minimise the risks of paying excessive tax due to double or multiple taxation on the same income and taxpayer. *Offensive tax planning* deals with tax planning strategies that lawfully optimise the after-tax income and capital flows of a transaction as it travels from the overseas source State ("host country") to the residence State ("home State") of the taxpayer.
- These plans consider the transaction costs, the management structure, business risks as well as the relevant anti-avoidance measures.
  - Therefore, the role of the international tax advisor varies widely depending on the nature of the cross-border transaction and how it is affected by the domestic laws (including tax laws) and tax treaties of the countries involved.
  - Judge Learned Hand in a famous tax case in the United States, viz., *George v. Helvering (1935) 69F 2d 809 (US),* commented: "Anyone may arrange his affairs so that his taxes shall be as low as possible; he is not bound to choose that pattern which best pays the treasury. There is not even a patriotic duty to increase one's taxes. Over and over again the Courts have said that there is nothing

sinister in so arranging affairs as to keep taxes as low as possible. Everyone does it, rich and poor alike and all do right, for nobody owes any public duty to pay more than the law demands."

Principles of International Tax Law: Concepts of International Tax Law

1. *Definition:* "International tax law refers to the principles derived from public international law that deal with tax conflicts involving cross-border transactions. These principles are based on the international tax aspects contained in the domestic tax law and the customary practices of countries, and tax treaties. Tax laws are not international. Besides tax treaties, there are no overriding international laws of taxation that are enforceable on taxing States.
2. The sources of international tax law include:
   - Multilateral international agreements, e.g., the Vienna Convention on the Law of Treaties—VCLT, secondary law of international communities of States, mutual agreement procedures for equitable settlement of conflict of legal systems.
   - Comprehensive bilateral double tax treaties, e.g., treaties and protocols, exchange of letters and notes, memoranda of understanding, and supplementary administrative agreements.
   - Limited bilateral double tax treaties, e.g. reciprocal declarations, specific treaties on shipping and airlines, death duties and taxes on gifts.
   - Customary international law and general principles of law, e.g., the principles of law recognised by civilised nations in their national legal systems, statute law, customary law and judicial decisions, and the practices of international organisations.
     - » It may be emphasised that the sources of international taxation law are the same as the sources of public international law. (See Robert Jennings and Arthur Watts, Oppenheim's International Law, 9th Ed., 1992; Ramon J. Jeffery, The Impact of State Sovereignty on Global Trade and International Taxation, 1999; Brian Arnold and Michael Mclntyre, International Tax Priemer, 2002.)

3. Double Taxation:
   - International tax law governs the taxing rights of sovereign nations.
   - These rights depend on their fiscal jurisdiction.
   - The term fiscal jurisdiction refers to both (i) the right of legislation, and (ii) the right of enforcement.
   - A State cannot enforce what it cannot legislate.
   - There are two schools of thought on fiscal jurisdiction based on differing perceptions of State sovereignty:
   1. The first believes that there is no restriction on the State's right to tax, and that it may be exercised without regard to other States.
   2. The other school maintains that the sovereign right to tax is confined to a territory having a "legally relevant connection" between the State and the taxpayer.
      - Be that as it may, both the schools/views accept that "connecting factors" give a State the right to tax. These connecting factors link the taxpayer personally to a particular tax jurisdiction.
   - *The domestic laws in countries normally apply the following international principles, based on connecting factors:*
   - **Residence Rule**: Unlimited taxation rights are granted to the country of residence or nationality, due to the *"personal attachment"* of persons. The country of residence or nationality may impose its taxes on the worldwide income of individuals or corporations due to the protection it offers to the tax subject.
   - **Source Rule:** Limited taxation rights are granted to the country of source due to the *"economic attachment"* of persons. The country of source reserves the right to tax the income that is derived from the economic activities within its territory.
      - Tax conflicts arise largely (but not only) due to this right of the residence/home/nationality State that subjects its residents to tax on their foreign source income.
   - As double taxation is generally considered undesirable, one of the objectives of international tax principles is to ensure that income is not taxed twice.
   - The term 'double taxation' implies "over-taxation" due to

overlapping taxing rights. Double or multiple taxation issues arise when the connecting factors grant competing taxing powers to two or more States on the same income.

- International double taxation may be *economic* or *juridical*.
- **Economic double taxation** refers to a double tax on the same income in the hands of different persons (e.g.: husband and wife, partnership and partner, company and shareholder, parent and subsidiary, etc.)
- **Juridical double taxation** deals with the same tax object and the same tax subject. It is the imposition comparable taxes by two or more States on the same taxpayer in respect of the same subject matter and for identical periods. ("legal identity of subjects")
- Juridical double taxation is the result of a conflict between two tax systems.
- Although the domestic tax systems in most countries provide for unilateral relief, juridical double taxation conflicts are largely resolved through tax treaties negotiated under the principles of international tax law accepted by sovereign States. Through their distributive rules that avoid double taxation and relief methods when it does arise, they ensure a fair distribution of global tax revenues among nations (inter-nation equity, i.e., double tax exemption or non-taxation).

4. Connecting Factor Conflicts:
   - The three key components of any taxable transaction are:
     (i) **Tax subject:** The identity of the taxpayer, or a person's relationship to the taxed object that creates a tax liability;
     (ii) **Tax object:** The identity of the subject matter, or the facts that cause the tax liability; and
     (iii) **Connecting factor:** There must be a "reasonable connection" between the taxing powers of the State, and the taxpayer or the transaction. Without a connecting factor between either the taxpayer or the business activity and the tax jurisdiction, a State cannot levy its tax.
   - Be that as it may, each country follows its own tax practices under its own legal system, and defines the connecting factors under its own laws.

- The varying connecting factor conflicts are:
- **Source-Source conflicts:** two or more countries claim the same income of a taxpayer as sourced in their country.
- **Residence-Residence conflicts:** two or more countries regard the same taxpayer as tax resident in their country.
- **Residence-Source conflicts:** the same income is taxed twice, first by the country where it is derived under its "source rule", and then in the country where the taxpayer resides under its "residence rule".
- **Income characterization conflicts:** two States characterize or classify the same income or capital differently and, therefore, apply differing tax provisions.
- **Entity conflicts:** an entity is characterized differently under the domestic laws of the two States and, therefore, it is subject to differing taxation.
- **Mismatching tax systems:** the two tax systems provide for differing rules for assessment, definition of taxable income, or computation of taxes.
    - The most common form of juridical conflict in international taxation relates to the Residence-Source taxation. A taxpayer satisfies a tax relationship in two States simultaneously. The unilateral tax rules under domestic law may relieve such tax conflicts, but tax treaties normally give a more favorable treatment.

5. Role of Tax Treaties: A treaty is an agreement between sovereign nations. Under international law, tax treaties carry the obligation to ensure that they have the force of domestic law. There are two principles that the tax treaty contracting countries may follow either, such as—
    1. **Monistic principle:** Some countries follow the monistic principle, under which the municipal law is linked and subordinated to the international law under the "doctrine of incorporation".
    2. **Dualistic principle:** Other countries follow the dualistic principle, which regards the international and municipal laws as separate and requires a specific domestic legislation under the "doctrine of transformation".

- Each State is free to decide its approach under its own constitutional laws to comply with its international obligations.
- In the backdrop of the above, thus, there are two groups of countries:

(i) **Direct effect:** treaties are self-executing and automatically become a part of the domestic law when they are ratified. The monistic principle provides that they are enforceable under domestic law without further legislation, e.g. France, Japan, Luxemburg, Netherlands, Portugal, Spain, Switzerland. Some countries require a formal or procedural executive or legislative act to incorporate them in domestic law, e.g. Austria, Belgium, Germany, United States.

(ii) **Indirect effect:** treaty provisions must be enacted into domestic law and require special legislative steps. Under the dualistic doctrine, it is usually the related statute, and not the treaty, which has the legal authority under the domestic law. The courts cannot enforce the treaty provisions until they are "transformed" into municipal law, i.e., Legislative Act or delegated legislation, e.g. Australia, Canada, Denmark, India, Israel, New Zealand, Norway, Sweden, United Kingdom.

- The treaty's "final provision: govern the timing.
- Generally, retrospective application of the new treaty provisions is not permitted if they would affect the taxpayer's rights adversely.
- Thus, tax treaties serve a dual purpose and have a parallel life. They are both "State to State" agreements under the international law and also part of the statutes under the domestic law. They are binding on the Contracting States under public international law. From the date of entry into force, but may be enforceable under the domestic law by the courts only after they are incorporated in the domestic or municipal law. Each State follows its own rules for the inclusion of the treaty under its law.
- Country Examples:
- ***India***: India follows the dualistic doctrine and tax treaties strictly require an Act of Parliament. See Article 51 of the Constitution of India; Section 90 of the Indian Income Tax Act, 1961; See *Union of India v. Azadi Bachao Andolan,* (2003) SC 56 ITR 563 (India).
- ***Assignment:*** *Explain the practice and procedure followed in India—Dualistic or Monistic doctrine; Law and Constitution; Case.*
- ***Is international tax law enforceable?***

6. International Tax Principles and Tax Treaties:
   – The two prevailing key taxing concepts in international taxation are the residence and source principles.
   – Both of them are based on the "benefit theory". Under this theory, taxes are payments for services (benefits) rendered by the State. Each jurisdiction has the right to tax derived from services rendered or benefits provided. The State of residence retains its rights to tax its citizens or residents on their worldwide income, while the State of source taxes the income derived within its own fiscal jurisdiction.
   – Taxation is more than just a fiscal issue. It is effected by political, social and economic factors. As a result, there are significant differences among States on the relevance of taxation (and fiscal goals in general) within their national policy. Each country tries to justify its own approach and sometimes impose it on others. A State's size and its place in the world economy and political order, influence these efforts. Under these circumstances, it may not be appropriate to apply a single treaty model under a "one-size-fits-all" approach to all countries.

- **Some of the principles underlying international tax law and tax treaties include:**

  (i) Equity and fairness—The tax system should be equitable and fair for taxpayers, i.e. inter-individual equity or relationship of taxpayers to each other. This principle requires equal taxation on taxpayers with equal income, regardless of sources, based on their ability to pay (**"horizontal equity"**), and the levy of progressively higher taxation on higher income (**"vertical equity"**). In the international context, the system should also enable each country to receive a fair share of the taxes generated by transactions involving their jurisdiction. This allocation of the worldwide tax base is achieved through a negotiated agreement or tax treaty between fiscal jurisdictions as equal partners with reciprocal appreciation of mutual taxing rights, i.e. inter-nation equity.

  (ii) Neutrality and efficiency—Neutrality refers to the relationship between the taxpayer and the State. A neutral tax system that does not interfere with market forces is regarded as a more efficient distributor of factors of production. Therefore, the concept of tax neutrality is often stated as one of the principles of international taxation. It requires that economic processes should not be affected by external influences, like taxation.

– Ideally, tax systems should be neutral as between investing at home or abroad (CEN=capital export neutrality) and as between investment by domestic and foreign investors (CIN=capital import neutrality).
– The overall objective is to promote free movement of capital.
– CEN is considered as a better approach by many developed countries with developed economy to achieve worldwide economic efficiency, i.e. allocation of economic resources to achieve optimal productivity. It favors taxation in the residence State with a grant of tax credit to relieve foreign taxes paid.
– CIN supports national efficiency and international competitiveness with only source taxation and full tax exemption in the residence State.
– However, in reality, unless there is a completely harmonised global tax system, full neutrality under both CEN AND CIN is impossible to achieve.

(iii) Promotion of mutual economic relations, trade and investment—Many countries (particularly developing countries with developing economy) regard this objective as more significant than the avoidance of double taxation. The primary purpose of tax treaties for them is to promote economic growth through foreign investment and technology. They are prepared to bear the loss of tax revenues due to tax incentives, e.g., double non-taxation, i.e. tax sparing credits, may be regarded as a justified cost to achieve non-fiscal objectives. As net capital importers, they are also more concerned with capital import neutrality—CIN.

- Developing countries concentrate as their policy tool to achieve their non-tax objectives, i.e. social-economic objectives to meet the ends of social-economic-political justice so that the distributive justice is achieved for all the resident-citizens equally without discrimination, e.g. Constitution of India.
- **Students are expected to examine the provisions of the Constitution of India.**
- In this sense, the tax policies and objectives of

developing countries may differ from those of developed countries.

- The developing countries regard direct taxation less as a means for financial resource mobilisation for the government and more as a tool to achieve higher economic growth. Tax levels may be kept low through incentives to enhance their competitiveness for capital, markets and technology. The lack of anti-avoidance measures like controlled foreign corporation and thin capitalisation may be acceptable and tax sparing as well as treaty shopping may be deemed as tax incentives. Tax competition is both widely practised and encouraged in these developing countries. **[Students are expected to examine the Indian policy in this perspective].**

(iv) Prevention of fiscal evasion—One of the stated objectives of Model Tax Treaties—OECD—is the prevention of tax evasion.

(v) Reciprocity—International taxation has the concept of reciprocity as one of its key principles. Reciprocity requires a holistic approach based on both fiscal and non-fiscal considerations to achieve a balanced allocation of taxing rights.

MODEL TAX CONVENTIONS HISTORICAL BACKGROUND

1. The first contemporary bilateral treaty on income and property was signed between Prussia and Austro-Hungary in 1899.
2. After the First World War, the League of Nations took the initiative to evolve an internationally acceptable double tax treaty—
   (a) In 1921 the Finance Committee of the Council of the League of Nations commissioned four eminent economists to study the issue of double taxation and tax avoidance.
   (b) Their 1923 Report regarded double taxation as a barrier to new foreign investment, and considered that function of the tax treaty was to promote such investment by removing this trade barrier.
   (c) The treaty fulfilled this goal by preventing double taxation. Thus, the encouragement of foreign investment was the end, and the avoidance of double taxation was the means to achieve it.

3. The Financial Committee of the League of Nations appointed in 1922 a group of international tax officials to study the administrative and practical aspects of international double taxation and tax evasion.
   (a) This group of experts finally presented several model tax treaties at a General Meeting of Government Experts held in October 1928 in Geneva.
   (b) In 1929, the Council of the League of Nations appointed a permanent Fiscal Committee, which produced a Model Convention in 1933, 1935, and eventually the draft Mexico Model in 1943. 1943 draft treaty included both the prevention of double taxation and the allocation of taxing jurisdiction. The objectives of this treaty were (and are) meant for the encouragement of foreign investment.
4. In March 1946, the Fiscal Committee met in London when a revised draft Model was discussed. The Mexico Draft Model approved source-based taxation and favored capital-importing countries. The London Draft Model gave more taxing rights to capital-exporting nations, particularly on dividends, interest, royalties, annuities and pensions.
5. The work of the League of Nations was taken over by the Fiscal Commission set-up by the Economic and Social Council of the United Nations (ECOSOC) in October 1946.
6. In 1951, The London Draft was abandoned in favor of the Mexico draft.
7. The Fiscal Commission suspended its work in 1954 as it failed to reconcile the taxing interests of the capital-exporting (or developed) and capital-importing (or developing) countries.
8. The Organisation for the European Economic Co-operation (OEEC) took over the initiative in the late fifties.
   (a) Its Fiscal Committee prepared four interim Reports from 1958 to 1961.
   (b) In 1963, the Fiscal Committee finally published the first Draft Double Taxation Convention on Income and Capital (OECD Model or OECD MC—Organisation for Economic Co-operation and Development).
      - Its recommendations were adopted by the Council of the OECD in July 1963.
      - A revised MC was published in 1977.
      - Subsequently, revised in 1992 and updated in 1994, 1995, 2000, 2003 and 2005.

- Since 1992, the MC and its Commentaries are published by the OECD Committee on Fiscal Affairs in an ambulatory form (loose leaf) to permit continuous future update.

9. The OECD, as a group of developed countries, had similar taxing interests and tax treaty policies. The OECD MC was based essentially on two premises:
   (a) the country of residence would eliminate double taxation through the credit method or the exemption method; and
   (b) the country of source, in response, would considerably restrict the scope of its jurisdiction to tax at source and reduce the rates of tax where jurisdiction was retained.
10. However, the above approach did not address sufficiently the concerns of developing countries.
    – OECD also recognized that its Model Treaty was not appropriate for capital-importing countries (developing).
    – Since income flows were largely from developing to industrialized countries, the revenue sacrifice was one-sided. This factor required greater allocation of taxing rights to the developing countries.
11. In the mid-1960s, the United Nations took renewed interest in the problem of double taxation "as a part of its action aimed at promoting the flow of foreign investment to developing countries".
    – In August 1967, ECOSOC decided to set-up an Ad Hoc Working Group to develop an appropriate framework for tax treaties between developed and developing countries and to provide guidance for their negotiation.
    – The Committee called the Ad Hoc Group of Experts on Tax Treaties between Developed and Developing Countries comprising independent tax experts was appointed in 1968.
    – The Committee's efforts led to the UN Model Treaty, viz., The UN Model Convention between Developed and Developing Countries ("UN MC") was issued in 1980 with its own commentaries—updated in 2001, 2003.
    – The term "UNMC" does not imply that contains formal recommendations of the United Nations.
    – The chronological history of the evolution of Model Tax Treaties over the years is as follows:

(a) League of Nations:
1928—Bilateral Convention for the prevention of Double Taxation in the Special Matter of Direct Tax;
1935—Double Taxation and Tax Evasion Convention for the Allocation of Business Income between States for the purpose of taxation;
1943—Bilateral Convention for the Prevention of the Double Taxation of Income with Protocol (Mexico Draft); and
1946—Bilateral Convention for the Prevention of the Double Taxation of Income and Property with Protocol (London Draft).

(b) Organisation for European Economic Co-operation/ Organisation for Economic Co-operation and Development (OECD):
1963—Draft Double Taxation Convention on Income and on Capital;
1977—Model Tax Convention on Income and on Capital; and
1992—Model Tax Convention on Income and on Capital as updated in 1994, 1995, 1997, 2000, 2003, and 2005 (OECD MC).

(c) United Nations MC:
1979—Manual for the Notification of Bilateral Tax Treaties between Developed and Developing Countries;
1980—UN Model Double Taxation Convention between Developed and Developing Countries;
2001—UN Model Double Taxation Convention between Developed and Developing Countries; and
2003—Manual for the Negotiation of Bilateral Tax Treaties between Developed and Developing Countries.

(d) United States of America (US MC):
1981—United States Model Income Tax Convention; and
1996—United States Model Income Tax Convention of September 20, 1996.

(e) Multilateral Tax Agreements:
- EU—Common Market
- SAARC—Common Market
- African Union—Common Market
  - » For foreign capital, patent, trademark, licences, royalties, dividends, and common economic interests
  - » *Objectives:* To eliminate internal trade and tariff barriers and create a Single Market
- Several European Countries established a Common Market under the Treaty of Rome, 1958 (EEC: European Economic Community)
- This EEC was superseded by the Treaty of European Union (also called EC Treaty or Treaty of Maastricht), November 1993 to create a Single European Community—EC
- The EC Treaty established a Single Economic and Monetary Union based on the four fundamental freedoms that guarantee free movement of goods, persons, services and capital under the Single European Act of 1987
- As from May 1, 2004, the EU comprises of twenty-five Member States
- EU has been successful in the harmonization of Value Added Tax (VAT)
- EU has one currency (except UK) Euro
- EU adopted regulations for a European Company (Societas Europaea) in October 2001 and became operational for use on October 8, 2004. European Company can be set-up by the creation of a holding company, or a joint subsidiary, or by merger of companies located at least two Member-States, or by conversion of an existing company set-up under national law, or acquisition of company
- The European Court of Justice (ECJ) to safeguard the above-mentioned four freedoms and to prevent tax discrimination against national of Member States.

13. Relief against Juridical Double Taxation:
14. Benefits of the Model Tax Treaties:
15. OECD MC and UNMC—Comments:

Problem I

- PHD House is a Chamber of Commerce of India and is situated with its head office in New Delhi, India. Its delegation recently visited Addis Ababa, Ethiopia and met, through diplomatic channels of India and Ethiopia, the Prime Minister and his Cabinet of Ethiopia. PHD delegation aspires to construct Hydroelectric Power Project in Ethiopia, which has sufficient and adequate potentialities of energy generation. The proposed project shall improve the power-energy of Ethiopia inasmuch as that it shall usher in an era of tremendous progress—industry and economic both. It shall generate employment opportunities for Ethiopian citizens. It shall increase the status of Ethiopia in the world economic market. Both India and Ethiopia are friendly countries. Ethiopian Government is eager to start this project with India. Indian Government seeks the advice to help her in drafting a bilateral treaty of taxation between India and Ethiopia.
- Draft a Bilateral Model Treaty in the backdrop of the following points:
    1. Who shall be involved in the Negotiation process of bilateral tax treaty under UNMC and /or OECD MC?
    2. Preamble of the bilateral tax treaty.
    3. Clauses of Incentives to the involving country India in Ethiopia in terms of land, tax exemption, avoidance of Double Tax on Income of PHD Chamber of Commerce as a Company and Indian Persons engaged by PHD Chamber of Commerce in Ethiopia in Source Country Ethiopia under Ethiopian Law and Indian Law.
    4. Clauses of incentive to the capital investing agency, i.e., PHD India, by the Government of India in terms of tax exemptions, etc. on Home/Residence Income and Source/ Host State income to protect the rights of PHD India regarding Double Taxation under the Domestic Tax Law of India.
    5. Clauses regarding dispute resolution through arbitral process, i.e., arbitration or "tie breaker" or "negotiation" between "competent authorities" of "tax authorities" of the contracting countries.
    6. Any other clauses with reference to UNMC and/or OECD MC.

Problem II

- Bajaj Auto Ltd., India (BALI) is one of the largest motorcycle manufacturer in the world with a pronounced focus in African Union that shall have exclusive distributor facilitation for Bajaj products in Eastern, Central and Western Africa, namely, Uganda, Rwanda, Kenya, Ethiopia, Sudan, Guinea Conakry, Sierra Leon, Liberia, Senegal, Cameron, Benin and Nigeria. BALI product range comprises motorcycles and three-wheelers with engine capacity ranging from 100cc to 220cc. BALI has a completely integrated Research and Development facility that is engaged in developing new age technologies and products that reinforce the company's leadership position. Some of the many path-breaking technology innovations from BALI are DTSi, ExhausTec and SNS suspension to name a few. The cornerstone of success in African Union (named above) shall be the "Boxer bike". The "Boxer bike" has been specially designed to meet market need of African countries named above. This bike is touted for its ruggedness, reliability and low operating cost as highlighted by its "Strong for Longer" tagline. With a strong service backbone, a Bajaj forte, customers are embracing the "Boxer bike" faster than ever before in India, SAARC countries, Dubai, South Africa, and shall meet the demands/aspirations of the "need-customers" in the above named countries of Africa, who shall have more reason to cheer with new product innovations in the offing. Boxer shall be a great business aid to African Union and also provide livelihood earning opportunities to many Africans. "Boxer bike" shall be taking above named African countries by storm if this project is launched.
- Draft a multilateral tax treaty:
  1. How would you be facilitators of Negotiation of multilateral tax treaty?
  2. Preamble of multilateral tax treaty.
  3. Clauses of "without trade and tariff barrier".
  4. Clauses of "Common Market".
  5. Clauses of VAT in Common Market.
  6. Clauses of African Court of Justice with its headquarter in South Africa, to protect the rights of consumers and distributors in the Common Market.
  7. Clauses of Arbitral Process, i.e., arbitration or "ties

breaker" or "negotiation" between "competent authorities" of "tax authorities" of countries.

8. Any other clauses with reference to multilateral tax treaty Model.

Private law or civil law as some scholars call it (not in the sense of civil law system) is that branch of law which deals relationship between private individuals, *viz.*, *res* or subject matter is private law and *lis inter-partes* or dispute or conflict between parties to the litigation. *Lis inter-partes* may involve *res* under mercantile law, commercial law, corporate law—contract law, partnership law, sale of goods law, company law—, transfer of property law, easement law, trust law, sale law, lease law, tenancy law, consumer protection law, estate law, real estate law, etc.

These laws involve contractual relationship, ownership issues, and possession issues; these laws may also involve issues in the nature of compensation and compensatory costs. Civil procedure code and evidence law take care of procedural niceties and angularities.

The criminal justice system in India encapsulates the fundamentals of substantive criminal law and procedural criminal law. Criminal law is a law that culls out the conceptual as well as definitional aspects of offences having the elements of deviance, *mens rea*, guilty mind, guilty intention, malice, accomplice, conspiracy and criminality. Conspiracy thou are hatched in secrecy and executed in darkness. Secrecy and suspicion have no shore to reach except committing crimes of any magnitude. Because, crime is a crime may be heinous or non-heinous. Offences are crimes against the State. State is meant to maintain law and order in the society. It is the duty of the State to ensure peace in the environ of the system and peaceful life of the people so that they enjoy the life and liberty with dignity. The quantum of punishment varies according to the nature of the offence. Therefore, State acts as prosecrutrix against the criminal. It is the genesis of criminal law jurisprudence that a criminal is presumed to be innocent unless proved guilty. Therefore, a criminal is provided with a defense councilor of his choice to defend his cause. Indian Penal Code, FERA, FEMA, COFEPACEA, National Security Act, MOCOCA, etc. deal with different varieties of offences forming crimes as acts of criminality. Criminal Procedure Code and Evidence Act relate to procedural niceties, complexities and interscities of procedural knots in criminal trials. Criminology and victimology are also inclusive in the criminal law jurisprudence of India. Social re-organization or re-socialization or rehabilitation of criminals is the important component of criminology.

Socialization and compensatory justice to the victims of crime is the genesis of victimology.

Hindu Law, Muslim Law, Christian Law, Parsi Law relate to Familial relationships such as marriage, divorce, judicial separation, maintenance, alimony, bigamy, polyandry, maintenance, welfare and custody of children, adoption, maintenance and welfare of old aged persons and senior citizens, etc.

Besides, POISE Laws—Power, Oil, Gas, Infrastructure, Shipping, Energy and Mining and Mineral Laws—have emerged as new areas in the Indian legal regime of legal education pedagogy. *Urja servam pratishthtam*: energy is the foundation of Universe. Energy is the source of life as well as development and growth. The concept of energy is as old as the concept of universe and person in law. There is a linkage between energy and economic growth of the countries world over including India—the emerging potential global power in the world. Thus, the progressive development of energy is the progressive development of person's life, liberty and sustainability. As such, power as an important source of energy is distinctly related to the life and liberty of persons. Want of energy or non-availability of energy or denial of energy facility to person amounts to denial of right to life and personal liberty. Indian Energy Laws cover a wide spectrum of POISE conceptual framework. POISE encapsulates Power, Oil and Gas, Infrastructure, Shipping, Energy and Mining and Mineral Laws and Policies. Power means and includes power generation, transmission, distribution, and trading. This aims at generally for taking measures conducive to development of electricity industry, promoting competition therein, protecting interest of consumers and supply of electricity to all areas, ensuring transparent policies regarding subsidies, promotion of efficient and environmentally benign policies, as a source and means of energy, which covers both conventional as well as non-conventional sources of energy—electricity generation by the use of different sources of power generation such as hydropower, oil and natural gas, coal, atomic energy, and alternative sources of power generation such as biogas, solar, wind, and bio-diesel—renewable and non-renewable. India depends heavily on oil and gas on its producers since her home products are insufficient to meet domestic needs and demands, and as such faces enormous challenges from OPES, US, EU, Iran, Russia, etc. How far world challenges carry impact on India's energy and power policy framework? How far national and supranational/international policies are interdependence for economic co-operation? Whether National Integrated Energy

Policy, 2006, finalized by the Planning Commission, Government of India duly approved by the Cabinet in 2008, is in tune with International Energy Policy, viz., UNFCCC (UN Framework Convention on Climate Change), UNCDM (UN's Clean Development Mechanism), EU Summit on Climate-Energy, 2008? These and other similar questions seek co-operation, competition and territorial as well as extra territorial disputes/conflicts (gas pipeline) in the competitive economic market of privatization and globalization. Decision-making process has achieved new dimensions in the form of regulatory boards/authorities/commissions, viz., petroleum and gas regulatory board, atomic energy regulatory board, electricity regulatory authority, etc., thus making dispute resolution mechanism fast-track in place of snail pace decision-making process. Road, rail, shipping, air (aviation) are the dimensions of infrastructure and the creation of infrastructure regulatory authority an innovative mechanism of policy-making and policy enforcement. Besides, these infrastructure sources work for person and cargo carriers and involve issues of compensatory justice in the eventuality of loss or damage. With the emergence of POISE regime there have emerged new challenges, viz., environmental, natural habitat, security, taxation, title to property and contractual issues like acquisition and merger, dispute resolution by informal methods in the nature of arbitration, mediation and conciliation—national and international scenario. In the backdrop of this, corporate laws and commercial laws need re-examination and re-visit to the understanding/ comprehension of new contractual policies/strategies in contractual relationships; contractual management—international agreements; corporate socio-legal responsibility; international investment law; concept of liability—contractual and tortuous; concept of arbitration, mediation and conciliation in national and international disputes/ conflicts resolution.

Chapter V

SOURCES OF LAW

There are two sources of law, viz., primary sources of law and secondary sources of law.

The primary sources of law are:

I. Constitution;
II. Legislation;
III. Ordinances;
IV. Precedents; and
V. Custom.

In India, in the case of Hindus and Muslims, personal laws (which are based on revealed truths), commentaries and customs constitute important primary materials to the extent to which they have not been displaced/replaced by statutes.

I. CONSTITUTION

In India like many other countries Constitution is supreme law/lex of the land and all the authorities, namely, legislative, executive and judiciary derive their powers from and act under the limitations imposed by the Constitution. Constitution consists of rules, which establish and regulate or govern the government.

The Constitution of India, in accordance with the federal principles, provides for government at the national (Union Government) and regional levels (State Governments).[1] The Supreme law-making power is vested in the Parliament, a bicameral legislature, of which the lower house—House of People, i.e., *Lok Sabha* is constituted of the representatives of the people elected on the basis of adult franchise, and the upper house—Council of States, i.e., *Rajya Sabha* mostly of the elected representatives of the State Legislature.[2] Parliament also controls the cabinet (Council of Ministers), on whose advise the President is to carry on the administration of the country. The pattern of State Governments is similar. The Governor, with a Council of Ministers to advise him exercises executive powers and the State Legislature performs the law-making function in the sphere allotted to the States under the Constitution. The Judiciary consists of the Supreme Court of India and the State High Courts, with several tiers of subordinate/trial/base courts. The Constitution also grants to the people certain Fundamental Rights, which act as limitation on the power of Government. Further, certain social objectives (Directive Principles of State Policy) are laid down, which the State is enjoined to pursue. Moreover, certain Fundamental Duties are cast upon the citizens of India to abide by the avowed and cherished goals enshrined in the Constitution of India so that the components of national heritage and culture of Indian Nation's pride are preserved, conserved and promoted.[3] Besides, the Constitution provides rules regarding Citizenship, Elections, Public Services, Official Language and several other matters. It is one of the most elaborate Constitution of the world.

1. See Articles 52-78 and 152-167 of the Constitution of India.
2. See Articles 79-104 and Fourth Schedule of the Constitution of India.
3. See Article 51-A of the Constitution of India.

A. Federal Structure

The following table provides the federal structure:

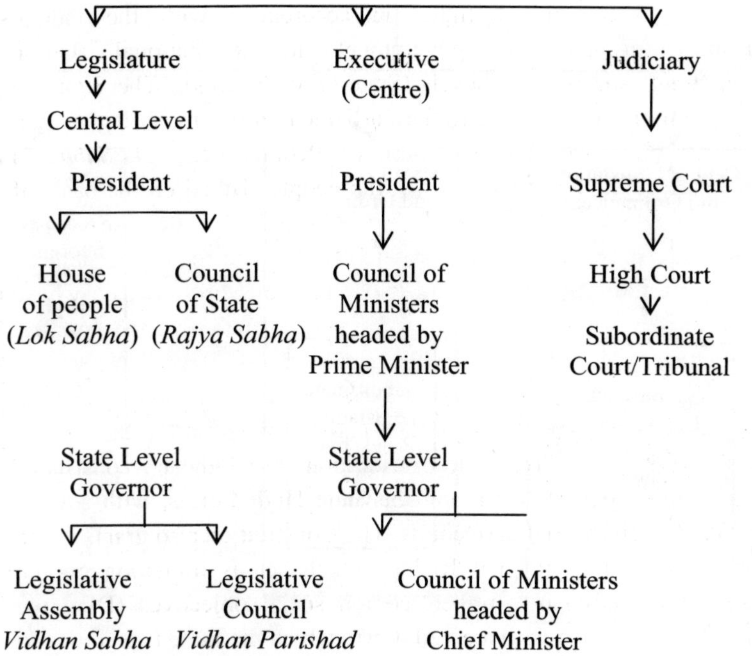

B. Hierarchy of Laws

In India, as seen earlier, Constitution is supreme law of the land. It has provided three organs of the State, namely, legislature for law-making, executive for enforcement of law, and judiciary for interpretation of the Constitution and the laws. The Supreme Court is the custodian and final interpreter of law. The following table gives the hierarchy of law:

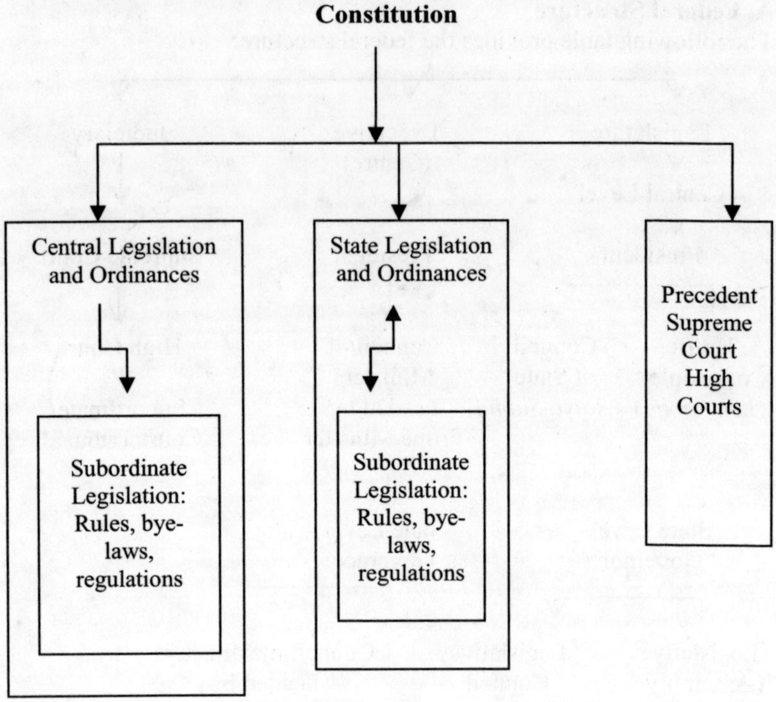

C. Salient Features of the Constitution

(i) Preamble

It provides to secure to its citizens

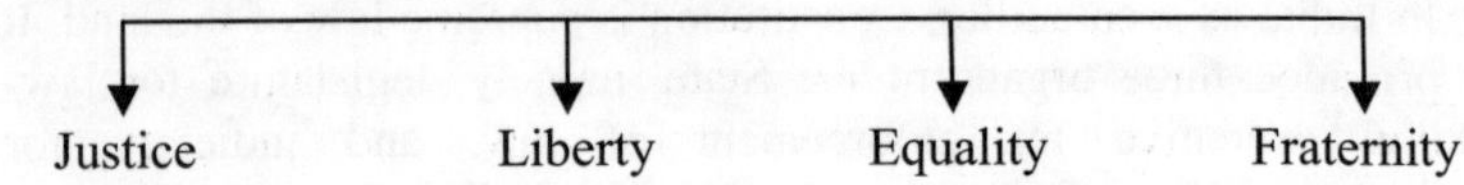

(ii) It proclaims India to be a democratic Republic

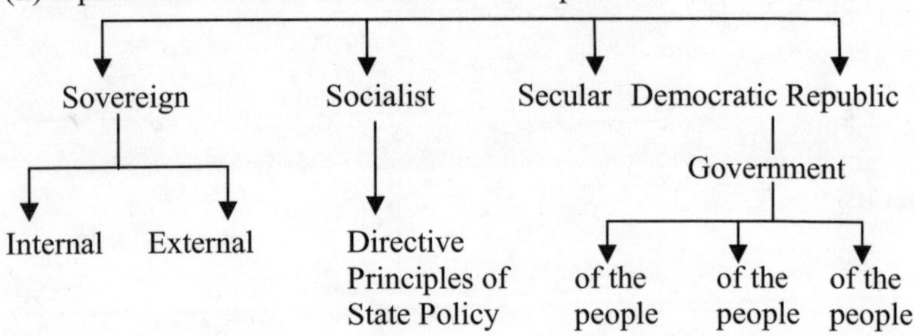

(iii) Nature:

1. Basically federal but with striking unitary.
2. Federal feature forms basic structure of the Constitution.
3. Federal Policies of system.

- Dual Govt.
- Distribution of Power Constitution
- Supremacy of Constitution
- Authority
- Rigidity of Court
- Written and Flexibility

***Fundamental Rights*: Part-III**

- Right to Equality Articles 14-18
- Right to Freedom Articles 19-22
- Right against exploitation Articles 23 & 24
- Right to freedom of Articles 25-28
- cultural & education right Articles 29-30
- Right to constitutional remedies Articles 32

Directive Principles of State Policy – Part IV – Articles 36-51
Fundament Duties – Article 51A

II. LEGISLATION

A. General

Legislation is another source of law. It consists of formal declaration of legal rules by a competent authority duly empowered by the Constitution. It lays down the general rules of conduct for the society. Legislation may also enact to modify or repeal the existing laws or to lay down new rights and duties. Under a Unitary Constitution, like Britain, law-making power for the whole country is vested in one central legislative body, while under a federal Constitution like that of the United States of America, this power is divided subject-wise between the central legislature on the one hand, and the regional legislatures on the other. In India, the law-making power of legislature is not unlimited. The Constitution of India lays down certain higher standards, like fundamental rights, to which the legislation has to conform. Any law inconsistent with such constitutional provisions is declared invalid and unenforceable by the courts.

1. Why Legislation

The following table indicates the purpose or object. Broadly speaking, there are two views:

Everything can be well fixed by a good law

Unwillingness to recourse by legislation except as a last resort

Legislative enactment becomes ***sine qua non*** for attainment of given policy objective

2. Who Legislates

Legislature

Executive

Monopoly of Parliament—19th century

Dominance of executive—20th century

3. Advantages and Disadvantages

Process of circulation of bills among the legislators give scope of public opinion

Judge made Law come as unexpected surprise

Defect in Precedent

Judge has to act more in accordance with law

Statute Law may not be so clear

Greater scope of Judicial discretion

4. Nature and Scope of Legislation

1. Legislation today means art of making-law.
2. It is a positive and artificial process opposed to natural law like custom and usage.
3. Legislation—enactment of law by a competent authority.

4. But sometimes Legislation means and includes every will of the legislature such as:

- Declaration of war or peace
- Rectifying a treaty with foreign state
- Change of calendar year of the country
- Law-making by defined person or body

5. Definition of Legislation

Prof. Dias: Law made deliberately in a set form by an authority which the courts have accepted as competent to exercise that function.

Prof. Gray: As formal utterances of the legislative organ of the society.

Jordan: Function of laws to control life and it is in the legislation that life becomes the act of law.

Salmond: The sources of law consist in the declaration of legal rules by the competent authority.

William C. Burton: As formulation of rules for the future through legislative process.

Dicey: As movement based on characteristics of human nature.

Bentham: Besides being an art it is also a science.

6. General and Restrictive Meaning

- Judge-made laws
- Particular rules of law
- Rights created by law between parties to the contract

- Enactment of law by competent authority which is accepted and applied in the court of law while administrative justice

7. Kinds of Legislation

- Direct
  Enactment and declaration of enforceable legal rules of behaviour by competent authority
- Indirect
  Legislation by Judicial interpretation of statutes and application of equitable principles

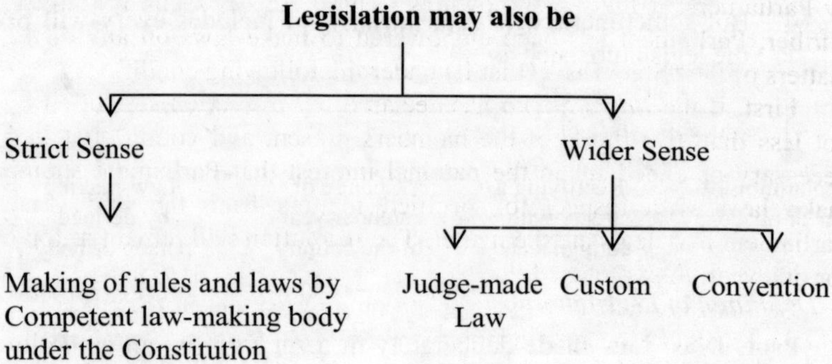

B. Central Legislation

The power to make laws for the whole or any part of the territory of India[4] is vested in the Union Legislature, called Parliament.[5] This power, however, extends only to such subjects of legislation as are enumerated in the 'Union List' (List I)[6] and 'Concurrent List (List III)[7] of the Seventh Schedule to the Constitution and such matters as are not enumerated in any one of the three lists in the Seventh Schedule, viz., residuary powers of legislation are vested with the Parliament of India.[8] Fundamental Rights[9] and Freedom of Inter-State Trade and Commerce[10] are other important provisions of the Indian Constitution imposing express limitations on the legislative power. The laws made

---

4. According to Article 245(2) of the Constitution of India which declares that no law passed by Parliament can be declared invalid on the ground that it would apply outside the territory of India.
5. This power is given under Article 245(1) of the Constitution of India.
6. Union List (List I) contains 97 items or entries of legislation, e.g., Defence of India; Foreign Affairs; Railways, Airways; Posts and Telegraph; Currency coinage and legal tender; Trade and Commerce with foreign countries; Banking; Insurance; Income Tax; Duties and Custom including export duties.
7. Concurrent List (List III) contains 47 items or entries of Legislation, e.g., Criminal Law; Criminal Procedure; Transfer of Property; Contracts; Civil Procedure; Education; Economics and Social Planning; Trade Union and Industrial and Labour Disputes; Price Control; Electricity.
8. Article 248 of the Constitution of India; see Constitutional Application Order, 1954 to Jammu and Kashmir.
9. As enumerated in Part III of the Constitution of India, Articles 12-35, and Article 35-A as applicable to the Permanent Residents of the State of Jammu and Kashmir by Presidential Order, 1954.
10. As provided in Part XIII of the Constitution of India.

by Parliament of India are known as Central Acts or Central Statutes. Further, Parliament has been empowered to make laws on any of the matters of the "State List" (List II) under the following conditions:

First, if the *Rajya Sabha* has declared, by resolution supported by not less than two-thirds of the members present and voting, that it is necessary or expedient in the national interest that Parliament should make laws with respect to specified matters from the State List, Parliament may legislate the matter. The resolution will remain in force for one year unless relaxed.[11]

Second, Parliament may legislate on any matters in the State List while a relevant proclamation of emergency is in force.[12]

Third, Parliament may legislate for two or more States by their consent, the legislation shall apply to those States and any others which adopt it afterwards.[13]

Parliament has been given residuary power to legislate on such matters as are not enumerated in any list of the Seventh Schedule.[14] The power to make laws or the whole or any part of the State is vested in the State Legislature, which may make laws on such subjects as are enumerated in the State List and Concurrent List. In case a law made by the State Legislature on the matters enumerated in the Concurrent List is inconsistent with a Union Law on the same matter, the State Law will be inoperative to the extent of the inconsistency.[15] This facilitation is covered under the doctrine of "Occupied Field", i.e., the Central Law will occupy the statutory domain in preference to State Law. There is, however, one exception. In case a law made by the State Legislature is inconsistent with the Union Law, the State Law will prevail over the Union Law if the same has been referred for the consideration of the President of India and it has received his assent.[16] State Legislatures, too, are subject to the limitations imposed by the fundamental rights and freedom of inter-State trade and commerce.[17]

C. State Legislation

The power to make laws for the whole or any part of the State is

---

11. Article 249 of the Constitution of India.
12. Article 250 of the Constitution of India.
13. Article 252 of the Constitution of India.
14. See Article 248 of the Constitution of India; see also Entry 97 of Union List (List I).
15. Article 254(1) of the Constitution of India.
16. Article 254(2) of the Constitution of India.
17. See Part III and Part XIII of the Constitution of India.

vested in the State Legislature, which may make laws on such subjects as are enumerated in the "State List" (List II)[18] and the "Concurrent List" (List III) of the Seventh Schedule to the Constitution of India. In case, however, a law made by a State Legislature on one of the matters enumerated in the Concurrent List, is inconsistent with the Central Act on the same matter, the State Law will be inoperative to the extent of inconsistency.[19] This is covered under the doctrine of "Occupied Field", which means that Central Law will occupy the field of legislation in preference to State Law. State Legislatures, too, are subject to limitations like those imposed by Fundamental Rights and Freedom of Trade and Commerce. The laws made by the State Legislature are known as State Acts or State Statutes.

D. Types of Legislation

Broadly speaking, Legislation may be divided into two categories:

1. Supreme legislation;
2. Subordinate legislation; and
3. Delegated Legislation.

1. Supreme Legislation

Supreme legislation is that which proceeds directly from a supreme or sovereign power in the State. It is supreme because no other authority can annul, modify or control it. Legislation by any other authority is subordinate legislation and is capable of being controlled by the supreme authority. In India, as already observed, the Constitution of India is the supreme law of the land. Constituent power is enjoyed by the Parliament of India alone under Article 368 of the Constitution of India. Quite apart from this there are Central and State legislations.

Supreme legislation is made either by the Parliament of India or the State Legislature as per the scheme of the Constitution of India. Supreme legislation is also known as 'Parent Act', and subordinate legislation is also known as 'Child Act'.

Subordinate forms of legislation derive their authority to legislate only by delegation, express or implied, of the supreme power. Central Government has rule-making powers under the Petroleum and Natural Gas Regulatory Board Act, 2006, the Electricity Act, 2003, the

18. State List (List II) contains 66 items or entries of Legislation, e.g., Public Order; Police; Local Government; Public Health and Sanitation; Agriculture; Forests; Taxes on Agricultural income; Taxes on Land and buildings.
19. Article 254 of the Constitution of India.

Telecommunications Act, 1996, the Competition Act, 2005 for the regulation of decision-making processes of Regulatory Boards or Commissions created under these Acts. Municipal corporations, university bodies, railway companies and clubs have got powers to make rules and orders governing themselves and their members.

2. Subordinate Legislation

It may broadly be categorized as under:

1. Colonial Legislation—Legislation by the legislature of the colonies or other dependencies of the Crown enjoying the powers of self-government is subject to the control of the Imperial Legislature. In view of the Statute of Westminster, 1931, the Dominion Legislature now enjoys sovereign power.
2. Executive Legislation—It is legislation by the executive of a State meant for supplementing the statutory provisions by the issue of more detailed regulations pertaining to the subject.
3. Judicial Legislation—It is the rule-making power of the courts for the regulation of their own procedure.
4. Municipal Legislation—The bye-law-making power of municipal authorities is another form of subordinate legislation.
5. Autonomous Legislation—Legislation by autonomous bodies like universities or railway companies is also termed subordinate legislation.

3. Delegated Legislation

Delegated Legislation is a kind of subordinate legislation. In a welfare State, the functions of the Legislature get enormously increased with the result that it becomes, rather impracticable, for the legislature to make laws on all matters in detail. The legislature, therefore, defines and lays down the fundamental principles and policies in the legislation and delegates powers to subordinate bodies or administrative authorities to lay down details. The body to which the power is delegated acts as the delegate of and within the limits of the power conferred by the legislature. This process is known as delegated legislation. Legislation so made is known by following names:

(i) Rules,
(ii) Regulations,
(iii) Schemes,
(iv) Notifications,
(v) Orders, and
(vi) Bye-laws.

However, beyond a certain limit there can be no delegation of power by the legislature. The majority judgment in *re*: *Delhi Laws Act*[20], settled that a legislature cannot delegate its essential powers of legislation which term includes its functions of laying down legislative policy in respect of a measure and its formulation as rules of conduct. This is the rule in India that the legislature cannot delegate its essential functions and/or features or powers to the executive, or the legislature cannot abdicate its domain to executive or administration, or what belongs to the legislature must be performed by the legislature alone, or executive convenience should not be a burden of beast for the legislature to hand down a *carte blenche* to the executive. The essential function of the legislature is the determination of the legislative policy and enacting that policy into a binding rule of conduct. This function—the laying down of policy and enacting it—cannot be delegated. But when the legislature has once laid down the policy and a standard is established by the statute, the executive may be given the power to make subordinate rules within that limit. Such delegation is not unconstitutional. In other words, where the law lays down the principles and affords guidance to the subordinate law-making authority, details may be left for being filled up by the executive or by other authorities vested with quasi-legislative power.[21]

Where a statute passed by the Union Parliament delegates power to administrative authorities in order to supplement the statute in necessary details, it is known as Central Delegated Legislation.

The Acts passed by the Parliament may delegate powers to the Central Government, the State Governments, and to other authorities. A few Acts which delegate powers to such authorities are Defence of India Act, 1939 (delegation to the Central Government, to Provincial Governments or to any other authority), the Essential Supplies Act, 1946 (delegation to the Central Government, Provincial Government), the Essential Commodities Act, 1955 (delegation to the Central Government, their officers), Central Sales Tax Act, 1956 (delegation to Central Government and State Governments), Workmen's Compensation Act, 1923 (delegation to the Central Government and the State Governments), the Central Administrative Tribunal Act, 1985 (delegation to the Central Government), The Petroleum and Natural Gas Regulatory Authority Board Act, 2006 (delegation to the Central Government), the Petroleum Act, 1934 (delegation to the Central Government), the Mines and Minerals (Development and Regulation)

20. A.I.R. 1951 S.C. 332.
21. See *Corporation of Calcutta v. Liberty Cinema*, A.I.R. 1965 S.C. 1107.

Act, 2010 (delegation to the Central Government and the State Governments), the Electricity Act, 2003 (delegation to the Central Government), the Telecommunication Act, 1996 (delegation to the Central Government).

Delegation of powers under the Central Acts is made to the local bodies of the centrally administered territories, viz., Union Territories, as enjoined in First Schedule of the Constitution of India, of Laccadive, Andaman, Nicobar, Chandigarh, Daman and Diu, etc.

Under Central Acts many public corporations or regulatory authorities in India have been established and they, being more or less independent statutory bodies, have been vested with wide rule-making powers regarding their organizational and business activities. The Central Acts also delegate powers to the Central Government to make rules in respect of public corporations. Under Section 59 of the Damodar Valley Corporation Act, 1948, the Central Government is empowered to make rules with respect to all or any of the matters of D.V.C. Similar instances may be found in the Indian Lac Cess Act, 1930 under Section 9; the Tea Act, 1953 under Section 50; and the Coir Industry Act, 1953 under Section 27.

Where a statute passed by a State Legislature delegates powers to administrative authorities in order to supplement the statute in necessary details, it is known as State Delegated Legislation.

State Governments, mostly in respect of their activities in relation to the items mentioned in List II of the Constitution of India, have been delegated powers under the Acts passed by their respective legislatures. Section 237 of U.P. *Kshettra Samittees* and Zila Parishads Act, 1961 delegates powers to the State Governments to make rules. Similarly, under the U.P. Panchayat Raj Act, 1947; the U.P. Municipalities Act, 1916; and the U.P. District Board Act, 1922, the State Government has been delegated powers to make rules. The local bodies created under these Acts have been delegated powers to make bye-laws. State Legislation may also delegate powers to public corporations. Under their respective State statutes, public corporations like U.P. Warehousing Corporation and Calcutta (now Kolkata) State Transport Corporation have been delegated powers to make rules.

The nature and extent of delegated legislation under the Central or State Acts and the rules, regulations, bye-laws, etc. made thereunder by the administrative authorities may be found in the Union Gazette or the State Gazette as the case may be.

III. ORDINANCES

In addition to the enactments passed by the Parliament or the State Legislatures the President of India and the Governor of a State may issue Ordinances when Parliament or the State Legislature are not in session. These Ordinances are issued by the President and the Governors and the laws made by the President or his delegate under Article 357(1)(a) of the Constitution partake legislative character and are made in the exercise of legislative power, within the contemplation of the Constitution.[22]

Subordinate Legislation or Delegated Legislation or Rule-making Power of the Administration or Quasi-Legislation:

Quite apart from this, most enactments delegate powers to the executive to make rules and regulations for the purposes of the Acts. These rules and regulations are periodically laid before the legislature (Union or State as the case may be). They are commonly known as subordinate legislation or delegated legislation or rule-making power of the administration or quasi-legislation and are another permanent source of law.

A. General

While accepting generally the democratic principle of law-making by popularly elected Legislature, the Indian Constitution also empowers the executive heads of the Union and the State Government—the President[23] and the Governor[24] to make, during the period the legislature is not in session, temporary laws by issuing ordinances.[25] The idea is to arm the government with power to make laws necessary to deal with a situation, which may suddenly and immediately need to be dealt.[26] The existing law may be inadequate for the purpose and resort to normal legislative process may mean unwarranted delay.[27] This power is to be distinguished from the power

22. See *A.K. Roy v. Union of India*, (1982) 1 SCC 271.
23. Article 123 of the Constitution of India.
24. Article 213 of the Constitution of India
25. Under the Government of India Act, 1935, the Governor-General and the Governors were given much wider powers to issue ordinances. In Britain and the United States of America, the Executive has no such power.
26. Dr. B.R. Ambedkar giving the reasons for vesting of extraordinary power in the President. See *C.A.D.*, Vol. VIII, p. 213.
27. See, for example, The Essential Services Maintenance Ordinance V of 1957, passed by the President to meet the emergency created by the notice of strike given by certain sections of government employees.

of the government to make laws under authority delegated by the Legislature.

B. Central Ordinances

The President of India may, when satisfied of the existence of circumstances requiring immediate action on his part, issue Ordinances. Law-making by ordinance can be resorted to by the President only when the Parliament is not in session. An ordinance ceases to operate at the expiration of six weeks after the Parliament reassembles, unless earlier withdrawn by the President or disapproved by both Houses of Parliament. In extent and scope, the ordinance-making power of the President is coextensive with the law-making power of Parliament. An ordinance can be promulgated as a law only on matters on which Parliament is competent to make laws and is subject to same limitations, which apply to legislative power of Parliament.

C. State Ordinance

The Governor of the State can issue, under the same circumstances an Ordinance on matters, on which State Legislature is competent to make laws. State ordinances, too, can be made only during the recess of State Legislature and remain in force upto the expiration of six weeks from the reassembly of the State Legislature, unless withdrawn earlier by the Governor or disapproved by the State Legislature.

A State ordinance has the same force and effect as an Act of State Legislature and is also subject to same conditions and limitations as operate on State Legislation.

IV. PRECEDENTS

A judicial precedent is another source of law. It enjoys high authority at all times and in all Common Laws countries.

In Anglo-Indian law, the theory of precedents has found acceptance—*jus receptum*. Before the independence, the highest court was the Privy Council and later the Federal Court. The decisions of these highest tribunals were binding on all the High Courts and courts subordinate to them in India. Under the Constitution of India, 1950, the Highest Court is the Supreme Court of India. Article 141 of the Constitution of India makes the law declared by the Supreme Court of India binding on all courts within the territory of India. However, the Supreme Court is not bound by its own decisions.[28] But the Supreme

---

28. *Bengal Immunity Co. v. State of Bihar*, A.I.R. 1955 S.C. 661.

Court would not ordinarily upset its own previous decision. However, in practice, the Supreme Court has observed that earlier decisions of the Court cannot be departed from unless there are extra ordinary or special reasons to do so.[29] If the earlier decision is found erroneous and is thus detrimental to the general welfare of the public, the Supreme Court will not hesitate in departing from it.[30] The Supreme Court may re-state its earlier law by culling out the issues clearly and erasing the uncertainties if the earlier law creates any confusion.[31]

The Supreme Court is not bound by the decisions of Privy Council or Federal Court. Observations of Krishna Iyer, J., in *K.C. Dora v. G. Annamanaidu*[32] are to the same effect. He stated:

> "Precedents should not be petrified nor judicial dicta divorced from the socio-economic mores of the age. Judges are not prophets and only interpret laws in the light of the contemporary ethos. To regard them otherwise is unscientific. My thesis is that while applying the policy of statutory construction we should not forget the conditions and concepts which moved the judges whose rulings are cited, nor be observed by respect at the expense of reason."

The Supreme Court has used these powers to venture into judicial activism going far beyond the traditional view that courts should only interpret the law and not make new law. Judgments of the Supreme Court on public interest litigation, protection of the environment and protection against arbitrary State action can be viewed in constitutional language of Article 142 more as judicial legislation as "flashing the flaming sword of its inspiration".[33]

The decisions of a High Court are binding on itself and on all the subordinate courts and tribunals within its jurisdiction in the State, over which High Court exercises territorial jurisdiction. However, judgments

---

29. A.I.R. 1976 S.C. 410.
30. *Sajjan Singh v. State of Rajasthan*, A.I.R. 1965 S.C. 845.
31. See *P.A. Inamdar v. State of Maharashtra*, (2005) 6 SCC 537; *T.M.A. Pai Education Foundation v. State of Karnatka*, (2002) 8 SCC 481; *Ashok Kumar Thakur v. Union of India*, (2008) 6 SCC 1.
32. A.I.R. 1974 S.C. 1061 at p. 1083.
33. See the words of Justice Vivian Bose in *Ram Jawaya Kapoor v. State of Punjab*, A.I.R. 1954 S.C.; *PUDR v. Union of India* (1982) 3 SCC 235; *D.S. Nakara v. Union of India*, (1983) 1 SCC 305; *Bandhua Mukti Morcha v. Union of India*, (1984) 3 SCC 161; *D.C. Wadhwa v. State of Bihar*, (1987) 1 SCC 378. The Apex Court has unequivocally emphasised upon its law-creative function, viz., "the childish fiction that the courts only find the law but do not make it must be done away with".

of one High Court are not binding on another High Court or on courts subordinate to another High Court.[34] They, however, have persuasive value only.

In a High Court, a single judge constitutes the smallest bench. A bench of two judges is known as Division Bench. Three or more judges constitute a Full Bench. A decision of such a Bench is binding on a smaller bench of the same High Court.

Thus, a decision by a Bench of a High Court should be followed by other Benches unless they have reason to differ from it in which case the proper course is to refer the question for decision to a Full Bench.

Judgments of foreign courts are also of persuasive value only. These judgments are normally cited in the Supreme Court and in the High Courts in the absence of Indian judgments on the point involved. Foreign judgments are seldom cited before the subordinate courts. Supreme Court of India, often to justify its decision on a given issue refers to the decisions of the Supreme Court of the United States of America, either to show analogy or for showing distinction.[35]

V. CUSTOM

In the early days, the custom occupied a key position. Indeed in some cases, it was the sole source of law. Over the period, its significance gradually diminished and legislation and judicial precedents became the main sources. Custom, as a source of law, involves the study of a number of its aspects: its origin and nature, its importance, reasons for its recognition, its classification and the essentials of a valid custom.[36]

Customs have played an important role in moulding the ancient Hindu Law. Most of the law given in *Smritis* and the *Commentaries* had its origin on customs. The *Smritis* have strongly recommended that the customs should be followed and recognized. Customs worked as a re-orientating force in Hindu Law. In modern India also, in personal laws, custom is an important source of law. Custom of the community or the personal laws of the parties have been accorded due recognition by both legislature and judiciary. Thus, the expression "law in force" in Articles 13 and 327 of the Constitution of India includes not only

34. *Bishnu Ramm v. Parag Saikia*, (1984) 2 SCC 488.
35. For instance, see *Christian Medical College Hospital Employees' Union v. Christian Medical College, Vellore*, and *State of Tamil Nadu v. Christian Medical College,* (1987) 4 SCC 691.
36. See Dr. B.N. Mani Tripathi, Jurisprudence (Legal Theory), 1992, p. 148.

statutory law, but also custom or usage having the force of law.[37] However, custom can be abolished by statute either by express words or by use of words inconsistent with continued existence of the custom.[38] Therefore, even if there was a custom that has been recognized by law with regard to a hereditary village office, that custom may have to yield to a fundamental right.[39]

The courts have relied upon the customs pleaded by parties while arriving at a decision. Parties in the court are also allowed to adduce evidence as to existing of any custom on which they place reliance in the suit.[40] For instance, the custom that the ancestral property is ordinarily inalienable especially amongst *Jats* residing in the Central District of Punjab, except for necessity and other permissible reasons, have been held to be valid.[41]

It is settled rule of procedural law of the country that in the matter of custom, a party has to plead in specific terms as to what is the custom pleaded by him. He cannot be permitted to prove a custom not pleaded by him.[42] Mohammadan Law, which is administered in respect of property and personal rights of the Muslims in India, is totally a customary law.[43] The courts in disputes and issues involving religious and charitable endowments completely fall back on usage and custom of the institution to give justice to the parties before them.[44] Usage of custom is not restricted to sphere of application to personal laws only but even labour law of the country take note of customs, practices, etc. to determine the number of paid festival holidays per year.[45] Family law of the country is totally a product of usual customs that are prevalent amongst members of the community.[46]

Tribal Customary Laws

The framers of the Constitution recognized the need for a separate

---

37. *Builders Supply Corpn. v. Union of India*, AIR 1965 SC 1061.
38. *Darshan Singh v. Ram Pal Singh*, 1992 Supp (1) SCC 191.
39. *Gazula Dasaratha Rama Rao v. State of A.P.*, AIR 1961 SC 564.
40. *Bhagat Singh v. Jaswant Singh*, AIR 1966 SC 1861.
41. *Bara Singh v. Kashmira Singh*, (1990) 4 SCC 711.
42. *Kochan Kani Kumjuraman Kani v Mathevan Kani Sankaran Kani*, (1971) 2 SCC 345.
43. *Bhagwati Prasad Sah v. Bhagwati Prasad Sah* (1964) 5 SCR 105.
44. *Bihar State Board Religious Trust v. Mahant Sri Biseshwar Das* (1971) 1 ACC 574.
45. *Bijli Cotton Mills (P) Ltd. v. Presiding Officer, Industrial Tribunal II* (1972) 1 SCC 840.
46. *Biswambhar Singh v. State of Orissa*, AIR 1954 SC 139.

political and administrative structure for the tribes. Special provisions were made to prevent encroachment on their land, personal rights and other customs. In spite of the assimilation of tribal communities into the system of the State laws, there remains in tribal society a large residual area of autonomy in many matters of civil and social nature. The tribal council functions effectively in such cases even today. Tribal customary laws are ubiquitous, existing in all tribal groups, cherished, adapted and regarded as intrinsic to tribal identity. This body of law survives even among the numerically small, fragile tribal communities, facing the threat of extinction or dwindling of numbers. In spite of the dwindling authority of the traditional jural authority, an attempt is made to preserve and uphold traditional norms.[47] The Supreme Court of India in *Madhu Kishwar v. State of Bihar*,[48] declined to declare the custom of inheritance/succession of the Scheduled Tribes, which deny tribal women right to succession as unconstitutional. The Apex Court observed that customs are prevalent and are being followed among the tribes in matters of succession and inheritance apart from other customs like marriage, divorce, etc. Customs became part of the tribal laws as a guide to their attitude and practice in their social life and not a final definition of law. They have accordingly nearly acquired the status of law. Under these circumstances, it is not desirable to grant general declaration that the custom of inheritance offends the Constitution.

Customs may be:

(i) *Customs without sanction* are those customs which are non-obligatory and are observed due to the pressure of public opinion. These are called as 'positive morality'.

(ii) *Customs having sanction* are those customs which are enforced by the State.

Requisites of a Valid Custom

In order that a custom may be legally valid it must conform to certain requirements laid down by law, which is as follows:

1. ***Reasonableness***: A custom must be reasonable. The authority of usage is not absolute but conditional on certain measure of conformity with justice, public policy and utility. It is reasonable if found to be in consonance with reason and its origin and continuance are capable of being explained. Thus, the *Sati Pratha* could not take the place of a legal custom due

47. K.S. Singh, Tribal Ethnography Customary Law and Change, Concept Publishing Co., New Delhi, 1993, pp.17-20.
48. (1996) 5 SCC 125 at p. 158, para 46.

to its being repugnant to the logical sense of justice and goodness in man. Similarly, 'child marriage' or 'polyandry' or 'monogamy' is not legal custom because of its repugnancy to law, logic, justice and goodness in man.

2. ***Conformity with statute law:*** No custom or prescription can take away the force of an Act of Parliament. The custom in order to be a source of law must not conflict with statute law.
3. ***Observance as of right***: It must have been observed as of right. Mere practice of a voluntary nature would not make custom valid.
4. ***Immemorial antiquity:*** A custom to be valid must be immemorial. Recent and modern custom is of no account. It must have been observed for such a long time that "the memory of man runneth not to the contrary".
5. ***Continuity:*** A custom to be valid must have continued, without interruption since time immemorial.
6. ***Peaceable enjoyment:*** It must have been peaceably enjoyed, as custom owes its origin to common consent.
7. ***Certainty:*** Custom to be source of law must be definite.

Chapter VI

HIERARCHY OF COURTS: AN OVERVIEW

The Indian Constitution though federal in character provides for unitary judicial system. The Supreme Court is the apex court of the country. The framers of our constitution have tried to secure independence of the Supreme Court and the Indian Judiciary on the lines of the American, Canadian and British Constitutions.

Under the Supreme Court, there exists High Court for every State/Union Territory. At present, the country is divided into 28 States and 7 Union Territories (UT).[1] There are 21 High Courts in the country, 5 having jurisdiction over more than one State/UT. In few states, due to large geographical area, benches are established outside the principal seat of a High Court.

Under High Courts, in each State/UT, there are subordinate courts. These represent the first tier of the entire judicial structure. In fact, each State/UT is divided into districts as units of administration and each district is further divided into talukas or tehsils comprising certain villages contiguously situated. These are administrative units. The court structure more or less corresponds with these administrative units except in urban areas.

On the criminal side, vertically moving downwards, the highest

---

1. http:// goidirectory.nic.in/fstateut.htm; The Constitution of India, Schedule I, 2012 Ed. (Eastern Book Company, Lucknow).

court is either the Sessions Court, presided over by a Sessions Judge or Court of District and Sessions Judges, who is also the administrative head. He assigns cases to the Additional Sessions Judges. Sessions Court has original, appellate and revision jurisdiction against orders passed by lower courts.

Subordinate to the Sessions Courts are the courts of Chief Judicial Magistrate and Additional Chief Judicial Magistrate. Each of these courts has one or more police stations assigned to it. The designated court decides criminal cases from those police stations. Below these are the courts of Judicial Magistrates. They deal with cases relating to breach of public peace, nuisance, dispute of immobile property likely to cause breach of peace.

On the civil side, vertically moving downwards in the hierarchy, we have at the peak, the principal civil court called the District Court presided over by District Judge. Further, there are the courts of additional district judges. Both the district judges and additional judges are vested with the same powers and appellate jurisdiction against the order or decree of courts subordinate to them.

Under the District Courts there are courts of Civil Judges (Senior Division) and Civil Judges (Junior Division). The "Senior" and "Junior" labels do not have anything to do with the powers of the judges but reflect the nature of the cases. These courts are vested with only original jurisdiction. Appeals against the judgment of the courts of civil judges, (senior or junior division) lie before the district judge, who either decides the appeal himself or assigns it to the court of additional district and session's judge or additional district judge, wherever exists under him.

In some State/UT, a court of munsif/district munsif-*cum*-magistrate/subordinate judge, class-III and the sub-judge, class-II are established at a taluk or tehsil level, instead of the courts of civil judges (junior division). Immediately above the district munsif's court in the hierarchy is the court of subordinate civil judge, class-I instead of the courts of civil judge (senior division).[2]

In addition to the regular criminal courts, there are special courts to deal with cases relating to narcotics, corruption, terrorist, consumer,[3] labour[4], environment,[5] family, etc.

2. 118th Report of the Law Commission of India, December 1986, at 1.
3. *Id.*, Chapter 3, p.72.
4. *Id.*, Chapter 4, p. 115.
5. *Id.*, Chapter 5, p. 157.

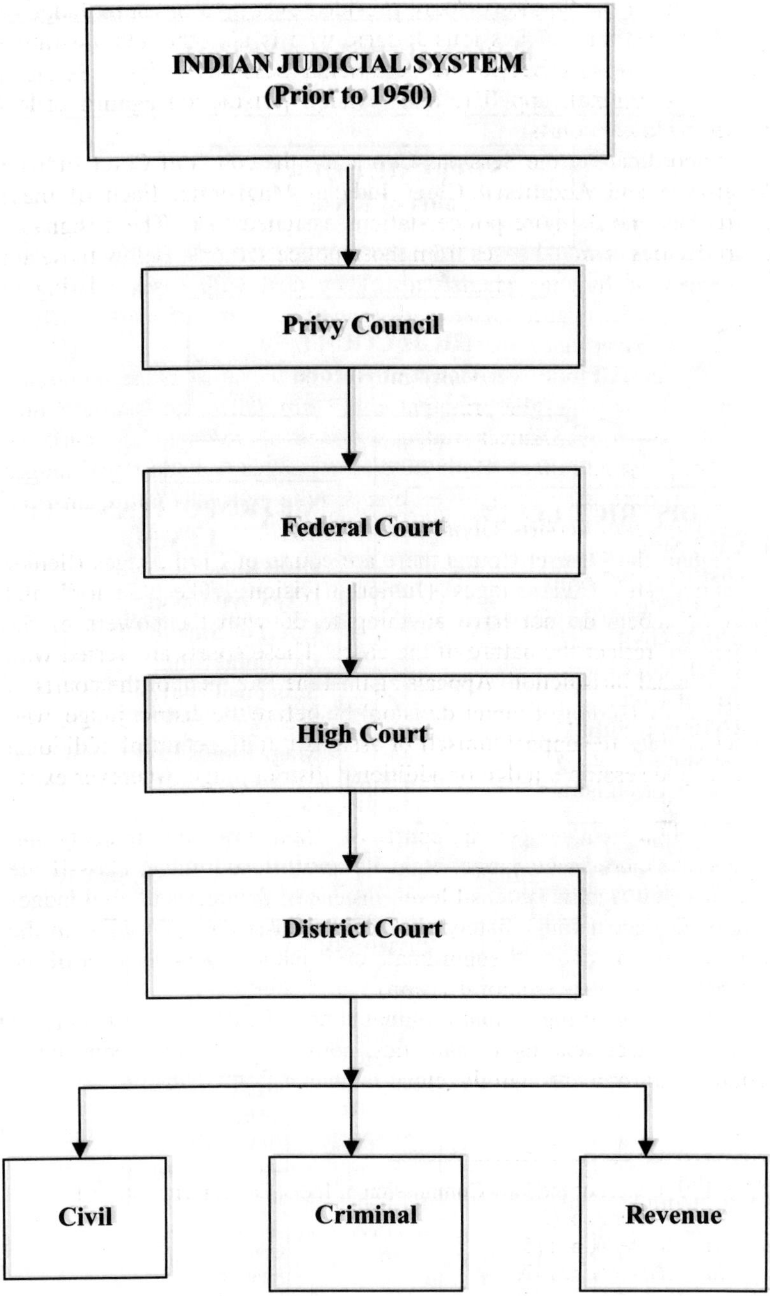
INDIAN JUDICIAL SYSTEM
(Prior to 1950)
Privy Council
Federal Court
High Court
District Court
Civil
Criminal
Revenue

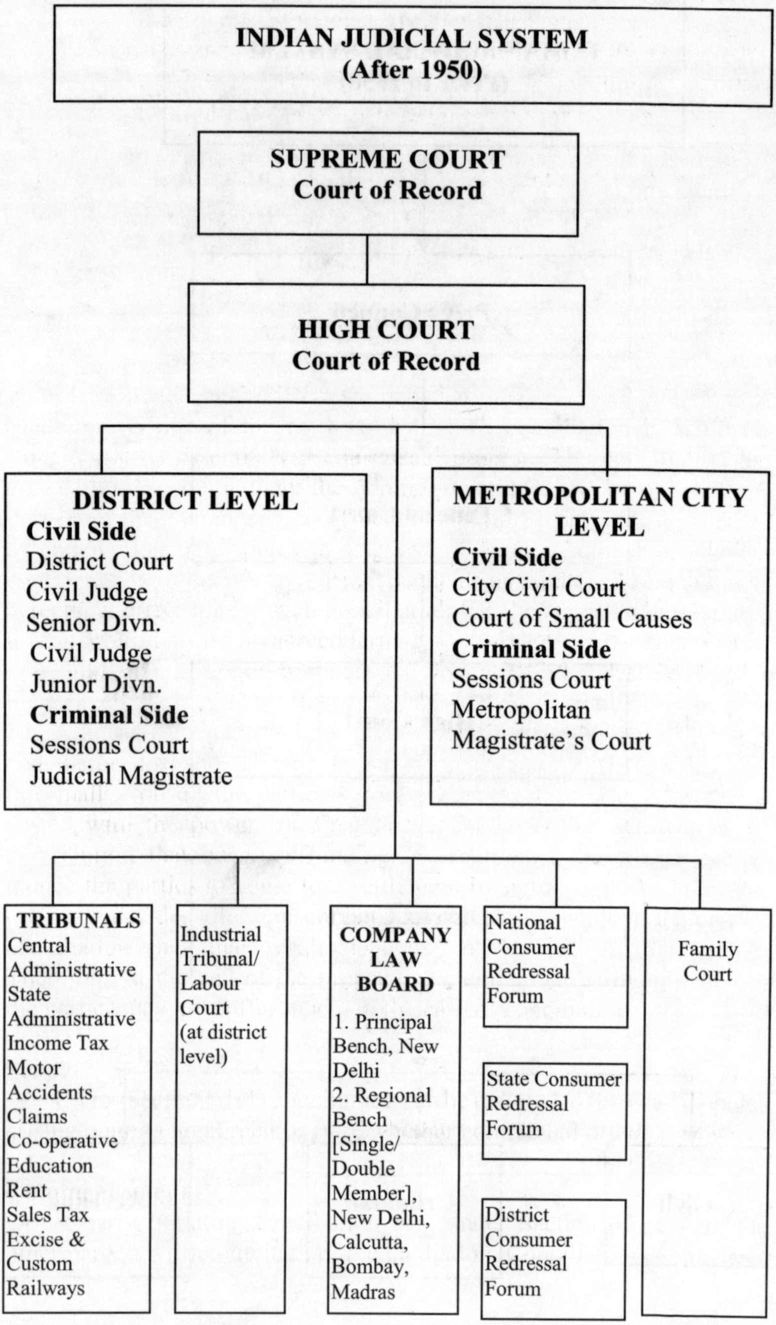
INDIAN JUDICIAL SYSTEM
(After 1950)
SUPREME COURT
Court of Record
HIGH COURT
Court of Record
DISTRICT LEVEL
Civil Side
District Court
Civil Judge
Senior Divn.
Civil Judge
Junior Divn.
Criminal Side
Sessions Court
Judicial Magistrate
METROPOLITAN CITY LEVEL
Civil Side
City Civil Court
Court of Small Causes
Criminal Side
Sessions Court
Metropolitan
Magistrate's Court
TRIBUNALS
Central Administrative
State Administrative
Income Tax
Motor Accidents Claims
Co-operative
Education
Rent
Sales Tax
Excise & Custom
Railways
Industrial Tribunal/ Labour Court (at district level)
COMPANY LAW BOARD
1. Principal Bench, New Delhi
2. Regional Bench [Single/ Double Member], New Delhi, Calcutta, Bombay, Madras
National Consumer Redressal Forum
State Consumer Redressal Forum
District Consumer Redressal Forum
Family Court

SUPREME COURT
(Court of Record)

Original Jurisdiction	**Appellate Jurisdiction**
I	**II**
1. between the Government of India and one or more States	1. Appeal in matters of interpretation of the Constitution
2. between the Government of India and any State or States on one side and one or more other States on the other	2. Appeal in Civil Cases
3. between two or more States	3. Appeal in Criminal Cases 4. Special leave to appeal

SUPREME COURT
(Court of Record)

Advisory Jurisdiction	**Writ Jurisdiction**
III	**IV**
If at any time it appears to the President that— (a) a question of law has arisen or is likely to arise; and (b) the question is of such a nature and such public importance that it is expedient to obtain the opinion of the Supreme Court upon it, he may refer the question for the advisory opinion of the court.	Art. 32 1. Habeas Corpus 2. Mandamus 3. Certiorari 4. Prohibition 5. Quo-warranto

Original Jurisdiction Civil Company Matters	**Appellate/ Revisional Jurisdiction**	**Reference Jurisdiction**	**Court of Record**
I	**II**	**III**	**IV**

Power of Superintendent over all courts	**Power to withdraw/ transfer cases**	**Power to issue writs**
V	**VI**	**VII Art. 226**

SUBORDINATE COURT

Civil Cases

Succession Certificate
(a) District Court
↓
(b) Civil Court

Land Acquisition

Matrimonial Cases

Letter of Administration

Probate

Guardianship cases

(a) Sessions Judge
(b) Chief Judicial Magistrate/Chief Metropolitan Magistrate
(c) Sub-Divisional Magistrate
(d) Judicial Magistrate/Metropolitan Magistrate

JUDICIAL MAGISTRATE

First Class | Second Class | Special Judicial Magistrate

TRIBUNALS AND OTHER QUASI-JUDICIAL BODIES

1	2	3	4	5	6	7
Labour	Tax Cases Sales Tax	Excise & Gold		Service	Motor	Environmental
Disputes		Control	Matters	Accident Cases	Disputes	
Labour Industrial National Court Tribunal	Income Tax Officer	Central Excise & Gold Control Tribunal	Central Admin. Tribunal	Motor Accident Claim Tribunal	National Environmental Tribunal	Sales Tax Officer
High Court	Income Tax Commissioner	State Admin. Tribunal		Sales Tax Commissioner		
Supreme Court	Income Tax Appellate Tribunal High Court Supreme Court	Joint Admin. Tribunal		Sales Tax Tribunal		

8	9	10	11	12	13	14	15	16
Company Cases	Unfair Trade Practices	Consumer Cases	Educational Disputes	Rent Cases	Railway Claims	Bank Cases	Family Courts	Petroleum & Natural Gas
Company Law Board	Mono-polies & Res-trictive Trade Forum Commission	National Consumer Redressal	Educational Tribunal	Rent Tribunal	Railway Claims Practices	Bank Tribunal	Petroleum Board	
	Competition Commission		State Redressal Consumer Forum	Rent Controller				Electricity Tribunal

ALTERNATIVE FORUM FOR RESOLUTION OF DISPUTES

- Lok Adalat (People's Court)
- Gram Panchayat
- Mediation
- Conciliation
- Arbitration
  - National
  - International
- Pension & Public Grievance Cells
- Court of Enquiry

Chapter VII

ALTERNATIVE FORUM FOR RESOLUTION OF DISPUTES: CONCILIATION, ARBITRATION, AND MEDIATION; LOK ADALATS—ASPECTS OF LEGAL METHOD

I. INTRODUCTION

Alternative dispute resolution as the name itself signifies is an alternative to the traditional judicial system. It seeks to involve people in the process of resolving their dispute, which is not possible in a formal and adversarial system. It offers wide range of choices in method, procedure, cost, representation and location. It is faster than judicial proceedings and reduces burdens on the courts.

Existing Models

In India a wide range of models exists for redressal of disputes. Among them mention may be made of the following authorities:

1. Tribunals, Commissions, Regulatory Authority Commission, etc.
2. Lok Adalats
3. Nyaya Panchayat
4. Conciliation
5. Mediation

6. Arbitration
7. Ombudsman
8. Fast Track Courts

II. TRIBUNALS

Tribunal System in India—Article 323-B of the Constitution empowers the legislature to establish tribunal, commissions, district boards, etc., for the adjudication or trial of any disputes, complaints or offences with respect to specified matters, even though various tribunals existed even prior to 1976 and the provisions for special leave to appeal and writs exists even prior to 1976. The tribunals, as alternative for settlement of special types of disputes are quicker, economical, and less formal and possess expertise in a subject compared to the courts.

Two decades after commencement of the Constitution of India, it was realized that the existing court system alone was insufficient to cater the needs of people and to deal with all types of disputes. The Constitution was accordingly amended and Article 323-B was added to authorize the legislature to establish tribunals, commissions, district boards, etc., for the adjudication or trial of any disputes, complaints or offences with respect to any matters.

Functions of the Tribunal

The functions and duties of the Tribunal are very much like those of a body discharging judicial functions, although it is not a court. The rules framed by the Tribunal require evidence to be taken and witness to be examined, cross-examined and re-examined. The Act constituting the Tribunal imposes penalties for incorrect statements made before the Tribunal. While the powers of the Tribunal in some respects are different from those of an ordinary civil court and it has jurisdiction and powers to give reliefs which a civil court administering the law of the land (for instance, ordering the reinstatement of a workman) does not possess in the discharge of its duties, it is essentially working as a judicial body. The fact that its determination has to be followed by an order of the Government which makes the award binding, or that in cases where Government is a party the legislature is permitted to revise the decision, or that the Government is empowered to fix the period of the operation of the award do not alter the nature and character of the functions of the Tribunal. Thus, the Tribunal is discharging functions very near those of a court, although it is not a court in the technical sense of the word. The main function of this tribunal is to adjudicate the disputes which imply that there must be two or more parties before it with conflicting cases, and that it has also to arrive at a conclusion as to how the dispute is to be ended.

Nature of Tribunal

The tribunal, to use the well-known legal maxim "all the trappings of a court, performs functions which cannot but be regarded as judicial. This is evident from the rules by which the proceedings before the tribunal are regulated. Generally speaking the proceedings before it commence on an application which in many respects is in the nature of a plaint. It has been vested with the same power as that of civil court under the Code of Civil Procedure when trying a suit, in respect of discovery, inspection, granting adjournment, reception of evidence taken on affidavit, enforcing the attendance of witness, compelling the production of documents, issuing commissions, etc. It is to be deemed to be a civil court within the meaning of Sections 480 and 482 of the Code of Criminal Procedure, 1973. It may admit and call for evidence at any stage of the proceeding and has the power to administer oaths. The parties appearing before it have the right of examination, cross-examination and re-examination and of addressing it after all evidence has been called. A party may also be represented by a legal practitioner with its permission.

In settling the Labour disputes the function of the tribunal is not confined to administration of justice in accordance with law. It can confer rights and privileges on either party which it considers reasonable and proper, though they may not be within the terms of any existing agreement. It has not merely to interpret or give effect to the contractual rights and obligations of the parties. It can create new rights and obligations between them which it considers essential for keeping industrial peace. An industrial dispute as has been said on many occasions is nothing but a trial of strength between the employers on the one hand and the workmen's organization on the other and the industrial tribunal has got to arrive at some equitable arrangement for averting strikes and lock-outs which impede production of goods and the industrial development of the country. The tribunal is not bound by the rigid rules of law.

Existing Tribunals

Name of the Tribunal	Name of Statute
1. (i) Central Administrative Tribunal (ii) State Administrative Tribunal (iii) Joint Administrative Tribunal	1. Administrative Tribunals Act, 1985
2. (i) General Courts Martial (ii) District Courts Martial (iii) Summary-General Courts Martial	2. Air Force Act, 1950
3. (i) General Courts Martial (ii) District Courts Martial (iii) Summary-General Courts Martial	3. Army Act, 1950
4. Banking Regulations Tribunal	4. Banking Regulation Act, 1949

Name of Tribunal	Name of Statute & Functions
5. Appellate Tribunal for Electricity	The Electricity Act, 2003 It has jurisdiction to hear appeals against the orders of the adjudicating officer, the Central Regulatory Commission, State Regulatory Commission and Joint Commission constituted under section 76(i) or 82 or 83 of the Act. The tribunal has also original jurisdiction to hear petitions under section 121 of the Act, it may issue directions to any Appropriate Commission for the performance of its statutory functions.
6. Railways Claims Tribunal	Railways Act, 1989 It has jurisdiction, powers and authority which was exercised by any Civil Court or a Claims Commissioner appointed under the provisions of the Railways Act,—(a) relating to the responsibility of the railway administrations as carriers under Chapter VII of the Railways Act in respect of claims for—(i) compensation for loss, destruction, damages,

Name of Tribunal	Name of Statute & Functions
	deterioration or non-delivery of animals or goods entrusted to a railway administration for carriage by railway, and (ii) compensation payable under Sections 124 and 124A of The Railways Act or the rules made thereunder; and (b) in respect of the claims for refund of fares or part thereof or for refund of any freight paid in respect of animals or goods entrusted to a railway administration to be carried by railway.
7. Income tax Appellate Tribunal	Income Tax Act, 1961 It has powers to decide other matters dealing with exercise of quasi-judicial powers of the tax administration such as, whether or not the tax assessment can be reopened by the Assessing Officer and thereby disturb finality of the assessment, whether or not registration as a charitable exemption has been correctly declined by the Administrative Commissioner, or whether or not a particular assessment order can be subjected to review by the Administrative Commissioner because of his perception that the order so sought to be revised is erroneous and prejudicial to the interest of the revenue. In so far as the matters in which appeals can be filed against the orders passed by the Administrative Commissioner, the ITAT is the first appellate authority.
8. Debts & Recovery Tribunal	The Recovery of Debts Due to Banks and Financial Institutions Act, 1993.
9. Customs Excise and Service Tax Appellate Tribunal	The Customs, Excise and Service Tax Appellate Tribunal.
10. National Company Law Tribunals	All the matters relating to companies which were earlier handled by various High Courts, CLB, BIFR and AAIFR will now be handled by the NCLT. Pending matters with the High Court and CLB will be transferred to NCLT.
11. National Green Tribunal	In June 2010, the National Green Tribunal Act has been established for handling cases involving environmental law.

Name of Tribunal	Name of Statute & Functions
12. Intellectual Property Appellate Board	Intellectual Property Appellate Board (IPAB) has been constituted by the Central Government in the Ministry of Commerce and Industry on 15th September 2003 to hear appeals against the decisions of the Registrar under the Trade Marks Act, 1999 and the Geographical Indications of Goods (Registration and Protection) Act, 1999.
13. Labour Tribunal	Like consumer, following alternative dispute settlement machinery exists for the resolution of labour disputes: (i) Labour court (ii) Industrial tribunal (iii) National tribunal (iv) Arbitration under section 10A

Quite apart from the aforesaid tribunals, there are several other tribunals, which, *inter alia*, include:

1. Election Tribunal.
2. Income Tax Tribunal under the Income Tax Act.
3. Central Administrative Tribunal under the Administrative Tribunal Act.
4. National Commission (State Commission, District Forum).
5. Election Tribunal under the Representation of People's Act.
6. Revenue Tribunal.
7. Rent Central Authority under Rent Control Act.
8. Excise Appellate Tribunal under Excise Act.
9. Commission for Religious Endowment.
10. Panchayat Court.

III. COMMISSIONS UNDER CONSTITUTION

The Constitution provides for following Commissions:

(i) National Finance Commission;
(ii) Election Commission;
(iii) Commission on Official Languages;
(iv) Union Public Service Commission and State Public Service Commissions;
(v) Commission for Backward Classes; and
(vi) National Commission for Scheduled Castes and Scheduled Tribes.

Commissions created by Statutes

(i) Press Council under the Press Council Act, 1965;
(ii) Inquiry Commissions under the Commissions of Inquiry Act, 1952;
(iii) National Commission for Women under the National Commission for Women Act, 1990;
(iv) National Commission for Minorities under the National Commission for Minorities Act, 1992;
(v) Human Rights Commission under the Protection of Human Rights Act, 1993;
(vi) National Commission for Backward Classes under the National Backward Class Commission Act, 1993;
(vii) National Commission for Backward Classes under the National Backward Class Commission Act, 1993;
(viii) Competition Commission under the Competition Act, 2002;
(ix) Electricity Regulatory Commissions under the Electricity Act, 2003;
(x) TRAI under the Telecom Regulatory Authority of India Act, 1995; and
(xi) IRDA under the Insurance Regulatory and Development Authority Act, 1999.

Commissions set-up by Government Resolution

(i) Planning Commission; and
(ii) Law Commission.

IV. REGULATORY AUTHORITY

1. Competition Commission of India under the Competition Act, 2002.
2. Central Electricity Regulatory Commission and State Electricity Regulatory Commission under the Electricity Act, 2003, Joint Commission.
3. Telecom Regulatory Authority of India under the Telecom Regulatory Authority (Telecom Dispute Settlement and Appellate Tribunal) of India Act, 1997.
4. Insurance Regulatory & Development Authority under Insurance Regulatory & Development Authority Act, 1999.
5. Petroleum & Natural Gas Regulatory Board under the Petroleum & Natural Gas Regulatory Board Act, 2006

V. LOK ADALATS

Lok Adalat is another mode of ADR. The Lok Adalats decide the dispute with utmost expedition to arrive at a compromise or settlement on the basis of principles of justice, equity, fair play and other legal principles, when no agreement is arrived.

Constitutional Mandate

Article 39A of the Constitution provides that the State shall secure that the operation of the legal system promotes justice on the basis of equal opportunity, and shall, in particular, provide free legal aid, by suitable legislation or schemes or in any other way, to ensure that opportunities for securing justice are not denied to any citizen by reason of economic or other disabilities.

In order to achieve the objective the Government appointed a Committee for Implementing Legal Aid Scheme [CILAS] to monitor and implement legal aid programs on uniform basis in all the States and Union Territories. The said Committee evolved a model scheme which was accordingly implemented by the Government. But on review certain deficiencies were found and it was considered desirable to constitute statutory legal authorities at the National, State and District levels so as to provide effective monitoring of legal aid programs.

For the disposal of large number of cases expeditiously and without much cost, Lok Adalats have been constituted and they have been functioning as conciliatory agencies.

Lok Adalat means people's court, in contrast to the regular law courts. Lok Adalats received statutorily sanction by the Legal Services Authorities Act, 1987. The Act seeks to provide free and competent Legal service to the weaker sections of the society to ensure that opportunities for securing justice are not denied to any citizen by reason of economic or other disabilities, and to organize Lok Adalats to secure that the operation of the legal system promotes justice on the basis of equal opportunity.

Legal Status and Powers of Lok Adalats

Under the Legal Services Authorities Act, 1987 the Lok Adalats have a sound statutory base. Sections 19-22 of the Legal Services Authority Act, 1987 deal with Lok Adalats. Let us turn to examine them.

Organization of Lok Adalats

Section 19(1) authorizes every State Authority, District Authority or the Supreme Court, Legal Services Committee of every High Court, Legal Services Committee or, as the case may be, Taluk Legal Services

Committee to organize Lok Adalts at such intervals and places and for exercising such jurisdiction and for such areas as it thinks fit.

Composition

Every Lok Adalat organized for an area shall consist of –

(a) Serving or retired judicial officer as Chairperson, and

(b) two members.

The experience and qualifications of other persons referred to in clause (b) of sub-section (2) of Lok Adaltas organized by the Supreme Court Legal Services Committee shall be such as may be prescribed by the Central Government in consultation with the Chief Justice of India.

The experience and qualifications of other persons referred to in clause (b) of sub-section (2) for Lok Adalats other than referred to in sub-section (3) shall be such as may be prescribed by the State Government in consultation with the Chief Justice of High Court.

Jurisdiction

Jurisdiction of the area as may be specified by the State Authority or the District Authority or the Supreme Court Legal Services Committee or the High Court Legal Services Committee, or as the case may be, the Taluk Legal Services Committee organizing such Lok Adalats.

A Lok Adalat shall have jurisdiction to determine and to arrive at a compromise or settlement between the parties to a dispute in respect of—

(i) any case pending before; or

(ii) any matter which is falling with the jurisdiction of, and is not brought before,

any court for which the Lok Adalat is organized.

However, no Lok Adalat shall have jurisdiction in respect of any case or matter relating to an offence not compoundable under any law.

Cognizance of Cases by Lok Adalats

(1) Where in any case referred to in clause (i) of sub-section (5) of section 19—

(i) (a) the parties thereof agree; or

(b) one of the parties thereof makes an application to the court, for referring the case to the Lok Adalat for settlement and if such court is *prima facie* satisfied that there are chances of such settlement; or

(ii) The court is satisfied that the matter is an appropriate one to be taken cognizance of by the Lok Adalat.

The court shall refer the case to the Lok Adalat.

However, no case shall be referred to the Lok Adalat under sub-clause (b) of clause (i) or clause (ii) by such court except after giving a reasonable opportunity of being heard to the parties.

Reference to Lok Adalat

The Authority or Committee organizing the Lok Adalat under sub-section (1) of section 19 may, on receipt of an application from any one of the parties to any matter referred to in clause (ii) of sub-section (5) of section 19 that such matter needs to be determined by a Lok Adalat, refer such matter to the Lok Adalat, for determination.

Duties of Lok Adalat

(1) Where any case is referred to a Lok Adalat the Lok Adalat shall proceed to dispose of the case or matter and arrive at a compromise or settlement between the parties.

(2) Every Lok Adalat shall, while determining any reference before it under this Act, act with utmost expedition to arrive at a compromise or settlement between the parties and shall be guided by the principles of justice, equity, fair play and other legal principles.

(3) Where no award is made by the Lok Adalat on the ground that no compromise or settlement could be arrived at between the parties, the record of the case shall be returned by it to the court, from which the reference has been received under sub-section (1) for disposal in accordance with law.

(4) Where no award is made by the Lok Adalat on the ground that no compromise or settlement could be arrived at between the parties, in a manner referred in sub-section (2), that Lok Adalat shall advice the parties to seek remedy in a court.

(5) Where the record of the case is returned under sub-section (5) to the court, such court shall proceed to deal with such case from the stage which was reached before such reference under sub-section (1).

Award of Lok Adalat

(1) Every award of the Lok Adalat shall be deemed to be a decree of a civil court or, as the case may be, an order of any other court and where a compromise or settlement has been arrived at, by a Lok Adalat in a case referred to it under sub-section (1) of section 20, the court-fee paid in such case shall be refunded in accordance with the Court Fees Act, 1870 (7 of 1870).

(2) Every award made by a Lok Adalat shall be final and binding on all parties to the dispute, and no appeal shall lie to any court against the award.

Section 22 provides: Powers of Lok Adalats

(1) Every Lok Adalat or Permanent Lok Adalat shall, for the purposes of holding any determination under this Act, have the same powers as are vested in a civil court under the Code of Civil Procedures, 1908 (5 of 1908) while trying a suit in respect of the following matters, namely:

(a) the summoning and enforcing the attendance of any witness and examining him on oath;
(b) the discovery and production of any document;
(c) the reception of evidence on affidavits;
(d) the requisitioning of any public record or document or copy of such record or document from any court or office; and
(e) such other matters as may be prescribed.

(2) Every Lok Adalat is also empowered to specify its own procedure for the determination of any dispute coming before it.

(3) All proceedings before a Lok Adalat shall be deemed to be judicial proceedings with the meaning of sections 193, 219 and 228 of the Code of Criminal Procedure, 1973.

Permanent Lok Adalats

In order to decongest the existing courts the Legal Services Authorities (Amendment) Act, 2002 seeks to provide the composition and establishment of permanent Lok Adalats. It shall consist of the Chairman of the status of a District Judge or an Additional District Judge or even higher status Judge and two other persons with adequate experiences in public utility services. The Lok Adalat shall have Jurisdiction to adjudicate matters connected with transport services of passengers or goods by air, road and water.

Who may Constitute?

Section 22B empowers: (i) The Central Authority or, as the case may be, every State Authority is required to establish Permanent Lok Adalats at such places and for exercising such jurisdiction in respect of one or more public utility services and for such areas as may be specified in the notification, (ii) postal, telegraph or telephone services; (iii) supply of power, light or water to the public by any establishment; (iii) public conservancy or sanitation; (iv) services in hospitals or dispensaries; and (v) insurance services.

Pecuniary Jurisdiction

The primary jurisdiction of the Permanent Lok Adalat is upto Rs.10 Lakhs. However, the Central Government may increase the monetary jurisdiction of pubic utility services by amendment in the rules only and without going to the Parliament.

Duties

Lok Adalat is required to adjudicate pre-litigative disputes and its awards will be binding within the meaning of Civil Procedure Code.

Cognizance of cases by Permanent Lok Adalat.—Section 22C provides that (1) any party to a dispute may, before the dispute is brought before any court, make an application to the Permanent Lok Adalat for the settlement of dispute. However, the Permanent Lok Adalat have jurisdiction of any matter. (2) Once an application is made to the Permanent Lok Adalat, no party to that application shall invoke jurisdiction of any court in the same dispute.

Where an application is made to a Permanent Lok Adalat under sub-section (1), it—

(a) shall direct each party to the application to file before it a written statement, stating therein the facts and nature of dispute under the application points or issues in such dispute under the application points or issues in such dispute and grounds relied in support of, or in opposition to, such points or issues, as the case may be, and such party may supplement such statement with any document and other evidence which such party deems appropriate in proof of such facts and grounds and shall send a copy of such statement together with a copy of such document and other evidence, if any, to each of the parties to the application;

(b) may require any party to the application to file additional statement before it at any stage of the conciliation proceedings; and

(c) shall communicate any document or statement received by it from any party to the application to the other party, to enable such other party to present reply thereto.

(3) When statement, additional statement and reply, if any, have been filed under sub-section (3), to the satisfaction of the Permanent Lok Adalat, it shall conduct conciliation proceedings between the parties to the application in such manner as it thinks appropriate taking into account the circumstance of the dispute.

(4) The Permanent Lok Adalat shall, during conduct of conciliation proceedings under sub-section (4), assist the parties in their attempt to reach an amicable settlement of the dispute in an independent and impartial manner.

(5) It shall be the duty of every party to the application to

cooperate in good faith with the Permanent Lok Adalat in conciliation of the dispute relating to the application and to comply with the direction of the Permanent Lok Adalat to produce evidence and other related documents before it.

(6) When a Permanent Lok Adalat, in the aforesaid conciliation proceedings, is of the opinion that there exist elements of settlement in such proceedings which may be acceptable to the parties, it may formulate the terms of a possible settlement of the dispute and give to the parties concerned for their observations and in case the parties reach at an agreement on the settlement of the dispute, they shall sign the settlement agreement and the Permanent Lok Adalat shall pass an award in terms thereof and furnish a copy of the same to each of the parties concerned.

(7) Where the parties fail to reach at an agreement under sub-section (7), the Permanent Lok Adalat shall, if the dispute does not relate to any offence, decide the dispute.

Procedure of Permanent Lok Adalat.—Section 22C Lays down the procedure to be followed by Permanent Lok Adalat. It says that the Permanent Lok Adalat shall, while conducting conciliation proceeding or deciding a dispute on merit under this Act will follow the principles of natural justice, objectivity, fair play, equity and other principles of justice. It is not be bound by the Code of Civil Procedure, 1908 and the Indian Evidence Act, 1872.

Award of Permanent Lok Adalat to be final.—Under Section (22E) every award of the Permanent Lok Adalat (1) made either on merit or in terms of a settlement agreement shall be final and binding on all the parties thereto and on person claiming under them, (2) shall be deemed to be a decree of a civil court, (3) shall be by a majority of the persons constituting the Permanent Lok Adalat, (4) shall be final and shall not be called in question in any original suit, application or execution proceeding. The Permanent Lok Adalat may transmit any award made by it to a civil court having local jurisdiction and such civil court shall execute the order as if it were a decree made by that court.

VI. NYAY PANCHAYATS

In India, *Panchayat* System is prevalent since ancient days. In village, the administration was carried out by a *Panchayat* headed by village headman who among others, were deciding petty civil, criminal and revenue cases. The respectable members of the village community formed the *Panchayat*, where the five preferred ones amongst them used to resolve the disputes by a process of conciliation and mediation.

Panchayat's decisions were generally honored and accepted by the village community. In the pre-British period, the *Panchayat* formed the key-stone of the village arch. However, during the British rule *Panchayats* were not permitted to function as autonomous and self-sufficient bodies. After India became independent *Panchayats* were revived and it began to function in all states.

The functions of *Pachayats* cover a wide range of activities, which may broadly be classified under four broad categories: (i) civic amenities; (ii) social welfare activities; (iii) development work; and (iv) judicial functions such as resolution of petty civil, criminal and revenue cases.

The dispensation under the Constitution of India, pertaining to *Panchayats*, was introduced by the Constitution (73rd Amendment) Act, 1992 w.e.f. 01-06-1993, by inserting Part-IX, from Articles 243 and 243(A) to 243(O) and Schedule-XI as organic parts of the Constitution. It enjoined the State to take steps to organize village *Panchayats* and endow them with such powers and authority as may be necessary to enable them to function as units of self-government. The 73rd Constitution Amendment lays down in broad outline, the constitution, composition, reservation of seats, duration, disqualification for membership, powers, authority and responsibilities of *Panchayat*, power to impose taxes, and several other related matters. Apart from the above, one of the highlights of the 73rd Amendment is the *Gram Sabha* (village assembly) for every *Panchayat.* When *Panchayat* dispenses justice it acts as *Nyaya Panchayat.*

The major characteristics of *Panchayat* are as under:

(i) *Panchayats* have become the institutions of local self-governance in rural areas, where people elect their own representatives.

(ii) The duration of the office of every *Panchayat* is five years, unless dissolved.

(iii) It is a community organization free from party affiliation.

(iv) It is not only a unit of local self-government but also an effective institution for securing social justice.

(v) For attaining the goal of social justice, express provision under the 73rd Amendment of the Constitution is made for reservation of seats for Scheduled Castes and Scheduled Tribes with the number of seats reserved, bearing, as nearly as possible, the same proportion to the total number of seats to be filled by direct election, as the population of the Scheduled Castes or the Scheduled Tribes in that *Panchayat* area bears to the total population of that area. Such seats are allotted by rotation to different constituencies in a *Panchayat*.

(vi) In order to give representation to women in *Panchayats*, as provided in the 73rd Amendment of the Constitution, one-third of the total number of seats are reserved for women.

(vii) *Panchayat* is required to prepare plans for economic development and social justice implement such sachems.

(viii) *Panchayat* may levy, collect and appropriate such taxes, duties, tolls and fees as specified in the law by the legislature of the state.

VII. CONCILIATION

There is not much difference between mediation and conciliation. Mediation is one of the methods by which conciliation is achieved. Conciliation is essentially a consensual process. The conciliation has got statutory sanction under the Arbitration and Conciliation Act, 1996. Part III of the Act consisting of Sections 61 to 81 provides for method of conciliation of disputes arising out of legal relationship, whether contractual or not. It is by an independent conciliator. The settlement agreement arrived at by such conciliation has the status and effect as if it is an arbitral award on agreed terms.

Unlike an arbitrator, a conciliator does not give a decision but his main function is to induce the parties themselves to come to settlement. An Arbitrator is expected to give a hearing to the parties, but a conciliator does not engage in any formal hearing, though he may informally consult the parties separately or together. The arbitrator is vested with the power for final decision and in that sense it is his contribution that becomes binding. In contrast, a conciliator has to induce the parties to come to a settlement by agreement. An arbitrator generally decides after consent between the parties while in the case of conciliation the final result depends on the will of the parties. Therefore, at the end of the proceedings, emotional harmony between the parties may not suffer much, in the case of conciliation.

Scope

Under Section 61(1) conciliation can be resorted to resolve "disputes arising out of a legal relationship, whether contractual or not".

Commencement

A party initiating conciliation can, under Section 62 send to the other party a written invitation to conciliation. Conciliation commences when the other party accepts in writing this initiation. If it does not accept it, then there will be no conciliation.

Composition

There will be only one conciliator, unless the parties agree to two or three. Where there are two or three conciliators, then as a rule, they ought to act jointly. Where there is only one conciliator, the parties may agree on his name. When three are two conciliators, each party may appoint one, and the parties may agree on the name of the third conciliator, who shall act as presiding conciliator.

Institutional Assistance

Parties may enlist the assistance of a suitable institution or person regarding appointment of conciliator. The institution may be required to recommend or to directly appoint the conciliator or conciliators. In recommending such appointment, the institutions, etc. shall have regard to the considerations likely to secure an "independent and impartial conciliator". In the case of a sole conciliator, the institution shall take into account the advisability of appointing a conciliator other than the one having the nationality of the parties.

Stages

Sections 65 to 73 lay down the procedure to be followed by the conciliator. Thus, the conciliator, when appointed, may request each party to submit a statement, setting out the general nature of the dispute and the points at issue. Copy of the same must be given to the other party. If necessary, the parties may be asked to submit further written statement and other evidence.

The conciliator shall assist the parties "in an independent and impartial manner", in their attempt to arrive at an amicable settlement. The conciliator is guided by the principles of "objectivity, fairness and justice". He has to give consideration to: rights and obligations of the parties; trade usages; and circumstances surrounding the dispute, including previous business practices between the parties. He may, at any stage, propose a settlement, even orally, and without stating the reasons for the proposal. He may invite the parties (for discussion) or communicate with them jointly or separately. For successful conciliation, parties themselves must, in good faith, co-operative with the conciliator and supply the needed written material, provide evidence and attend meetings. If the conciliator finds that there exist "elements of a settlement which may be acceptable to the parties", then he shall formulate the terms of a possible settlement and submit the same to the parties for their observation. On receipt of the observations of the parties, the conciliator may re-formulate the terms of a possible settlement in the light of such observation. If ultimately a settlement is reached, then the parties may draw a sign on written settlement agreement. At their request, the conciliator can help them in drawing up the same.

Legal Effect

The settlement/agreement signed by the parties shall be final and binding on the parties. It is to be authenticated by the conciliator. It has the same status and effect as if it were an arbitral award rendered by the arbitral tribunal on agreed terms. The net effect is that the settlement can be enforced as a degree of court under section 36 of the Act.

Role of the Parties

Under section 72, a party may submit to the conciliator his own suggestions for the settlement of a dispute. Such suggestions may be submitted by him either on his own initiative or on request of the conciliator.

Procedure

The conciliator is not bound by the Code of Civil Procedure or the Evidence Act. The conciliator is to be guided by the principles of objectivity, fairness and justice. He may conduct the proceedings in such manner as he considers appropriate, taking into account the circumstances of the case; wishes expressed by the parties; and need for speedy settlement.

Disclosure and Secrecy

Factual information received by the conciliator from one party should be disclosed to the other party, so that the other party can present his explanation, if he so desires. But information given on the conditions of confidentiality cannot be so disclosed. This obligation extends also to the settlement agreement except where disclosure is necessary for its implementation and enforcement.

Admissions

In any arbitral or judicial proceedings (whether relating to the conciliated dispute or otherwise the party shall not rely on, or introduce as evidence views expressed or suggestion made by the other party for a possible settlement; admissions made by the other party in the course of conciliation proceedings proposal made by the conciliator; and the fact that the other party had indicated his willingness to accept a settlement proposal.

Parallel Proceedings

During the pendency of conciliation proceedings, a party is debarred from initiating arbitral or judicial proceedings on the same dispute, except "such proceedings as are necessary for preserving his rights".

Conciliator Not to Act as Arbitrator, etc.

Unless otherwise agreed by the parties, the conciliator cannot act as arbitrator, representative or counsel in any arbitral or judicial proceedings in respect of the conciliated dispute. Nor can he be "presented" by any party as a witness in such proceedings.

VIII. MEDIATION

Mediation is a simple relatively inexpensive form of dispute resolution by communication. Successful mediation as an alternative method of dispute resolution, in all of these contexts, is mediation because it has the following five elements:

1. An Impartial Third Party Facilitator

The third party neutral, the mediator, is the person who makes the entire process work. As long as there is a neutral facilitator, the parties can trust that they have some safety and are not being abused by an interested party. All of these programs work because the mediator in them is known to either be neutral or supportive of the parties and not an involved party.

2. A Third Party who Protects the Integrity of the Proceedings

The mediator preserves the integrity of the proceedings in all ways. The entire Mediation processes are "confidential" means that the mediation process doesn't become part of the public record as does a court trial.

3. Good Faith from the Participant

Both the behavior and integrity of the neutral are important in creating, and preserving good faith.

4. The Presence of the Parties

All parties necessary to resolve the problems should interact with the mediator. It is the parties who are being resolved as much as it is the problem that is being settled.

5. An Appropriate Site or Venue

Venue must be acceptable for all the relevant parties.

IX. ARBITRATION

Before 1996, arbitration was regulated by the Arbitration Act, 1940. This Act dealt with only domestic arbitration but not International Arbitration. The enforcement of foreign award was covered by the Arbitration and Protocol Act, 1937 and the Foreign Award (Recognition and Enforcement) Act, 1961. However, two Acts (except Section 3) merely laid down the conditions for enforcement of foreign awards in India.

Even though the Arbitration of 1940 Act was a good piece of legislation in actual practice it was felt by all concerned that it was ineffective. Dealing with the issue the Supreme Court in *M/S Guru Nanak Foundation v. M/S Rattan Singh & Sons*[1] observed:

> "In terminable, time consuming, complex and expensive court procedures impelled jurists to search for an alternative forum, less formal, more effective and speedy for resolution of disputes avoiding procedural claptrap and this led them to Arbitration Act, 1940. However, the way in which the proceedings under the Act are conducted and without an exception challenged in Courts, has made lawyers laugh and legal philosophers weep. Experience shows and law reports bear ample testimony that the proceedings under the Act have become highly technical accompanied by unending prolixity, at every stage providing a legal trap to the unwary. In formal forum chosen by the parties for expeditious disposal of the disputes has by the decision of the courts been clothed with "legalese" of unforeseeable complexity."

Eight years later, the Supreme Court in *Food Corporation of India v. Joginderpal Mohinderpal*[2] emphasized the need for simplification of the law of arbitration:

> "We should make the law of arbitration simple, less technical

1. (1981) 4 SSC 634.
2. 2 (1987) 3 SSC 394.

and more responsible to the actual realities of the situations but must be responsive to the canons of justice and fair play and make the arbitrator adhere to such process and norms which will create confidence, not only by doing justice between the parties, but by creating sense that justice appears to have been done."

The Arbitration & Conciliation Act, 1996 seeks to consolidate and amend the law relating to domestic arbitration, international commercial arbitration and enforcement of foreign arbitral awards as also defines the law relating to conciliation and for matters connected therewith or incidental thereto.

The Act of 1996 covers both international and domestic arbitration, i.e., where at least one party is not an Indian national and also arbitrations where both parties are Indian nationals respectively.

The Act is based on the Model Law, a set of 36 Articles, which was drafted to govern all international arbitrations by a working group of the UN and was finally adopted by the U.N. Commission on International Trade Law (UNCITRAL) on June 21, 1985.

Objectives of the Act

The main objectives of the Act are as under:—

(i) to comprehensively cover international and commercial arbitration and conciliation as also domestic arbitration and conciliation;

(ii) to make provision for an arbitral procedure which is fair, efficient and capable of meeting the needs of the specific arbitration;

(iii) to provide that the arbitral tribunal gives reasons for its arbitral award;

(iv) to ensure that the arbitral tribunal remains within the limits of its jurisdiction;

(v) to minimize the supervisory role of courts in the arbitral process;

(vi) to permit an arbitral tribunal to use mediation, conciliation or other procedures during the arbitral proceedings to encourage settlement of disputes;

(vii) to provide that every final arbitral award is enforced in the same manner as if it were a decree of the court;

(viii) to provide that a settlement agreement reached by the parties as a result of conciliation proceedings will have the same status and effect as an arbitral award on agreed terms on the substance of the dispute rendered by an arbitral tribunal; and

(ix) to provide that, for purposes of enforcement of foreign awards, every arbitral award made in a country to which one of the two international Conventions relating to foreign arbitral awards to which India is a party applies, will be treated as a foreign award.

THE ARBITRATION AND CONCILIATION ACT, 1996

The above Act seeks to consolidate and amend the law relating to domestic arbitration, international commercial arbitration and enforcement of foreign arbitral awards as also to define the law relating to conciliation and for matters connected therewith or incidental thereto.

Scope of the Act

The Act is divided into four parts, namely:

(i) Domestic Arbitration,

(ii) Enforcement of certain foreign awards,

(iii) Conciliation, and

(iv) Supplementary provisions.

Section 37 provides that an appeal shall lie from certain orders. No second appeal will lie from an order passed in an appeal. However, the right to appeal to the Supreme Court is not affected. Section 38 deals with deposits to be made by the parties in relation to arbitral proceedings. The arbitral is empowered to fix the amount of deposit or supplementary deposit as an advance for the costs of arbitration.

Lien on arbitral award and deposits as to costs: Section 39 provides that the arbitration agreement, the arbitral tribunal shall have a lien on the arbitral award for any unpaid costs of the arbitration.

Arbitration agreement not to be discharged by death of party thereto: Section 40 provides that an arbitration agreement shall not be discharged by the death of any party thereto either as respects the deceased or as respects any other party, but shall in such event be enforceable by or against the legal representative of the deceased.

Provisions in case of insolvency: Under Section 41, where it is provided by a term in a contract to which an insolvent is a party that any dispute arising thereout or in connection therewith shall be submitted to arbitration, the said term shall, if the receiver adopts the contract, be enforceable by or against him so far as it relates to any such dispute.

Jurisdiction: Under Section 42 court alone shall have jurisdiction over the arbitral proceedings and all subsequent applications arising out of that agreement and the arbitral proceedings shall be made in that court and in no other court.

Limitations: Section 43 provides that the Limitation Act, 1963 (36 of 1963), shall apply to arbitrations as it applies to proceedings in court. Section 33 empowers the arbitral tribunal to make connection in or give interpretations of awards and for making additional awards under certain conditions.

RECOURSE AGAINST ARBITRAL AWARD

Application for setting aside arbitral award: Section 34 lays down the following grounds for setting aside arbitral award:

(a) The party making the application furnishes proof that—

(i) a party was under some incapacity; or

(ii) the arbitration agreement is not valid under the law to which parties have subjected it or, failing any indication thereon, under the law for the time being in force; or

(iii) the party making the application was not give proper notice of the appointment of an arbitrator or of the arbitral proceedings or was otherwise unable to present his case; or

(iv) the arbitral award deals with a dispute not contemplated by or not falling within the terms of the submission to arbitration, or it contains decisions on matters beyond the scope of the submission to arbitration:

Provided that, if the decision on matters submitted to arbitration can be separated from those not so submitted to arbitration can be separated from those not so submitted, only that part of the arbitral award which contains decisions on matters not submitted to arbitration may be set aside; or

(v) the composition of the arbitral tribunal or the arbitral procedure was not in accordance with the agreement of the parties, unless such agreement was in conflict with a provision of this Part from which the parties cannot derogate, or, falling such agreement, was not in accordance with this Part; or

(b) The court finds that—

(i) the subject-matter of the dispute is not capable of

settlement by arbitration under the law for the time being in force, or

(ii) the arbitral award is in conflict with the public policy of India.

An application for setting aside may not be made after 3 months have elapsed from the date on which the party making that application had received the arbitral award or, if a request had been made under section 33, from the date on which that request had been disposed of by the arbitral tribunal, however if the court is satisfied that the applicant was prevented by sufficient cause from making the application within the said period of three months it may entertain the application within a further period of thirty days, but not thereafter.

The court may, where it is appropriate and it is so requested by a party, adjourn the proceedings for a period of time determined by it in order to give the arbitral tribunal an opportunity to resume the arbitral proceedings or to take other action as in the opinion of arbitral tribunal will eliminate the grounds for setting aside the arbitral award.

Finality and Enforcement of Arbitral Awards

Finality of arbitral awards.—Section 35 requires that an arbitral award shall be final and binding on the parties and persons claiming under them respectively.

Enforcement.—Under Section 36 where the time for making an application to set aside the arbitral award under section 34 has expired, or such application having been made, it has been refused, the award shall be enforced under the Code of Civil Procedure, 1908 (5 of 1908) in the same manner as if it were a decree of the court.

Decision-making by panel of arbitrators.—Section 29 provides for decision-making by arbitrators and providers that unless the parties have otherwise agreed, in all arbitral proceedings with more than one arbitrator, decision, making by arbitral tribunal shall be by a majority of all its members.

Settlement.—(1) Section 30 provides it is not incompatible with an arbitration agreement for an arbitral tribunal to encourage settlement of the dispute and, with the agreement of the parties, the arbitral tribunal may use mediation, conciliation or other proceedings at any time during the arbitral proceedings to encourage settlement.

(2) If, during arbitral proceedings, the parties settle the dispute, the arbitral tribunal shall terminate the proceedings and, if requested by the parties and not objected to by the arbitral tribunal, record the settlement in the form of an arbitral award on agreed terms.

(3) An arbitral award on agreed terms shall be made in accordance with section 31 and shall state that it is an arbitral award.

(4) An arbitral award on agreed terms shall have the same status and effect as any other arbitral award on the substance of the dispute.

Form and contents of arbitral award.—(1) An arbitral award shall be made in writing and shall be signed by the members of the arbitral tribunal.

(2) For the purposes of sub-section (1), in arbitral proceedings with more than one arbitrator, the signatures of the majority of all the members of the arbitral tribunal shall be sufficient so long as the reason for any omitted signature is stated.

(3) The arbitral award shall state the reasons that no reasons upon which it is base, unless—

(a) the parties have agreed that not reasons are to be given, or

(b) the award is an arbitral award on agreed terms under section 30.

(4) The arbitral award shall state its date and the place of arbitration as determined in accordance with section 20 and the award shall be deemed to have been made at that place.

(5) After the arbitral award is made, a signed copy shall be delivered to each party.

(6) The arbitral tribunal may, at any time during the arbitral proceedings, make an interim arbitral award on any matter with respect to which it may make a final arbitral award.

(7) (a) Unless otherwise agreed by the parties, where and in so far as an arbitral award is for the payment of money, the arbitral tribunal may include in the sum for which the award is made interest, at such rate as it deems reasonable, on the whole or any part of the money, for the whole or any part of the period between the date on which the cause of action arose and the date on which the award is made.

(b) A sum directed to be paid by an arbitral award shall, unless the award otherwise directs, carry interest at the rate of eighteen per centum per annum from the date of the award to the date of payment.

(8) Unless otherwise agreed by the parties,—

(a) the costs of an arbitration shall be fixed by the arbitral tribunal;

(b) the arbitral tribunal shall specify—

(i) the party entitled to costs,

(ii) the party who shall pay the costs,

(iii) the amount of costs or method of determining that amount, and

(iv) the manner in which the costs shall be paid.

Section 31

Termination of proceedings.—(1) The arbitral proceedings shall be terminated by the final arbitral award or by an order of the arbitral tribunal under sub-section (2).

(2) The arbitral tribunal shall issue an order for the termination of the arbitral proceedings where—

(a) the claimant withdraws his claims, unless the respondent objects to the order and the arbitral tribunal recognizes a legitimate interest on his part in obtaining a final settlement of the dispute,

(b) the parties agree on the termination of the proceedings, or

(c) the arbitral tribunal finds that the continuation of the proceedings has for any other reason become unnecessary or impossible.

(3) Subject to section 33 and sub-section (4) of section 34, the mandate of the arbitral tribunal shall terminate with the termination of the arbitral proceedings.

Correction and interpretation of award; additional award.—Section 22 deals with the language to be used in arbitral proceedings. While the parties have freedom to agree upon the language or languages to be used in arbitral proceedings, if they fail to do so, the arbitral tribunal will determine the language or languages to be used in the arbitral proceedings.

Statements of claim and defense.—(1) Section 23 within the period of time agreed upon by the parties or determined by the arbitral tribunal, the claimant shall state the facts supporting his claim, the points at issue and the relief or remedy sought, and the respondent shall state his defense in respect of these particulars, unless the parties have otherwise agreed as to the required elements of those statements.

(2) The parties may submit with their statements all documents they consider to be relevant or may add a reference to the documents or other evidence they will submit.

(3) Unless otherwise agreed by the parties, either party may amend or supplement his claim or defense during the course of the arbitral proceedings, unless the arbitral tribunal considers it inappropriate to allow the amendment or supplement having regard to the delay in making it.

Hearing and written proceedings.—(1) Section 24 provides unless otherwise agreed by the parties, the arbitral tribunal shall decide whether to hold oral hearings for the presentation of evidence or for oral argument, or whether the proceedings shall be conducted on the basis of documents and other materials:

Provided that the arbitral tribunal shall hold oral hearings, at an appropriate stage of the proceedings on a request by a party, unless the parties have agreed that no oral hearing shall be held.

(2) The parties shall be given sufficient advance notice of any hearing and of any meeting of the arbitral for the purposes of inspection of documents, goods or other property.

(3) All statements, documents or other information supplied to, or applications made to the arbitral tribunal by one party shall be communicated to the other party, and any expert report or evidentiary document on which the arbitral tribunal may rely in making its decision shall be communicated to the parties.

Default of a party.—Under section 25 unless otherwise agreed by the parties, where, without showing sufficient cause—

(a) the claimant fails to communicate his statement of claim in accordance with sub-section (1) of section 23, the arbitral tribunal shall terminate the proceedings;

(b) the respondent fails to communicate his statement of defense in accordance with sub-section (1) of section 23, the arbitral tribunal shall continue the proceedings without treating that failure in itself as an admission of the allegations by the claimant; and

(c) a party fails to appear at an oral hearing or to produce documentary evidence, the arbitral tribunal may continue the proceedings and make the arbitral award on the evidence before it.

Expert appointment by arbitral tribunal.—(1) Under Section 26 unless otherwise agreed by the parties, the arbitral tribunal may—

(a) appoint one or more experts to report to it on specific issues to be determined by the arbitral tribunal, and

(b) require a party to give the expert any relevant information or to produce, or to provide access to, any relevant documents, goods or other property for his inspection.

(2) Unless otherwise agreed by the parties, if a party so requests or if the arbitral tribunal considers it necessary, the expert shall, after delivery after delivery of his written or oral report, participate in an oral hearing where the parties have the opportunity to put questions to him and to present expert witnesses in order to testify on the points at issue.

(3) Unless otherwise agreed by the parties, the expert shall, on the request of a party, make available to that party for examination all documents, goods or other property in the possession of the expert with which he was provided in order to prepare his report.

Court assistance in taking evidence.—(1) Section 27 provides the arbitral tribunal, or a party with the approval of the arbitral tribunal, may apply to the court for assistance in taking evidence.

(2) The application shall specify—

(a) the names and addresses of the parties and the arbitrators;

(b) the general nature of the claim and the relief sought;

(c) the evidence to be obtained, in particular,—

(i) the name and address of any person to be heard as witness or expert witness and a statement of the subject-matter of the testimony required; and

(ii) the description of any document to be produced or property to be inspected.

MAKING OF ARBITRAL AWARD AND TERMINATION OF PROCEEDINGS

Rules applicable to substance of dispute.—(1) Where the place of arbitration is situate in India,—

(a) in an arbitration other than an international commercial arbitration, the arbitral tribunal shall decide the dispute submitted to arbitration in accordance with the substantive law for the time being in force in India;

(b) in international commercial arbitration,—

(i) the arbitral tribunal shall decide the dispute in accordance with the rules.

(2) Where the mandate of an arbitrator terminates, a substitute arbitrator shall be appointed according to the rules that were applicable to the appointment of the arbitrator being replaced.

(3) Unless otherwise agreed by the parties, where an arbitrator is replaced under sub-section (2), any hearings previously held may be repeated at the discretion of the arbitral tribunal.

(4) Unless otherwise agreed by the parties, an order or ruling of the arbitral tribunal made prior to the replacement of an arbitrator under this section shall not be invalid solely because there has been a change in the composition of the arbitral tribunal.

JURISDICTION OF ARBITRAL TRIBUNALS

Competence of arbitral tribunal to rule on its jurisdiction.—(1) Section 16 of the arbitral tribunal may rule on its own jurisdiction, including ruling on any objections with respect to the existence or validity of the arbitration agreement, and for that purpose—

(a) an arbitration clause which forms part of a contract shall be treated as an agreement independent of the other terms of the contract; and

(b) a decision by the arbitral tribunal that the contract is null and void shall not entail *ipso-jure* the invalidity of the arbitration clause.

(2) A plea that the arbitral tribunal does not have jurisdiction shall be raised not later than the submission of the statement of defense, however, a party shall not be precluded from raising such a plea merely because that he has appointed, or participated in the appointment of, and arbitrator.

(3) A plea that the arbitral tribunal is exceeding the scope of its authority shall be raised as soon as the matter alleged to be beyond the scope of its authority is raised during the arbitral proceedings.

(4) The arbitral tribunal may, in either of the cases referred to in sub-section (2) or sub-section (3), admit a later plea if it considers the delay justified.

(5) The arbitral tribunal shall decide on a plea referred to in sub-section (2) or sub-section (3) and, where the arbitral tribunal takes a decision rejecting the plea, continue with the arbitral proceedings and make an arbitral award.

(6) A party aggrieved by such an arbitral award may make an application for setting aside such an arbitral award in accordance with section 34.

Interim measure ordered by arbitral tribunal.—(1) Under Section 17 unless otherwise agreed by the parties, the arbitral tribunal may, at the request of a party, order a party to take any interim measure of protection as the arbitral tribunal may consider necessary in respect of the subject matter of the dispute.

(2) The arbitral tribunal may require a party to provide appropriate security in connection with a measure ordered under sub-section (1).

CONDUCT OF ARBITRAL PROCEEDINGS

Equal treatment of parties.—Under section 18 the parties shall be treated with equality and each party shall be given a full opportunity to present his case.

Determination of rules of procedure.—Section 19 provides for determination of rules of procedure for conduct of arbitral proceedings. While the arbitral tribunal is not bound by the Code of Civil Procedure, 1908 or the Indian Evidence Act, 1872, the parties are given freedom to agree on the procedure to be followed by the arbitral tribunal in conducting its proceedings.

Place of arbitration.—(1) Section 20 deals with the question of determining the place of arbitration. While the parties are given freedom to agree on the place of arbitration, where they fail to agree, the place of arbitration will be determined by the arbitral tribunal having regard to the circumstances of the case, including the convenience of the parties.

Commencement of arbitral proceedings.—Under Section 21 unless otherwise agreed by the parties, the arbitral proceedings in respect of a particular dispute commence on the date on which a request for that dispute to be referred to arbitration is received by the respondent.

Language.—(1) Section 22 requires request by one party from the other party to so agree the appointment shall be made, upon request of a party, by the Chief Justice or any person or institution designated by him.

(2) Where, under an appointment procedure agreed upon by the parties,—

(a) a party fails to act as required under that procedure; or

(b) the parties, or the two appointed arbitrators, fail to reach an agreement expected of them under that procedure; or

(c) a person, including an institution, fails to perform any function entrusted to him or it under that procedure;

a party may request the Chief Justice or any person or institution designated by him to take the necessary measure, unless the agreement on the appointment procedure provides other means for securing the appointment.

(3) A decision on a matter entrusted by sub-section (4) or sub-section (5) or sub-section (6) to the Chief Justice or the person or institution designated by him is final.

(4) The Chief Justice or the person or institution designated by him, in appointing an arbitrator, shall have due regard to—

(a) any qualifications required of the arbitrator by the agreement of the parties, and

(b) other considerations as are likely to secure the appointment of an independent and impartial arbitrator.

(5) In the case of appointment of sole or third arbitrator in an international commercial arbitration, the Chief Justice of India or the person or institution designated by him may appoint an arbitrator of a nationality other than the nationalities of the parties where the parties belong to different nationalities.

(6) The Chief Justice may make such scheme as he may deem appropriate for dealing with matter entrusted by sub-section (4) or sub-section (5) or sub-section (6) to him.

(7) Where more than one request has been made under sub-section (4) or sub-section (5) or sub-section (6) to the Chief Justices of different High Courts or their designates, the Chief Justice or his designate to whom the request has been first made under the relevant sub-sections shall alone be competent to decide on the request.

(8)(a) Where the matters referred to in sub-sections (4), (5), (6), (7), (8) and (10) arise in an international commercial arbitration, the reference to 'Chief Justice' in those sub-sections shall be construed as a reference to the 'Chief Justice of India'.

(b) Where the matters referred to in sub-sections (4), (5), (6), (7), (8) and (10) arise in any other arbitration , the reference to "Chief Justice" in those sub-sections shall be construed as a reference to the Chief Justice of the High Court within whose local limits the principal Civil Court referred to in clause (e) of sub-section (1) of section 2 is situate and, where the High Court itself is the Court referred to in that clause, to the Chief Justice of that High Court.

Ground for challenge.—(1) Section 12 not only imposes the obligation upon the arbitrator but also provides the ground of challenge. Thus it provides, when a person is approached in connection with his possible appointment as an arbitrator, he shall disclose in writing any circumstances likely to give rise to justifiable doubts as to his independence or impartiality.

(2) An arbitrator, from the time of his appointment and throughout the arbitral proceedings shall, without delay, disclose to the parties in writing any circumstances referred to in sub-section (1) unless they have already been informed of them by him.

(3) An arbitrator may be challenged only if—

(a) circumstances exist that give rise to justifiable doubts as to his independence or impartiality, or

(b) he does not possess the qualification agreed to by the parties.

(4) A party may challenge and arbitrator appointed by him, or in

whose appointment he has participated, only for reasons of which he becomes aware after the appointment has been made.

For a Challenge procedure.—(1) Subject to sub-section (4), the parties are free to agree on a procedure for challenging an arbitrator.

(2) Failing any agreement referred to in sub-section (1), a party who intends to challenge an arbitrator shall, within fifteen days after becoming aware of the constitution of the arbitral tribunal or after becoming aware of any circumstances referred to in sub-section (3) of section 12, send a written statement of the reasons for the challenge to the arbitral tribunal.

(3) Unless the arbitrator challenged under sub-section (2) withdraws from his office or the other party agrees to the challenge, the arbitral tribunal shall decide on the challenge.

(4) If a challenge under any procedure agreed upon by the parties or under the procedure under sub-section (2) is not successful, the arbitral tribunal shall continue the arbitral proceedings and make an arbitral award.

(5) Where an arbitral award is made under sub-section (4), the party challenging the arbitrator may make an application for setting aside such an arbitral award in accordance with section 34.

(6) Where an arbitral award is set aside on an application made under sub-section (5), the court may decide as to whether the arbitrator who is challenged is entitled to any fees.

Failure or impossibility to act.—(1) The mandate of an arbitrator shall terminate if—

(a) he becomes *de jure* or *de facto* unable to perform his functions or for other reasons fails to act without undue delay; and

(b) he withdraws from his office or the parties agree to the termination of his mandate.

(2) If a controversy remains concerning any of the grounds referred to in clause (a) of sub-section (1), a party may, unless otherwise agreed by the parties, apply to the court to decide on the termination of the mandate.

(3) If, under this section or sub-section (3) of section 13, an arbitrator withdraws from his office or a party agrees to the termination of the mandate of an arbitrator, it shall not imply acceptance of the validity of any ground referred to in this section or sub-section (3) of section 12.

Termination of mandate and substitution of arbitrator.—(1) In addition to the circumstances referred to in section 13 or section 14, the mandate of an arbitrator shall terminate—

(a) where he withdraws from office for any reason; or
(b) by or pursuant to agreement of the parties.

Extent of judicial intervention.—Section 5 says notwithstanding anything contained in any other law for the time being in force, in matters governed by this Part, no judicial authority shall intervene except where so provided in this Part.

Administrative assistance.—In order to facilitate the conduct of the arbitral proceedings, the parties, or the arbitral tribunal with the consent of the parties may arrange for administrative assistance by a suitable institution or person.

X. OMBUDSMAN

The institution of ombudsman is slowly gaining momentum in India. Keeping in view the time constraints, the economy and the resources involved in regular courts some of the institutions have preferred to have an ombudsman for settlement of disputes arising against their institution. In this process, two developments are visible:

(i) Setting up of grievance redressal machinery, a step in this direction;
(ii) Setting up of the Office of Lokpal at the centre level; and
(iii) Setting up of the offices of *Lok Ayukta* at the state level.

Grievance Redressal Machinery

From 1996 onwards a consensus engaged in the government on effective and responsive administration culminating in the Chief Minister's Conference in May 1997. One of the major decisions of the conference was to formulate and operationalise grievance redressal machinery at the Centre and in the states in sector which deals with a large public interface such as railways, telecom, posts, public distribution systems, hospitals, revenue, electricity and petroleum among other. Pursuant to this decision, nodal agencies are marked for handling public grievances at the Public Wing of the Prime Minister's Office, the Department of Administrative Reforms & Public Grievances, Ministry of Personnel, the Department of Pensions, and the Directorate of Public Grievances in the Cabinet Secretariat.

XI. FAST TRACK COURTS

A novel experiment aimed at clearing the massive backlog in court cases has just begun in the country with the setting up of 'fast track' courts in various States under the Constitution of India, 1950 for the purpose of setting up of 1734 Fast Track Courts in various States. The allocated funds were to be used by the various State Governments in a time bound period of five years. The Law Commission had also suggested that for disposal of pending cases, the States may consider re-employment of retired Judges for a limited period. Since the Fast Track Courts were to be *adhoc* in the sense that they would not be permanent addition to the number of Courts within a particular State, the Constitutional validity of setting up of such Fast Track Courts came up for consideration before the Supreme Court in *Brij Mohan Lal* v. *Union of India*,[3] primarily on the ground that there was no Constitutional sanction for the appointment of retired Judges and also on the ground of non availability of effective guidelines and requisite infra-structural facilities.

Commenting on the anxiety of all concerned about quick dispensation of justice, the Supreme Court referred to its earlier judgment in *All India Judges Association* v *Union of India*[4] wherein the Supreme Court had already held: "An independent and efficient judicial system is one of the basic structures of our Constitution. If sufficient number of judges are not appointed, justice would not be available to the people, thereby undermining the basic structure. It is well known that justice delayed is justice denied. Time and again the inadequacy in the number of judges has adversely been commented upon. Not only have the Law Commission and the Standing Committee of Parliament made observations in this regard, but even the head of the judiciary, namely, the Chief Justice of India has had more occasions than once to make observations in regard thereto under the circumstances, we feel it is our constitutional obligation to ensure that the backlog of the cases is decreased and efforts are made to increase the disposal of cases. Apart from the steps which may be necessary for increasing the efficiency of the judicial officers, we are of the opinion that time has come for protecting one of the pillars of the Constitution, namely, the judicial system, by directing increase, in the first instance, in the judge strength from the existing ratio of 10.5 or 13 per 10 lakh people to 50 judges for 10 lakh people. We are conscious of the fact that overnight these vacancies cannot be filled. In order to have additional judges, not only the posts will have to be created but infrastructure required in the form of additional court rooms, building, staff, etc. would also have to be made available. We are also aware of the fact that a large number of vacancies as of today from amongst the sanctioned strength remain to be filled. We, therefore, first direct that the existing vacancies in the

3. 2002-4 SCALE 433.
4. JT-2002-3-SC-503.

subordinate courts at all levels should be filled, if possible, latest by 31st March, 2003, in all the States. The increase in the Judge strength to 50 judges per 10 lakh people should be effected and implemented with the filing up of the posts in a phased manner to be determined and directed by the Union Ministry of Law, but this process should be completed and the increased vacancies and posts filled within a period of five years from today. Perhaps increasing the judge strength by 10 per 10 lakh people every year could be one of the methods which may be adopted thereby completing the first stage within five years before embarking on further increase, if necessary.

The Eleventh Finance Commission recommended a scheme for creation of 1734 Fast Track Courts in the country for disposal of long pending Sessions and other cases. The Ministry of Finance sanctioned an amount of Rs. 502.90 crores as "special problem and up-gradation grant" for judicial administration. The scheme was for a period of 5 years. The Finance Commission Division (FCD), Ministry of Finance released funds directly to the State Governments under the scheme of Fast Track Courts, it is the primary responsibility of the State Governments to establish these courts in consultation with the concerned High Courts.

The FTCs were established to expeditiously dispose of long pending cases in the Sessions Courts and long pending cases of under trial prisoners.

The Government accorded its approval for the continuation of 1562 Fast Track Courts that were operational as on 31.3.2005 for a further period of 5 years, i.e. up to 31st March, 2010 with a provision of Rs. 509 crores as a 100 per cent central assistance. The Department of Justice is monitoring the scheme. These FTCs have disposed of 21.16 lakh cases out of the 28.84 lakh cases transferred to them so far.

This Department has requested State Governments and the High Courts to earmark at least one FTC in each District to exclusively deal with cases involving senior citizens, abuse of women and the disabled.

The Central assistance under the above said scheme is limited to an approved norm, i.e. Rs. 4.80 lakh per court per annum (recurring) and Rs. 8.60 lakh (non-recurring). Any expenditure incurred by the State in excess as recurring and/or non-recurring expenditure would have to be borne by the State Government. During the financial year 2005-06, an amount of Rs.100.00 crore has been released to the States (Annexure I).

During the financial year 2006-07, an amount of Rs.102.93 crore was released to the State Governments (Annexure-II). During the year 2007-08, an amount of Rs. 57.20 crore was released (Annexure-III).

A statement indicating the number of Fast Track Courts established and the cases transferred to them and disposed of is attached as Annexure-IV.

Annexure I

Statement showing amount released during 2005-06 under Fast Track Courts

(Rs. in lakhs)

Sl. No.	*Name of the state*	*Sanctioned under recurring expenditure*	*Sanctioned under non-recurring expenditure*	*Total sanctioned*
1.	Andhra Pradesh	412.80	137.70	550.50
2.	Arunachal Pradesh	14.40	4.80	19.20
3.	Assam	96.00	32.00	128.00
4.	Bihar	720.00	240.30	960.30
5.	Chhattisgarh	148.80	49.60	198.40
6.	Goa	24.00	8.00	32.00
7.	Gujarat	796.80	266.00	1062.80
8.	Haryana	76.80	25.60	102.40
9.	HP	43.20	14.40	57.60
10.	Jharkhand	427.20	142.60	569.80
11.	Karnataka	446.40	149.00	595.40
12.	Kerala	148.80	49.60	198.40
13.	Madhya Pradesh	316.80	105.70	422.50
14.	Maharashtra	897.60	299.60	1197.20
15.	Manipur	9.60	3.20	12.80
16.	Meghalaya	14.40	4.80	19.20
17.	Mizoram	14.40	4.80	19.20
18.	Nagaland	9.60	3.20	12.80
19.	Orissa	196.80	65.60	262.40
20.	Punjab	86.40	28.80	115.20
21.	Rajasthan	398.40	133.00	531.40
22.	Tamil Nadu	235.20	78.50	313.70
23.	Tripura	14.40	4.80	19.20
24.	U.P.	216.00	72.00	288.00
25.	Uttarakhand	1162.01	387.79	1549.80
26.	West Bengal	571.20	190.60	761.80
	Total	**7498.01**	**2501.99**	**10000.00**

Annexure II
Statement showing amount released during 2006-07 under the Fast Track Courts

(Rs. in lakhs)

Sl. No.	*Name of the state*	*Sanctioned under recurring expenditure*	*Sanctioned under non-recurring expenditure*	*Total sanctioned*
1.	Andhra Pradesh	412.80	0	412.80
2.	Arunachal Pradesh	14.40	0	14.40
3.	Assam	96.00	0	96.00
4.	Bihar	720.00	0	720.00
5.	Chhattisgarh	129.60	0	129.60
6.	Goa	24.00	0	24.00
7.	Gujarat	715.20	64.70	1355.90
8.	Haryana	33.60	0	33.60
9.	HP	43.20	37.00	43.57
10.	Jharkhand	226.00	0	226.00
11.	Karnataka	340.80	270.00	610.80
12.	Kerala	148.80	0	148.80
13.	Madhya Pradesh	215.40	0	215.40
14.	Maharashtra	801.60	300.00	1101.60
15.	Manipur	9.60	0	9.60
16.	Meghalaya	14.40	0	14.40
17.	Mizoram	14.40	3.28	17.68
18.	Nagaland	9.60	8.58	18.18
19.	Orissa	196.80	0	196.80
20.	Punjab	48.00	0	48.00
21.	Rajasthan	398.40	355.24	753.64
22.	Tamil Nadu	235.20	0	235.20
23.	Tripura	3.80	0	3.80
24.	U.P.	2107.20	968.49	3075.69
25.	Uttarakhand	216.00	0	216.00
26.	West Bengal	571.20	0	571.20
	Total	**7746.00**	**2546.66**	**10292.66**

Annexure III
Statement showing amount released during 2007-08 under the Fast Track Courts

(Rs. in lakh)

Sl. No.	*Name of the state*	*Sanctioned under recurring expenditure (2007-08) (Rs. in lakhs)*	*No. of FTCs for which grants sanctioned*
1.	Andhra Pradesh	412.80	86
2.	Arunachal Pradesh	14.40	3
3.	Assam	96.00	20
4.	Bihar	720	150
5.	Chhattisgarh	129.6	27
6.	Goa	24	5
7.	Gujarat	715.2	119
8.	Haryana	33.6	14
9.	H.P.	226	0
10.	Jharkhand	226	48
11.	Karnataka	340.8	48
12.	Kerala	148.8	31
13.	Madhya Pradesh	215.4	66
14.	Maharashtra	801.6	163
15.	Manipur	9.6	2
16.	Meghalaya	14.4	0
17.	Mizoram	14.4	3
18.	Nagaland	9.6	2
19.	Orissa	196.8	33
20.	Punjab	48	17
21.	Rajasthan	398.4	83
22.	Tamil Nadu	235.2	49
23.	Tripura	3.8	0
24.	U.P.	2107.2	242
25.	Uttarakhand	216	36
26.	West Bengal	571.2	119

Annexure IV
Status of Fast Track Courts, May 2008

Sl. No.	*States*	*No. of Fast Track Courts functional*	*Total cases transferred since inception*	*Total cases disposed since inception*	*No. of cases pending*	*As on*
1.	Andhra Pradesh	108	177854	145680	32174	May '08
2.	Arunachal Pradesh	3	3045	1048	1997	May '08
3.	Assam	20	49960	36861	13099	May '08
4.	Bihar	150	78495	29178	49317	March '05
5.	Chhattisgarh	31	41939	32762	9177	March '06
6.	Goa	121	522914	313201	209713	May '08
7.	Gujarat	3	5208	4114	1094	Aug. '07
8.	Haryana	14	31258	20795	10463	Apr. '08
9.	Himachal Pradesh	8	20711	15754	4957	May '08
10.	Jammu & Kashmir	0	0	0	0	
11.	Jharkhand	49	74767	61268	13499	March '08
12.	Karnataka	43	120586	97731	22855	March '08
13.	Kerala	38	77028	63373	13655	May '08
14.	Madhya Pradesh	65	188655	143218	45437	March '08
15.	Maharashtra	154	408774	276650	132124	March '08
16.	Manipur	2	2430	2211	219	March '08
17.	Meghalaya	3	849	498	351	March '08
18.	Mizoram	3	1491	1080	411	March '08
19.	Nagaland	2	633	499	134	March '08
20.	Orissa	32	44560	36542	8018	March '08
21.	Punjab	16	54027	26423	27604	April '08
22.	Rajasthan	83	112081	90986	21095	April '08
23.	Sikkim	0	0	0	0	
24.	Tamil Nadu	49	334724	301266	33458	Dec. '07
25.	Tripura	3	4421	4311	110	May '08
26.	U.P.	10	72817	67245	5572	May '08
27.	Uttarakhand	240	346369	266599	79770	Dec '07
28.	West Bengal	150	108866	76289	32577	April '08
	Total	**1400**	**2884462**	**2115582**	**768880**	

Chapter VIII

LEGAL CULTURE, HUMAN VALUES AND PROFESSIONAL ETHICS

I. PROLOGUE

Legal Culture involves the relationship between law, language, civility and cultural values. Legal culture is an evolutionary process like the relationship between law, language and culture. This relationship involves the culture of interpretation of law in terms of its language and culture, which may have certain inherent qualities and/or infirmities in a system. Quite apart from the evils while interpreting the laws, in many Commonwealth Asian countries the English judges invoked and applied the principles of English common law which were highly technical in nature and were not consistent with customs, habits, circumstances and culture of such countries. The English judges influenced by their own culture background, training and experience applied in the process of interpretation the English law, which governed the British people and whose civilization and culture was entirely different from several Commonwealth Asian countries, including India. This was not justifiable. Said Stone:

> "At this point, indeed, when a precedent ceases to be used to illustrate a probably just result to another context for comparison with the present and is taken an ultimate formulation independent of its former context to be transposed as a premise for deductions to the present context precedent ceases to be a rational means towards judgment. It becomes symbol and a devise which conceals rather than determines the

process of judgment. Precedent becomes rather pegs on which to hang judgment than an explanation of the process of reaching it. While this is not itself an evil, it is likely to become one at the point when the peg chosen for hanging the present decision was manufactured in a difficult factual context and with a different purpose from the instant case. An ... assessment whether context are sufficiently similar to justify use of the same peg for decision is essentially a process of evaluation."[1]

Be that as it may, "it was inevitable that the common law which so profoundly governed the English system of laws and which had found its way into the Indian jurisprudence either in the shape of statutory codification of judicial decisions or unwritten principles of English law applied *ad hoc* from time to time to Indian circumstances should leave its ineffaceable mark on the Indian system of law generally and also on the method of administration of justice in British India"[2]. Indeed some countries of Commonwealth Asia have body of laws and systems of administration of justice which were developed in England in the golden era of Benthamite *laissez faire* and is, *prima facie*, not conducive to the attainment of socialistic pattern of changing society. Lest the very foundation of Rule of Law is shaken, it is imperative that the gap between the preferred values of the society and its values being fostered by our laws is abridged.

II. RELATIONSHIP BETWEEN LANGUAGE AND CULTURE

Language is the effective medium through which one can ably convey one's feeling to others. It is also a reflection of the development of culture. Indeed language does not exist apart from culture. However, difficulty arises in a society or country, like India, where there are diverse languages and cultures, namely, pluralism. In such countries one may find different languages having same culture or different cultures but same language. Thus, Edward Sapir observed that "totally unrelated languages share in one culture, closely related languages —

1. Stone, J., The Province and Function of Law, 3rd Reprint, 1961, pp. 192-93.
2. Setalvad, M.C., The Role of English Law in India, Hebrew University, 1966, p. 18.

even a single language belong to distinct cultural spheres".[3] He added that a common language cannot indefinitely set the seal on a common culture when the geographical, political and economic determinants of the culture are no longer the same throughout the area.[4] Earlier he said:

> Historians and anthropologists find that language and culture are not in parallel fashion, that their areas of distribution intercross in the most bewildering fashion, and that the history of ach is apt to follow distinctive course.[5]

He added:

> The language may even die out in its primary area and live on among people violently hostile to the persons of its original speakers[6].

Thus, language and culture are not necessarily co-related. This does not, however, mean that they never are.[7] Quite apart from this, sometimes culture influences the language. Thus, when there is a cultural borrowing here is likelihood that the associated words may be borrowed too.[8] Thus, when the early Germanic people or northern Europe first learned of wine culture[9], and of paved street[10] from their commercial or war like contract with the Romans, it was only natural that they should adopt the Latin word (language) for the strange behaviour.[11]

III. RELATIONSHIP BETWEEN LAW AND LANGUAGE

Law, like language, is a slow process of evolution. Like language (which accepts words from foreign or other languages where it is either not possible to find equivalent word in that language or foreign word is current coin) law and judicial process, in the absence of established norms in each branch led the courts and Legislature to borrow the laws and practices of foreign countries and common law. May be this is

3. Edward Sapir, Language, Harcourt, Brace & Worler, Inc., New York, 1949, p. 213.
4. *Ibid.*, at p. 215.
5. *Ibid.*, at p. 207.
6. *Ibid.*, at p. 208.
7. *Ibid.*, at p. 215.
8. *Ibid.*, at p. 193
9. For example, Vium, English Wine, German Wein.
10. Unfamiliar types of road strate (via), English street, German Strasse, and Ghase.
11. *Supra* note 61.

primarily because of the influence of British rule for centuries over Commonwealth Asia. Like law, the language has also undergone phenomenal changes due to expansion of their social functions to meet the changing needs of society. Moreover, the influence of westerns is common both to languages and law in Commonwealth Asia. In these countries like language which is influenced by English and French the common law has greatly influenced the Commonwealth Asia and Australia and have been incorporated in their statutes, judicial decisions and other practices, viz., legal pluralism. Like law, the trend of borrowing languages led to the hybrid system in languages.

The language planning and the making of law have many things in common. Like making of law, the language planning undergoes development. It involves various processes, viz., selection, elaboration, codification and implementation. In the process of selection of language it is perhaps necessary that the language must be such which can be developed. The elaboration of language development has two conflicting approaches, namely, (i) the term should be coined only through the internal creation, (ii) the loan words be accepted particularly for those items where it is not possible to find the equivalent word in that language. But there is another dimension to this view, namely, words from foreign languages which have become current coin should be retained partly because they are current coin and partly because the more common words one have with the rest of the world. This would, as said earlier, lead to code mixing and hybrid in language. Codification is based on the socio-cultural connected with the developmental status of the language. Codification of the 'morphological system'[12] is essential for the productive coining of new terms in the language. This poses problems like the number of graphemes[13] to be used and the phonological[14] rules to be followed. The adoption and implementation of the language depends upon the political or national status of that language. The problem of implementation of a language is all the more so in multilingual countries where English language is more acceptable than other native languages.

---

12. Linguistics: The structure of words in a language, including patterns of infections and derivation; the study of the structure of words in a language; Biology: the study of the forms and structure of organism.
13. Letter representing phoneme; a written symbol, letter, or combination of letters that represents a single sound.
14. Study of language's pattern of speech sounds, the study of the pattern of speech sounds used in a particular language.

Law, like language, may also be codified. Indeed, there is a leaning towards codification of all laws in several Commonwealth Asian countries. According to Salmond the law has its formal source in legislation, case law having its source in precedent, customary law having its source in agreement. To this Keeton adds Equity and professional opinion having only persuasive sources. The purpose of legislation, judicial decision, convention and other legal acts is to influence men's behaviour and direct them in certain ways. The legal language must be viewed primarily as a means to an end. It is an instrument of social control and social intercourse. It may be called as 'directive language' in contrast to a 'reporting language'.[15]

Language of law is significant not only for interpretation of law but also from the view point of its implementation. It is through the use of words that one can legislate the rules of conduct. But if the words are misused communication becomes difficult, if not impossible. But the meaning of words changes according to the context in which they are used. Thus, Greek Philosopher Heraclitus observed that "you cannot point to the same river twice". The meaning of the words like river is in a constant state of flux.[16]

Like language implementation of law is key for its success. Summer points out five techniques of law, which may be used to implement social policies, namely, the use of law: (i) to remedy grievances among members of society; (ii) as a penal instrument with which to prohibit and persecute prescribed behaviour; (iii) for managing various governmental public benefits such as education and welfare policies; (iv) to give effect to certain private arrangements between members of a society, such as the provisions of the law of contract; and (v) as an instrument to promote certain defined activities.[17]

IV. LANGUAGE AND LEGAL EDUCATION

What should be the medium of instructions in Law in

15. K. Olivecrona, "Legal Language and Reality (Essay in the honour of Pound)", (Ed. Newman) (1962), p. 151, cited in Lord Lloyd of Hampstea, Introduction to Jurisprudence, Sherens & Sons, London, 1972, p. 530.
16. See A.G. Chloros, Law and Society, Law (Ed. Greeveson, R.H.), Routledge and Kegan Paul, London, 1967, p. 17.
17. R. Summers, The Techniques Element of Law, (1971) 59 Def. Law Rev., referred in Phil Harris, An Introduction to Law, Weidenfeld and Nicolson, London, 1980, p. 4.

Commonwealth Asian countries like Bangladesh, India, Malaysia, Sri Lanka and Pakistan where the most widely spoken languages are something other than English? The issue is not amenable to easy solution particularly where treatises, commentaries, law reports, law books and the law themselves have been written in English language. Further, it is feared that neglect or removal of English would place these countries away from commercial, intellectual, cultural, and economic world of today which is predominantly a free economic market dominated by privatization and globalization. This would mean isolation from the main current of knowledge and development, and, *inter alia*, deprive one for want of knowledge in English from studying, teaching and practicing law in foreign countries. The problem becomes all the more complex in a country having several languages and dialects. There is another side of the problem. It has been rightly said that it is neither desirable nor feasible to impose English upon students of law who can neither think nor express themselves in English. In such a situation meaningful use of case or discussion method in English is not feasible. Further, they cannot effectively make legal analysis and present the case before the law courts and tribunals or even before other legal institutions.[18] The only alternative in that situation would be to develop legal material, legal glossary, Law Reports, statutory material, and treatises in the language widely spoken in the country. However, it is felt that the language of law cannot continue to be English forever, in several Commonwealth countries. However, even in these countries English may continue as an associate language. This would be helpful particularly to those who wish to pursue legal studies in English. It would also help them to pursue legal studies in foreign universities, international forums, and conferences/seminars/workshops and would open wide vistas of legal knowledge assimilation as well as dissemination.

V. LAW AND CULTURE

At all times and in every society, at every stage of development, there have been a set of culture whatever may be its nature and scope to regulate the social relationship. However, several Commonwealth

18. Julius G. Getman, The Development of Indian Legal Education: The impact of the Language Problem, 21 J. Leg. Ed. (1968-69), p. 517; see also Jill Cottrell, 10+2+5: A change in Structure of Indian Legal Education, 36 J. Leg. Ed., (1986), p. 381; K.L. Bhatia, Legal Language and Legal Writing, Universal Law Publishing, 2010.

Asian countries, including India, are said to be multi-ethnic society in which there are large number of ethnic groups which vary in size from highly localized caste and tribal groups to great language and religious groups.[19] Some of these countries like India also have minority groups based on religion, scheduled castes, scheduled tribes, and socially and economically backward classes.[20] The Constitution of India makes special provisions for the advancement of this section of society and also makes provisions for their job reservation. But despite the constitutional and judicial admonition of caste in the affairs of the State and public life, caste has remained the most stubborn factor in real social interchange in Indian society. Most of the caste conflict, agitation and litigation about reservation revolve around the reservation of seats and posts.[21] The colonial policy of isolation kept the tribal people away from the mainstream of Indian life. This led Gandhiji to emphasize their development in order to ensure their integration with the rest of the country. The Constitution of India seeks to protect the tribal economic interests, safeguard their way of life, and ensure their development, so that they might take their legitimate place in the general life of the community.[22] But the tragedy is that while development of tribal personality is basic to the Indian Constitution, these tribes suffer in the name of development, of course, capitalistically and globally.[23] "Law cannot go it alone and paper legislation is paper tiger even as paper sub-plans are literary cosmetics and implementation processes statistical counterfeit. It is pity, the scheduled caste/scheduled tribe Commission is a toothless functionary and can deplore but cannot enforce."[24]

The law represents the nexus between the values (or supposed values) of society. A rule of law may have its formal source in legislation, judicial decisions or custom. But the rule of law that is so codified in legislation, or pronounced and applied by a judicial decision

---

19. See Brass, P.R., Language, Religion and Politics in Northern India, 1975, p. 14.
20. Members of Scheduled Castes and Scheduled Tribes are those citizens who belong to the castes, races, or tribes specified as scheduled by the President of India under Articles 341 and 342 in the Constitution of India.
21. See Parmanand Singh, Reservation Crisis in India: Need for National Consensus, 1987, Kn. L.J., 45.
22. See P.G. Krishnan, Constitution and Tribal Welfare, (1985) C.U.L.R., 53.
23. See V.R. Krishna Iyer, Tribal Uplift and the Rule of Law, (1985) C.U.L.R., 9.
24. *Ibid.*, p. 7.

or embodied in custom involves competing values.[25] Law, therefore, must adopt concrete, culture-specific forms to be effective. It must serve the ends of society by maintaining social equilibrium in the multi-cultural society.[26]

Religion and law remained intermingled in the cultural history of mankind for a long time and in many countries. India, it has been observed, is a country where many religions and cultures have flourished simultaneously.

In the pre-colonial period Indian legal culture was governed by Hindu Law, which according to Myne has "the oldest pedigree of any known system of jurisprudence."[27] *Dharma* (Law) governs the universe.[28] It is king of kings. Nothing is superior to *Dharma* law. The law aided by the power of the king enables the weak to prevail over the strong.[29] Even kings are subordinate to *Dharma*, the rule of law.[30] *Dharma* ordained that king cannot legislate.[31] Originally, Hindu Law was territorial in character being applicable to all the inhabitants of India but after the advent of the Muslims, it could no longer claim to be absolutely territorial; it was confined to Hindu community alone. Under the Islamic culture regulated by Muslim Law, every Muslim ruler was required to rule in conformity with the tenets of their sacred law, the *Quran*, which lays down the broad principles governing the social life of the Muslims.[32] Likewise, Western legal system also according to Berman, "have their sources in religious rituals, liturgies and doctrines of the eleventh and twelfth centuries reflecting new attitudes towards death, sin, punishment, forgiveness, salvation as well as new assumptions concerning the relationship of the divine to the human and

---

25. See Bakshi, P.M., "Development and Deviance: The Law's Response", The Other side of Development, (Ed. K.S. Shukla), Sage Publication, New Delhi, 1987, p. 207.
26. See Sack, Minchin, 1986, p. 18.
27. See Sarkar, U.C., "Universality of Personal Laws with special reference to Marriage", 1 K.L.J., 1971, p. 15.
28. See K.L. Bhatia, The Concept of Dharma: Corpus Juris of Law and Morality—A Comparative Study of Legal Cosmology, 2010, Deep & Deep Publications, New Delhi, Chapters I & III.
29. Sarvadhikari, History of Hindu Law, 1980, p. 10.
30. Radhakrishnan, S., The Principal Upanishads, p. 170.
31. Jois, M. Rama, Legal and Constitutional History of India, Vol. I, 1984, p. 13.
32. *Ibid.*, at p. 4, Vol. II.

of faith to reason."[33]

With the growth of culture in the age of peace and prosperity, there is a rise in the level of law. A progressive society, said Sir Henry Maine, "has to keep adapting the law to fresh social and economic conditions, and legislation has proved in modern times the essential means of attaching this end, however imperfectly."[34] But in times of war, economic difficulties, ravages by diseases and natural calamity, or in degraded morals in prevailing societies, we find a fall on the graph of legal evaluation.[35]

Whatever may be the relationship between law and culture, legal culture has become rapidly proliferating not only in legal philosophy but also in comparative law, legal sociology, legal psychology and legal anthropology.[36] Legal culture is an alternative to social and cultural background of law in general and values and attitudes connected with law[37] (modeled after political culture).

VI. CROSS-CULTURAL QUESTIONS

The Basic Issues

The basic issues which are of vital importance for proper understanding and appreciation of the cross-cultural questions by lawyers of 21st century are: (i) Why they need to know the cross-cultural questions and for what ends? (ii) What are the arena of cross-cultural issues? and (iii) What the new lawyers niche law students need to know of cross-culture? Let us turn to discuss them.

Why to Know

With the expansion of international trade, establishment of WTO, international co-operation, influence of western culture and adoption of the common law system for solving problems (legal or otherwise) at international level it is indispensible for new lawyers to know cross-cultural issues, foreign law, social system and political set-up. Moreover, understanding of the inter-relations between the law and the

---

33. Berman, H.J., Law and Revolution: The formation of Western Legal Tradition, 1983, p. 165.
34. Lord Lloyd of Hampstead, Introduction to Jurisprudence, 1972, p. 565; Maine did not admire judicial legislation in English Law and disfavoured codification. But he was essentially an evolutionist.
35. Sethna, M.J., The Essentials of an Ideal Legal System, 1968, p. 12-B.
36. Masaji, Legal Pluralism in and across Legal Culture, Rechtstneorie Monismus Order, p. 297.
37. *Ibid.*

society as well as formulation of legal norms requires the knowledge of cross cultural issues. Indeed, Law cannot be understood without regard to the relation of social life. As Cardozo said, somewhere between the worship of the past and exaltation of the present, the path of safety must be found. Indeed, in the era of globalization the lawyers cannot champion reforms unless they know the cross cultural issues.

What are the Arena of Cross-Cultural Issues

The civilization of a country is well reflected by its social institutions, political set-up and legal systems. Law is an instrument of social change and is a reflection of societal values. However, most, if not all, the countries of Commonwealth Asia and Australia, which were under the colonial occupation for centuries have been greatly influenced by alien culture. The impact of western culture may be seen in several Commonwealth Asian countries even after their attaining independence. Though not fully integrated in the western social system several Commonwealth Asian countries imported western model of sophisticated technology, western concept of planning and attainment of social change and among others the common law system which includes supremacy of law, notion of equality and liberty as well as the systems of checks and balances to ensure separation of functions of the three organs of the Government.

What to Know and Contribute

In a country where a foreign culture, political set-up or legal system has either been imported, incorporated or influenced it becomes necessary for the new lawyers (the niche law students), to know such political, social and legal system and evaluate its impact. To analyze the impact of incorporation or influence of foreign socio-legal system a study of the social process, history, social system, effect of law in, and on, the social process, history, social system, effect of law in, and on, the society by the new lawyers becomes necessary. The aim is primarily to assess the actual working of social and legal order in terms of the satisfaction of the people who are governed by it. As a constructive review, it helps the lawyer to monitor the success or failure of a given law, locate the bottlenecks, if any, and finally revise the position. It is a preliminary step to law reform. Further, the new lawyers should not merely know the cross-cultural issues but be able to carefully evaluate the impact of import or assimilation at the foreign culture. Moreover, there is a need to evolve strategies for developing new social and cultural order best suited to the community formulate policy and make plans to meet the challenges of cross-culture; raise public awareness about the impact of importing foreign culture; and look afresh the entire cross-cultural issues. Such an understanding becomes essential to understand the current social and cultural mores of the society and in turn helps in better solving the contemporary problems both at national and international levels.

The Task

It is unfortunate that very little work has been done in this area in Commonwealth Asian countries. It is high time for the Law Schools in India to undertake teaching and research programs and bring out literature on the subject. Moreover, effort should be made to collect systematic information on cross-cultural issues, gain new insights in the new technique and methodology.

The Needs of Development

Development is a process of social, economic, political and cultural changes. It is also a process of transformation of the dominant organization of production, distribution and consumption. It connotes qualitative, structural and normative changes in both economy and polity and includes the idea of deliberately planned action designed to fundamentally alter those structures with the objective of improving the quality of life of the entire social community. It implies a process of social change from massive poverty, hunger and malnutrition to egalitarian sufficiency, eradication of social evils, inequality and abuses, injection of scientific spirit into a semi-feudal society, protection against discrimination and exploitation, and commitment to, and capabilities of the rule of law. The needs of development being dynamic one laid down. It varies from country to country and time to time, with varying stages of economic development political outlook and social set-up. Whatever may be the scope of the development, it is now realized in almost all the countries of the world that development is an indispensable chapter for international program.

The development is, however, not without any limitation. Thus, development cannot be asserted at the expense of the community or even at the expense of neighbouring States whose prospects may be jeopardized. Indeed, such development must be socially and politically accountable.

Law is a part of social milieu and must be brought to bear on the people's vital needs of development. It provides a convenient, dynamic and viable frame-work for the society and is expected to evolve a compromise between stability and change.

What the Niche Lawyers-in-the-making need to Know?

The primary functions of the niche lawyers-in-the-making in modern era is not only to promote but to play a positive role in shaping policies and making programs for rapid socio-economic development. They must also carve out the possible areas for analytical enquiry and survey and also identify their root causes. Further, they are required to ensure a proper balance between competing interests. For example, to fulfil this task the niche young would be lawyers are required to know why development is needed for the transformation of society and how to strike at the 'root of poverty, hunger, illiteracy, ignorance and sickness'. At the same time, they should be conversant with the problems of population, pollution, poverty, gender, consumers' justice and legal aid and legal advice. They must also have perspective that development is socially and politically accountable. Further, they should be aware of legal regulation of industrial hazards both at national and international levels. Moreover, they must know the scope and coverage of mechanism for compensation particularly in context of industrial disaster such as *Bhopal Gas Leakage case*. Quite apart from the aforesaid perspectives the new lawyers would-be need to know the concept and theories of development, choice of target and technologies for development, human rights, rule of law, legal principles for environmental pollution and sustainable development, the role of law and judiciary in development, and the emerging trends in the relativism of common law-civil law synergic merger and acquisition as well as jurisdictional preferences. These are quite essentials in the spheres of novel areas of litigation or arbitral process such as cyber laws, cyber crimes, like cyber piracy, telecommunications, POISE Laws, international trade law, international taxation, merger and acquisition, corporate laws, etc. This shall be a milestone in the building of a roadmap for "experiential learning."

VII. HUMAN VALUES

Human Values is a broad and dynamic concept. It varies from person to person, time to time and place to place. It is extremely important not only for the society but also the family, individual, neighbours, workers/employees at work.

Some of the major issues relating to human values are enumerated in the Covenant on Civil and Political Rights which includes:

The right to life, Freedom from torture and inhuman treatment, Freedom from slavery and forced labour, Right to liberty and security,

Right of detained persons to be treated with humanity, Freedom from imprisonment for debt, Freedom of movement and of choice of residence, Freedom of aliens from arbitrary expulsion, Right to a fair trial, Protection against retroactivity of the criminal law, Right to recognition as a person before the law, Right to privacy, Freedom of thought, conscience and religion, Freedom of opinion and of expression, Prohibition of propaganda for war and of incitement to national, racial or religious hatred, Right of peaceful assembly, Freedom of association, Right to marry and found a family, Rights of the child, Political rights, Equality before the law, Rights of minorities.

In addition to the aforesaid rights the Universal Declaration of Human Rights also include: Rights of detained persons to be treated with humanity, Freedom from imprisonment for debt, Prohibition of propaganda for war and of incitement of hatred, Rights of the child, Rights of minorities. Out of the aforesaid human values we propose and discuss some of them in detail.

1. Sex Discrimination

Women constitute almost fifty percent of the world's population. However, it is unfortunate that despite of their hard labour they at least in the past have been suppressed and kept under subordination of men, used for man's pleasure and subjected to discrimination because they happen to be women. The inequality of women is a innovation of man. Said Justice Krishna Iyer:

> "Womanhood as a biological division based on sex, has been exploited by historical distortions, although nature never meant any necessary inferiority. Differentiation is not subordination and social exploitation on the score of sex or of colour or creed is human injustice. A dialectical understanding of social relations over the past ages discloses how man has used religion, culture, muscle power and female modesty for aggressive exploitation, sexually, economically and politically."

2. Child Labour

Child Labour is another exploited section of labour force. They are not only denied of their childhood and education and have no time to rest. Indeed they expose unsafe working conditions and are not protected. They face long-term physical, intellectual and emotional stress. They face an adulthood and illiteracy.

3. Bonded Labour

Bonded labourers constitute one of the most exploited sections of the rural labour. It is the "relic of feudal exploitative system". Till recently, there existed in our country a system of usury under which the debtor, his descendants or dependents, had to work for the creditor without reasonable wages or with no wages in order to repay the debt. "At times, several generations work under bondage for the repayment of the paltry sum which had been taken by some remote ancestor. The interest rates were exorbitant and such bondage could not be interpreted as a result of a legitimate contract or agreement. This system implies infringement of basic human rights and destruction of the dignity of human labour".

4. Contract Labour

For several years contract labour has been paid low wages, employed for longer hours of work and on sub-contract basis, placed in insanitary working conditions and denied benefits and facilities equal to their counterparts who are employed under regular contract of service. Further, there is no security of tenure. Instances are not lacking where contract labour has been victimized. Moreover, contract labourers are not entitled to other benefits and amenities such as provident fund, gratuity, bonus, privilege leave, medical facilities, subsidized food and housing to which the regular workmen of the company are entitled. Thus, there is wide disparity in emoluments and working conditions between contract labour and direct labour and he is not treated at par with direct lab our.

5. Migrant Labour

The basic cause of migration is lack of employment opportunities. Even after the abolition of slavery they worked as indentured labour for plantation of mines. However, the present century brought the abolition of indentured system. Be that as it may, the system of employment of inter-State migrant labour is an exploitative system prevalent in Bihar, Madhya Pradesh, Orissa and Rajasthan and some other States. In these States they are recruited from various parts of the State through contractors or agents known as Sardars/Khatadars for work outside the State in large construction projects. But in the process of migration and during their employment they are exploited by contractors, middle-men, employers and public functionaries, who come in contact with them. Generally speaking, it has been reported that these migrant labourers become the victim of payment of low wages in human working conditions, forcing them to work against their will. They are subjected to physical assault when they want to run away or show any slackness in work or protest against in human working conditions. One also witnesses casual assault on women workers, selling them to other employers, keeping them in bondage, concealing death and injuries from appropriate legal/administrative authorities, and even cheating them by paying wages much less than what they were promised.

Chapter IX

CONSTITUTIONAL ASPECTS OF LEGAL METHOD

Constitutional aspects of legal method concern the process of the constitution in the making, its adoption, its enforcement and its working with the democratic experiences since its inception about which the law students, in the beginning of their legal study career, must know, imbibe and emulate the constitutional culture-value-politics-morality-conviviality behaviour in order to have sound base in the basic law of the country which lays down the basic unamendable as well as inalterable features of the Indian Nation. The Constitution of India is the soul of our country. The Constitution of India like all constitutions of the globe is the heir of the past and the testator of the future.[1] It is the aspiration of the posterity to live with the sustainability of human dignity. It in unequivocal terms reflects that the Constitution of the Indian Sovereign, Socialist, Secular, Democratic, Republic is the product not of a political revolution but of the endeavors, hard work, research and deliberations of a body of eminent representatives of the WE THE PEOPLE OF INDIA who sought to improve upon the existing systems of administration, makes a retrospect of the constitutional development indispensable for a proper understanding of this Constitution.[2] These give an in-depth as well as correct insight of

---

1. See Ivor Jennings, *Some Characteristics of the Indian Constitution*, 1953, p. 56.
2. See D.D. Basu, *Introduction to the Constitution of India*, p. 3.

the proper understanding of the Constitution of India, which has been dealt with the Constitutional Perspective.[3] Rule of law to serve the rule of life, judicial review to check and correct ultra vires virus, secularism, constitutional remedies, the State not to be an impediment but imperative organism in the promotion as well as protection of the basic rights/fundamental rights/human rights/social rights, the State as the promoter of fundamental duties, federalism, judicial process in upholding the constitutionality of compatible legislations, *locus standi*, devolution of powers and progressively safeguarding the principle of occupied field, maintain checks and balances in Parliament-Executive relationship, progressive and not static interpretation of the Constitution as well as legislations in terms of settled principles of common law as well as our own rules of *Mimansa* are the genesis of the Constitution of India. The constitutional practice and procedure mostly depend on the genesis of the said paradigms, which are imperative constitutional values to the upholding of constitutional culture, constitutional morality, constitutional ethics, and constitutional politics in developing synergetic constitutional comity in the furtherance of unity in diversity.

CONSTITUTIONAL PERSPECTIVE—THE GENESIS: AN OVERVIEW

Constitution of India is the soul of our country India that is Bharat—the union of states. It is supreme lex of India. It is a symbol of Unity in Diversity.

It was adopted on 26th of November 1949. It came into force on 26th of January 1950. The date 26th January was chosen to commemorate the declaration of Independence of 1930. This date is celebrated as Republic Day each year.

It contains 395 articles divided into 24 parts (now 488), and Schedules (now 12), and 96 amendments till 2011, for a total 117,369 words in English Language version. It has an official Hindi language version.

The Constitution of India was drafted and adopted by the Constituent Assembly of India, which was constituted under the Cabinet Mission Plan, 1946.

The Cabinet Mission Plan, 1946, at the initiative of British Prime

3. The sources are CAD; D.D. Basu, *Commentaries on The Constitution of India; V.N. Shukla*, Edited by M.P. Singh, *The Constitution of India*; M.P. Jain, *The Constitution of India*; H.M. Seervai, *The Constitution of India.*

Minister Clement Atlee, finalized plans for the transfer of power through British Raj to Indian Leadership and provide India with Independence in the Commonwealth of nations.

The Cabinet Mission, 1946 discussed the framework of the Constitution and laid down in some detail the Constitution drafting body.

Elections for the 296 seats assigned to the British Indian provinces for the Constitution drafting body, viz., Constituent Assembly of India were completed by August 1946.

Besides, there were representatives of the Princely Native Indian States.

With Native Indian States including four representative members of Princely State of Jammu & Kashmir—Sheikh Mohd. Abdullaha, Mirza Abzal Beg, Maulana Masoodi, and M.R. Baigra. On the Independence of India on August 15, 1947, the Constituent Assembly became a fully sovereign body and began its work on 9 December, 1946.

The first meeting of the Constituent Assembly of India took place in Constitutional Hall (now Central Hall of the Parliament and also the first seating place of the Supreme Court of India), New Delhi, on Monday, the 9th December 1946 at Eleven of the Clock.

The members of the C.A. were elected representatives under the Cabinet Mission Plan 1946 as well as nominated members from the Princely States which joined the Union of India after signing the Instrument of Accession under The Indian Independence Act, 1947.

The C.A. in its first meeting elected its Temporary Chairman proposed by Acharya J.B. Kriplani requesting Dr. Sachidananda Sinha to be the temporary Chairman who gratefully acceded to the request and acknowledged that he would cherish throughout his rest of the life this signal honour. Later on Dr. Rajendra Prasad was its permanent Chairman and Dr. B.R. Ambedkar was the Chairman of the Constitution Drafting Committee which comprised of 7 members including Sir B.N. Rau as its Constitutional Advisor.

Two significant tasks it did on the first day: *First,* the policy statement of Dr. Sinha on the framing of the Constitution for India by the Indians for the Indians in Independent India. *Second,* the Objectives Resolution of Pt. Jawaharlal Nehru. Dr. Sinha's policy statement was a direction for the Constitution Drafting Committee which was to prepare the Draft Constitution for the consideration, debate and adoption by the Constituent Assembly of India. The policy statement was regarding the devising of the Constitution on the basis of "The Constitution of India

—Yesterday, Today and Tomorrow".

He said that the constitutions which we could turn with some advantage were that of France, USA including first 10 amendments, Canada, Switzerland, besides unwritten constitutional law of UK evolved and developed on the basis of Conventions. He emphasized that Our Future Constitution should not be on the basis of the past experiences of Britishers' Experimentations from Charters to Indian Councils Acts and Government of India's Acts as working constitutions for India handed down by British Parliament with saddest experiences. The Future Constitution should be based on the aspirations and expectations of Indians.

He also expressed that our Future Constitution should be on the foundation of Mahatma M.K. Gandhi's statement, made so far back as 1922, and who was the architect of this Assembly. Mahatmaji wrote:

> "Swaraj will not be a free gift of the British Parliament. It will be a declaration of India's full self-expression ... of the people of India ... expressed through the freely chosen representatives."

Pandit Jawahar Lal Nehru moved *"OBJECTIVES RESOLUTION: AIMS AND OBJECTS"* in the Constituent Assembly of India met in the Constitution Hall, New Delhi, at Eleven of the Clock, under the Chairmanship of Dr. Rajendra Prasad. In his opening remarks as a prelude to the Objectives Resolution, he expressed:

"Governments do not come into being by State Papers. Governments are, in fact, the expression of the will of the people. We have met here today because of the strength of the people behind us and we shall go as far as the people not of any party or group but the people as a whole — shall wish us to go. We should, therefore, always keep in mind the passions that lie in the hearts of the masses of the Indian people and try to fulfil them. The Resolution that I am placing before you is in the nature of a pledge.

Resolution:

"(1) This Constituent Assembly declares its firm and Sovereign Republic and to draw up for her future Governance a Constitution;

(2) WHEREIN the territories that now comprise British India. The territories that now form Indian States, and such other parts of India as are outside British India and the States as well as such other territories as are willing to be constituted into Independent Sovereign India shall be a Union of them all;

(3) WHEREIN the said territories, whether with their present

boundaries or with such others as may be determined by the Constituent Assembly and thereafter according to the Law of the Constitution, shall possess and retain the status of autonomous Units, together with residuary powers, and exercise all powers and functions of government and administration, save and except such powers and functions as are vested in or assigned to the Union, or as are inherent or implied in the Union or resulting therefrom;

(4) WHEREIN all powers and authority of the Sovereign Independent India, its constituent parts and organs of government, are derived from the people;

(5) WHEREIN shall be guaranteed and secured to all the equality of status, of opportunity and before the law; vocation, association and action;

(6) WHEREIN adequate safeguards shall be provided for minorities, backward and tribal areas, and depressed and other backward classes;

(7) WHEREIN shall be maintained the integrity of the territory of the Republic and its sovereign rights on land, sea, and air according to Justice and the law of civilized nations; and

(8) This ancient land attains its rightful and honoured place in the world and make its full and willing contribution to the promotion of world peace and the welfare of mankind".

Since its first meeting on 9th December, 1946, the Constituent Assembly took 2 years, 11 months and 7 days till 26th day of November, 1949 — the last day of debates, finalization, adoption; and signature of the Constitution of India by all the members or Founding Fathers of the Constitution on 24 January, 1950. It came into effect on 26th day of January, 1950. This date was chosen to commemorate the declaration of Independence of 1930 as a Republic Day. During this period the Constituent Assembly has altogether held eleven sessions.

Out of these eleven sessions the first six were spent in passing the Objectives Resolution and the consideration of the Reports of Committees on Fundamental Rights, on Union Constitution, on Union Powers, on Provincial Constitution, on Minorities and on the Scheduled Areas and Scheduled Tribes. The seventh, eighth, ninth, tenth and the eleventh sessions were devoted to the consideration of the Draft Constitution. These eleven sessions of the Constituent Assembly have consumed 165 days. Out of these, the Assembly spent 114 days for the consideration of the Draft Constitution.

The Drafting Committee was elected by the Constituent Assembly on 29th August, 1947. It held its first meeting on 30th August, 1947. Since 30th August it sat for 141 days during which it was engaged in the preparation of the Draft Constitution. The Draft Constitution consisted of 243 Articles and 13 Schedules. In its final form, the Draft Constitution contained 395 Articles and 8 Schedules. The total number of amendments tabled was approximately 7,635. Of them, the total number of amendments actually moved in the House were 2,473. The total expenditure came to Rs. 63,96,729. 53,000 visitors were admitted to the Visitors' gallery. From First Amendment (1951) to last amendment (96th amendment 2011), it now contains 448 Articles,[4] 12 Schedules, and 117,369 words in the English language version.

These facts are mentioned to comprehend the genesis of the Constitution of India. Besides, at one stage it was being said that the Constituent Assembly had taken too long a time to finish its work that it was going on leisurely and wasting public money. It was said to be a case of Nero fiddling while Rome was burning. There seems no justification for this complaint. Constitution is not the birth of days or minutes or seconds; it requires investment of perceptions, concepts, visions and comprehension. "Where there is no vision the people perish." Illustrations: USA, May 25, 1787 to September 17, 1787, i.e. within 4 months; Canada October 10, 1864 to March 1867, i.e., 2 years 5 months; Australia March 1891 to July 9, 1900, i.e., consuming 9 years.

Drafting Committee was charged as a Drifting Committee. It shows a contempt for the Drafting Committee, which had had to gain insights in-depth of the working of democratic constitutions at the global level as per the policy directions of the Chairman, as mentioned above, before it could finalize the Draft Constitution for the consideration of the Constituent Assembly. Dr. B.R Ambedkar in his concluding speech remarked: "If hereafter things go wrong, we will have no body to blame except ourselves. There is nothing wrong with the Constitution. It is the man who is vile."

Dr. Rajendra Prasad concluded the proceedings of the Constituent Assembly in these prophetic words: "It acquires life because of the men who control it and operate it, and India needs today nothing more than a set of honest men who will have the interest of the country before them. It requires men of strong character, men of vision, men who will not sacrifice the interests of the country at large for the sake of smaller

4. However, in view of some scholars/lawyers there are 395 articles in the Indian Constittution

groups and areas and who will rise over prejudices which are born of these differences. We can only hope that the country will throw up such men in abundance. Let us launch on this new enterprise of running our Independent Republic with confidence, with truth and non-violence and above all with heart within and God over head. THAT THE CONSTITUTION AS SETTLED BY THE ASSEMBLY BE PASSED. THE MOTION WAS ADOPTED WITH PROLONGED CHEERS."

- The Constituent Assembly met in sessions open to public, for 166 days, spread over a period of two years, eleven months, and seven days before adopting the Constitution of India on 26th November, 1949.
- After many deliberations and some modifications, the 308 Members of the Constituent Assembly signed two hand written copies of the document one each in Hindi and English on January 24th, 1950.
- On January 26th, 1950, the Constitution of India became *the law of all the Indian Land* [India that is Bharat shall be union of states: Art.1, Schedules 1 and IV: 28 states, 7 Union Territories: Part A, B, C states done away with the States Reorganization Act] *and for the "We the people of India"*.
- In its over 60 years of enactment, the Constitution of India has been amended by 96 amendments.
- The Constitution of India is not *static lex*, because a static law is like a dead wood that makes the system hard and its structure rigid and inflexible inasmuch as dead wood.
- It is a living organism, it is dynamic and receptive of a living thought and may vary greatly, without losing its colour, content and basic sacrosanct character, according to the circumstances and the felt necessities of time in which it is used.

Our Supreme Court has not only been interpreting it, but expounding the Constitution inasmuch as keeping it out of legalese as well as legal archaisms.

Our Constitution is based on *two schools of thoughts*:—
One, that it is a *beautiful patchwork*, an ably conceived and drafted document, showing creative, if not an original, approach to the nation's constitutional needs, we cannot justly doubt.
And, *second* that the Indian Constitution, though *Euro-American* in appearance, *is native in its spirit*. (M.P. Singh)

Be that as it may, we know that our patchwork heritage is strength, not a weakness, because, though being far from perfection, it has withstood Unity in Diversity, sustaining diversified democracy rooted in Constitutional culture, Constitutional morality, Constitutional politics embedded in equality and rule of law.

Therefore, to save the Indian Constitution from being defaced and defiled, we need set of honest men who control it having the interests of the country before them. [Good and sustainable Governance; incorruptible].

Influence of Euro-American Constitutional legal models on the Indian Constitution:

British Constitution:

- Parliamentary—Executive form of government
- The idea of single citizenship
- The idea of the rule of law [Equality before the laws]
- Institution of speaker and his role
- Law-making procedure
- Procedure established by Law.

United States of America Constitution:

- Charter of Fundamental Rights, which is similar to the United States Bill of Rights [Equal protection of the laws]
- Federal structure of Government [Independent and Reciprocal dependence]
- Power of Judicial Review and Independence of the Judiciary
- President as Supreme Commander of Armed Forces
- Due process of Law.

Irish Constitution:

- Directive Principles of State Policy [Social and Economic Rights]

French Constitution:

- Ideals of Liberty, Equality and Fraternity

Canadian Constitution:

- A quasi-federal and quasi-Unitary government (a federal system with a strong Central Government and reciprocal dependence)
- The idea of Residual Powers.

Australian Constitution:

- Freedom of trade and commerce within the country and between the States [Concepts of intra-state and inter-state]

- Powers of Indian Parliament to make laws for implementing treaties, even on outside normal federal jurisdiction.

Malaysian Constitution:

- The idea of the Concurrent list

Japan Constitution:

- Fundamental Duties

Weimar Constitution Germany:

- Emergency Provisions

The Genesis:

- Our Constitution's spirit is the Preamble, which is the Backbone of our Constitution.
- It is the guiding spirit for Indian Nation on the touchstone of Basic Features of our Constitution.
- Preamble indicates the language and expressions of the Constitution as its ***Vision Mission*** and not in a rigid or exhaustive sense.
- This is the Genesis on which the edifice of the Constitution is made.

Preamble

We the people of India having solemnly resolved *to Constitute* India into a SOVEREIGN SOCIALIST SECULAR DEMOCTATIC REPUBLIC and *to secure* to all its citizens:

JUSTICE, social, economic and political;

LIBERTY of thought, expression, belief, faith and worship;

EQUALTY of status and opportunity and *to promote* among them all;

FRATERNITY *assuring* the dignity of the individual and the unity and integrity of the Nation;

IN OUR CONSTITUENT ASSEMBLY this twenty-sixth day of November, 1949, do HEREBY ADOPT, ENACT AND GIVE TO OURSELVES THIS CONSITUTION.

1. Fundamental Right [Arts. 12-35A]

Special privileges to the permanent residents of J&K by Constitution [Application of J&K] orders 1950 and 1954, inserted by Presidential Order and not by an Act of Parliament: genesis of Art. 370.

2. Affirmative Action [Art. 15(3)]

Women and children; 15(4): SC, ST, OBC, (creamy layer), 15(5): (93rd amendment) SEBC [Concept of Under-served/Under-privileged/ marginalized/deprived/neglected sections/segments of the society or Compensatory justice or permissible discrimination or distributive justice].

3. Fundamental Duties

[Art. 51-A: 42nd amendment, 1976]

4. Directive Principles of State Policy

Social and Economic Rights [Arts. 36-51]

5. Citizenship: Single Indian Origin

Citizenship Act, 1956 [Arts. 5-11]

6. Nature of Indian Federations

(a) Union of States: [Arts. 1-4 and Schedules I & IV]

(b) Legislative Relations [Three lists: Union list: 97 subjects, State list: 66 subjects, Concurrent list: 47 subjects, Residuary powers: Centre] Reciprocal Dependence and not Independence.

7. Doctrine of Basic Structure

[*Kesavananda Bharathi; Minerva Mills; Waman Rao; S.R. Bommai*].

8. Independence of Indian Judiciary

(a) Judicial Review [Arts. 32 and 226]

(b) Judicial Activism

(c) Public Interests Litigation: *pro bono publico*, *actio popularis*, from personal injury to public interest injury litigation

(d) S.C. Collegium of justices headed by CJI. Selection of Judges for H.Cs. and S.C.; a mechanism to move againt corrupt Judges where impeachment fails: An upright Judge has more regard to justice than to men: *Yogyao vicarka purushmanpeksheiy nyaya manusarti* [*Hitokti*].

Separation of Power

The executive power of the Union is vested in the President.[5] Similarly, the executive power is vested in the Governor in so far as the executive power of the state is concerned.[6]

Executive Powers and Functions of the Union and States

In terms of the executive powers and functions of both the Union and States, the Articles listed below and many other provisions of the Indian Constitution provide for the same.

Article	***Short Title***
72	Power of President to grant pardons, etc., and to suspend, remit or commute sentences.
73	Extent of executive power of the Union.
76	Attorney-General for India.
77	Conduct of business of the Government of India.
111	Assent to Bills.
117	Special provisions as to financial Bills.
123	Power of President to promulgate Ordinances during recess of Parliament.
124	Establishment and constitution of Supreme Court.
143	Power of President to consult Supreme Court.
144	Civil and judicial authorities to act in aid of the Supreme Court.
155	Appointment of Governor.
156	Term of office of Governor.
216	Constitution of High Courts.
223	Appointment of acting Chief Justice.
224	Appointment of additional and acting Judges.
162	Extent of executive power of State.
163 (2)	Council of Ministers to aid and advise Governor.
165	Advocate-General for the State.
166	Conduct of business of the Government of the State.
174	Sessions of the State Legislature, prorogation and dissolution.

5. Article 53—'The executive power of the Union shall be vested in the President and shall be exercised by him directly or through officers subordinate to him in accordance with this Constitution.'
6. Article 153—'The executive power of the State shall be vested in the Governor and shall be exercised by him directly or through officers subordinate to him in accordance with this Constitution'.

Article	***Short Title***
176	Special address by the Governor.
192	Decision on questions as to disqualifications of members.
200	Assent to Bills.
207	Special provisions as to financial Bills.
213	Power of Governor to promulgate Ordinances during recess of Legislature.
239	Administration of Union territories.
239AB	Power of administrator to promulgate Ordinances during recess of Legislature.
239B	Special provisions with respect to Delhi.
240	Power of President to make regulations for certain Union territories.
263	Provisions with respect to an inter-State Council.
280	Finance Commission.
292	Borrowing by the Government of India.
293	Borrowing by States.
316	Appointment and term of office of members.
318	Power to make regulations as to conditions of service of members and staff of the Commission.
331	Representation of the Anglo-Indian community in the House of the People.
333	Representation of the Anglo-Indian community in the Legislative Assemblies of the States.
339	Control of the Union of over the Administration of Scheduled Areas and the welfare of Scheduled Tribes.
340	Appointment of a Commission to investigate the conditions of backward classes.
341	Scheduled Castes.
342	Scheduled Tribes
344	Commission and Committee of Parliament on official language.
350B	Special Officer for linguistic minorities.
352	Proclamation of Emergency.
353	Effect of Proclamation of Emergency.
354	Application of provisions relating to distribution of revenuers while a Proclamation of Emergency is in operation.

Article	*Short Title*
355	Duty of the Union to protect States against external aggression and internal disturbance.
356	Provisions in case of failure of constitutional machinery in States.
357	Excise of legislative powers under Proclamation issued under Article 356.
358	Suspension of provisions of Article 19 during emergencies.
359	Suspension of the enforcement of the rights conferred by Part III during emergencies.
360	Provisions as to financial emergency.
372A	Special provision with respect to the State of Nagaland.
373	Power of President to make order in respect of persons under preventive detention in certain cases.
392	Power of the President to remove difficulties.

The aforesaid provisions pave way for a series of executive powers and functions to be performed by the President and the Governors under the Indian Constitution. The specific executive functions are also mentioned in Articles 85, 87, 103, 192 and 258A.

Legislative Powers and Functions of the Union Parliament and State Legislatures

The legislative powers and functions of both the Union Parliament and State Legislatures are provide under Articles listed below[7] and many other provisions of the Indian Constitution.

Article	*Short Title*
241	High Courts for Union territories.
245	Extent of laws made by Parliament and by the Legislatures of States.
246	Subject-matter of laws made by Parliament and by the Legislatures of States.
247	Power of Parliament to provide for the establishment of certain additional courts.
248	Residuary powers of legislation.
249	Power of Parliament to legislate with respect to a matter in the State List in the national interest.

7. http://lawmin.nic.in/coi/contents/htm accessed on 10 Nov. 2011 at 11:29.

Article	Short Title
250	Power of Parliament to legislate with respect to any matter in the State List if a Proclamation of Emergency is in operation.
252	Power of Parliament to legislate for two or more States by consent and adoption of such legislation by any other State.
253	Legislation for giving effect to international agreements.
265	Taxes not to be imposed save by authority of law.
267	Contingency Fund.
271	Surcharge on certain duties and taxes for purposes of the Union.
275	Grants from the Union to certain States.
276	Taxes on professions, trades, calling and employments.
286	Restrictions as to imposition of tax on the sale or purchase of goods.
302	Power of Parliament to impose restrictions on trade, commerce and intercourse.
303	Restrictions on the legislative powers of the Union and of the States with regard to trade and commerce.
304	Restrictions on trade, commerce and intercourse among States.
307	Appointment of authority for carrying out of the purpose of Articles 301 to 304.
309	Recruitment and conditions of service of persons serving the Union or a State.
312	All-India services.
312A	Power of Parliament to vary or revoke conditions of service of officers of certain services.
321	Power to extend functions of Public Service Commissions.
323A	Administrative tribunals.
323B	Tribunals for other matters.
327	Power of Parliament to make provision with respect to elections to Legislatures.
328	Power of Legislature of a State to make provision with respect to elections to such Legislature.
345	Official language or languages of a State.

Article	*Short Title*
357	Exercise of legislative powers under Proclamation issued under Article 356.
368	Power of Parliament to amend the Constitution and procedure therefor.
370	Temporary provisions with respect to the State of Jammu and Kashmir.
371	Special provision with respect to the States of Maharashtra and Gujarat.
372	Continuance in force of existing laws and their adaptation.

Judicial Powers and Functions

The judicial powers and functions are provided under Articles listed below and many other provisions of the Indian Constitution.

Article	*Short Title*
124	Establishment and constitution of Supreme Court.
131	Original jurisdiction of the Supreme Court.
132	Appellate jurisdiction of Supreme Court in appeals from High Courts in certain cases.
134	Appellate jurisdiction of Supreme Court in regard to criminal matters.
135	Jurisdiction and powers of the Federal Court under existing law to be exercisable by the Supreme Court.
136	Special leave to appeal by the Supreme Court.
137	Review of judgments or orders by the Supreme Court.
138	Enlargement of the jurisdiction of the Supreme Court.
139	Conferment on the Supreme Court of powers to issue certain writs.
140	Ancillary powers of Supreme Court.
141	Law declared by Supreme Court to be binding on all courts.
142	Enforcement of decrees and orders of Supreme Court and orders as to discovery, etc.
143	Power of President to consult Supreme Court.
214	High Courts for States.
215	High Courts to be courts of record.
216	Constitution of High Courts.

Article	Short Title
217	Appointment and conditions of the office of a Judge of a High Court.
220	Restriction on practice after being a permanent Judge.
221	Salaries, etc., of Judges
222	Transfer of a Judge from one High Court to another.
223	Appointment of acting Chief Justice.
224	Appointment of additional and acting Judges.
225	Jurisdiction of existing High Courts.
226	Power of High Courts to issue certain writs.
227	Power of superintendence over all courts by the High Court.
229	Officers and servants and the expenses of High Courts.

Apart from providing the powers and functions of the three branches of the government, both at the centre and at states, the Constitution also provides for a series of provisions to check the arbitrary exercise of such powers and functions by any one of these three branches. Thus, the doctrine of 'checks and balances' that is derived from the existence of the doctrine of 'separation of powers' or 'separation of functions' is also present under the Indian Constitution.

Provisions to Check Transgression of Powers

Some of the provisions that seek to check the powers and functions of the three branches of the government whenever they transgress the constitutionally provided limits are listed below:

Article	Short Title
117	Special provisions as to financial Bills.
121	Restriction on discussion in Parliament.
122	Courts not to inquire into proceedings of Parliament.
151	Audit reports.
207	Special provisions as to financial Bills.
211	Restriction on discussion in the Legislature.
212	Courts not to inquire into proceedings of the Legislature.
217	Appointment and conditions of the office of a Judge of a High Court.
222	Transfer of a Judge from one High Court to another.

247	Power of Parliament to provide for the establishment of certain additional courts.
262(2)	Adjudication of disputes relating to waters of inter-State rivers or river valleys.
274	Prior recommendation of President required to Bills affecting taxation in which States are interested.
280	Finance Commission.
281	Recommendations of the Finance Commission.
292	Borrowing by the Government of India.
323	Reports of Public Service Commissions.
324	Superintendence, direction and control of elections to be vested in an Election Commission.
329	Bar to interference by courts in electoral matters.
338	National Commission for Scheduled Castes.
352	Proclamation of Emergency.
353	Effect of Proclamation of Emergency.
354	Application of provisions relating to distribution of revenues while a Proclamation of Emergency is in operation.
356	Provisions in case of failure of constitutional machinery in States.
357	Exercise of legislative powers under Proclamation issued under article 356.
358	Suspension of provisions of Article 19 during emergencies.
360	Provisions as to financial emergency.
365	Effect of failure to comply with, or to give effect to, directions given by the Union.

Public Interest Litigation

- *Pro bono Publico*
- *Actio popularis*
  (An action that a member of the general public brings in the interest of public welfare)
- For the Public Good
- *Actio popularis*

(An action that a member of the general public brings in the interest of public welfare)

Access to Justice

- Distributive Justice
- Economic Justice
- Social Justice
- Human right to human dignity (Women; Police atrocities and custodial death; under-trials languishing in jails for a longer period longer than the period of punishment)

- Third party litigation
- Not for own right
- But for the rights of others who on account of purse poverty and right ignorance/illiteracy can't have access to justice—Doors of Court are ajar for them
- Underprivileged
- Marginalized
- Deprived
- Underserved

Movement

- From — To
- Personal/private injury litigation (strict *locus standi*) — Public injury litigation (Liberalisation/relaxation of *locus standi*) Origin, growth and development of public interest litigation
  - — Article 32: Constitution: Supreme Court of India
  - — Article 226: Constitution: High Court of a State
  - — Article 142: Constitution: Supreme Court of India: Expounding the Constitution

Jurisdiction

- Epistolary Jurisdiction : A letter addressed to the Judge of S.C. or H.C. is treated as a writ petition
- *Mumbai Kamgar Union* : explain
- PIL/SAL/PAL, i.e., Public Interest Litigation/Social Action Litigation/Private Attorneys at Law.
- 25 mentally ill and insane living in thatched homes and charred to death: explain directions issued by the Supreme Court.

PIL Write

- Cases: State's duty: Equal wages for equal work; Narmada, Ganges water; Housing colony and park for children; ecology, environment, deforestation; Sustainability.
- M.C. Mehta cases: Explain: Olem Gas leakage; State Public Trustee (Kamal Nath); Asiad '82; Salal Hydroelectric; Hussainara Khatoon; Bhagalpur blinding; etc.
- 77 years old man languishing in Assam jail as an under-trial for 54 years for an alleged offence grievous hurt under section 326 IPC for which punishment is 10 years, languished in jail for 54 years without trial, ordered to be released with a compensation of 3 lacs; could this meager amount re-compensate his prime youth lost as an under-trial in jail for the offence which police failed to put on trial for want of evidence?

Danger

- Is PIL a pill for every ill?
- Personal, popularity, publicity litigation.
- Judges should discipline PIL that it does not go wild—Judicial Restraint.

Chapter X

LEGAL REASONING: JUDGE-MADE LAW

Legal reasoning is what the Judge says, in the decision-making process, is the law in the real sense, says Holmes. This process is gained by experience in espousing explanation to cause and effect. Legal reasoning is about the human faculty of reason or rationality in the decision-making process. Legal reasoning means the process by which rational beings (lawyers, judges) espouse specific reasons or reasonable explanations of cause and effect. Thus, legal reasoning is a consideration or ratio which explains or justifies the rendition of justice. In this process, legal reasoning is a mental faculty or ability of the humans involved in the decision-making process that is able to generate conclusions from premises of facts (cause) and effects (law). Legal reasoning is thought to be more rational in discovering what truth is and what false is and separating truth from false in a legal conviviality, which potentially is in conflict with reason.

The concept of legal reasoning is closely related to the concept of language and logic, as reflected in *Greek logos*, the root of *logy* (logic), which translated into *Latin* became known ratio and in French came to be acknowledged *raison* from which the English language word 'reason' was derived. In *Indic Vidhi Shastra* language it is acknowledged as *Yukti* and *Pramana*—the genesis of legal reasoning and also the genesis of rules of Mimansa—the rules of interpretation.

In the backdrop of the above, the lawyers and the judges have their unique approaches to the resolution of disputant legal problems. The unique approach followed by them in resolving disputes is "laws" about "determining the law". And, the most significant laws, in practical terms, is the "law of precedent" or "*stare decisis*" or "*ratio decidendi*" in this perspective, which is the genesis of legal reasoning.

Professor Goodhart, a learned author on this subject, has a *proprio vigore* submitted the assertion that "the *ratio decidendi* (reason of deciding) of a case can be defined as the material facts of the case plus the decision thereon."[1] To explain his definition, Goodhart has suggested a helpful formula: "Suppose that in a certain case, e.g. *Rayland v. Fletcher*,[2] facts A, B and C exist, and suppose that the court finds that facts B and C are material and fact A immaterial, and then reaches conclusion X (e.g. judgment for the plaintiff or judgment for the defendant). Then the doctrine of precedent enables us to say that in future case in which facts B and C exist, or in which facts A, B and C exist, the conclusion must be X. If in a future case facts A, B, C and D exist, and the fact D is held to be material, the first case will not be a direct authority, though it may be of value as an analogy."[3]

However, Professor Glanville William presents, in practical terms, the explanation of the doctrine of precedent or *stare decisis* in this jurisprudential language: "What the doctrine of precedent declares is that cases must be decided the same way when their material facts are the same. Obviously, it does not require that all the facts should be the same. We know in the flux of life all the facts of a case will never recur, but the legally material facts may recur and it is with these that the doctrine of precedent is concerned."[4]

Be that as it may, Professor Gall, a Canadian Professor of Public Law, presents in an unequivocal expression: "*Stare decisis* is the abbreviation of the *Latin* language phrase *stare decisis et non quieta movere*, which in English legal language means 'to stand by decisions and not to disturb settled matters' or 'stick to what has already been settled or decided or adjudicated upon'."[5] According to the principle of *stare decisis* the decision of the highest court or superior court or the Apex Court acts as a binding authority on the High Courts or higher

1. Goodhart, Determining the Ratio Decidendi of a Case, Essays in Jurisprudence and the Common Law, 1931, p. 1.
2. (1868) L.R. 3 H.L. 330.
3. *Supra* note 118.
4. Glanville William, Learning the Law, 9th Ed., 1973, at pp. 67-68.
5. Gerald L. Gall, The Canadian Legal System, 2nd Ed., 1983, at p. 220.

courts and the trial courts and not *vice versa*.[6] The decision of a higher court within the same State jurisdiction acts as binding authority on subordinate courts or trial courts or basic courts within the same State jurisdiction. However, the decision of a higher court of another State jurisdiction acts as persuasive authority and not binding authority. The degree of persuasiveness depends upon various factors, viz., the nature of the other State jurisdiction, the date of the precedent case of the other State jurisdiction on the assumption that the more recent the precedent case the more reliable it will be as a binding-persuasive authority for a given proposition in the dispute.[7] Be that as it may, the judge's reputation may affect the degree of persuasiveness of the authority.[8]

In the backdrop of the above scholastic arguments, it seems that the doctrine of precedent or *stare decisis* or *ratio decidendi* is justified on the focal desirability of stability and certainty in the law, which, without staleness, is imperative in the administration of justice. Stability and certainty in the law depend upon the notions of justice and fairness. Justice Benjamin N. Cardozo has unequivocally expressed: "It will not do to decide the same question one way between one set of litigants and the opposite way between another. If a group of cases involves the same point, the parties expect the same decision. It would be a gross injustice to decide alternate cases on opposite principles. If a case was decided against me yesterday when I was a defendant, I shall look for the same judgment today if I am a plaintiff. To decide differently would raise a feeling of resentment and wrong in my breast; it would be an infringement, material and moral, of my right."[9]

"Adherence to precedent", opined Friedman "must then be the rule rather than exception if litigants are to have faith in the even-handed administration of justice in the courts."[10]

It, thus, discerns that the doctrine of *stare decisis* or precedent or *ratio decidendi* is closely related to justice and fairness and reverse shall constitute injustice. Observes an American legal philosopher: "The paradigm case of injustice is that in which there are two similar individuals in similar circumstances and one of them is treated better or

---

6. *Ibid.*, see also Article 141 of the Constitution of India.
7. *Ibid.*
8. *Ibid.*
9. Benjamin N. Cardozo, The Nature of the Judicial Process, 1921, at pp. 9-50.
10. Friedman, Stare Decisis at Common Law and under Civil Code, (1953) 31 Can. Bar Rev. 722.

worse than the other. In this case, the cry of injustice rightly goes up against the responsible agent or group; and unless that agent or group can establish that there is some relevant dissimilarity after all between the individuals concerned and their circumstances, he or they will be guilty as charged."[11]

Though the doctrine of precedent is sustainable for the sake of stability and certainty in the law, but it should not be at the cost of justice, because the old precedent (the law) may lead to staleness eventually causing injustice and unfairness in the administration of justice in the courts. This happens because the lawyers and the judges are trained in the lawyering-language of precedent. Be that as it may, staleness should not be a stumbling block or impediment in the framework of an innovation out of the old parched law. Therefore, to come out of the cobweb or nightmare of staleness, we may not amiss the legal auguring of Lord Denning in this perspective: "If lawyers hold to their precedents too closely, forgetful of the fundamental principles of truth and justice which they should serve, they may find the whole edifice comes tumbling down about them. Just as the scientist seeks for truth, so the lawyer should seek for justice. Just as the scientist takes his instances and from them builds up his general propositions, so the lawyer should take his precedents and from them build up his general principles. Just as the propositions of the scientist fail to be modified when shown not to fit all instances, or even discarded when shown in error, so the principles of the lawyer should be modified when found to be unsuited to the times or discarded when found to work injustice."[12]

It, thus, discerns that new precedents should be formed out of the staleness or discarded or old parchment of the dead or outdated law to meet the ends of justice.

The practice of following the precedents or stare decisis/*ratio decidendi* in India is enjoined in Article 141 of the Constitution of India, which reads that law declared by the Supreme Court shall be binding on all courts in India. The practice and procedure of precedent as binding authority is similar as explained above, i.e. the modern practice of precedent is followed which is not detriment to the welfare of 'We the People of India'. This is clear from the judicial decisions that too rigid adherence to precedent may lead to injustice and may also unduly restrict the proper development of law. It has been recognized that nothing prevents to depart from the previous decision when it

11. William K. Frankena, Ethics, 2nd Ed., 1973, at p. 49.
12. The Rt. Hon. Lord Denning, The Discipline of the Law, 1979, at pp. 9-50.

appears right to do so. In *Bengal Immunity Co. v. State of Bihar*[13] the Supreme Court held that "there is nothing in the Indian Constitution which prevents the Supreme Court departing from its previous decision if it is convinced of its error and its beneficial effect on the general interest of public. ... The Supreme Court should not lightly dissent from its previous decisions. Its power of review must be exercised with due care and caution and only for advancing the public well-being in the light of surrounding circumstances of each case brought to its notice but it is not right to confine its power within rigidly fixed limits. If on a re-examination it comes to the conclusion that the previous majority decision was plainly erroneous then it will be its duty to say so and not to perpetuate its mistake."

Thus, it discerns that the doctrine of precedent or *stare decisis* is not an inflexible rule of law. It does not permit to perpetuate errors of the Apex Court to the detriment of the general welfare of the public. Besides, the doctrine has hardly any application to an isolated and stray decision of the Court projected to be followed in a very recently case, which has not been followed by a series of earlier decisions-based thereon.

In *I.C. Golaknath* v. *State of Punjab*[14] while applying the rule of 'prospective overruling', the Supreme Court reversed its earlier two decisions, viz., *Shankari Prasad v. Union of India*[15] and *Sajjan Singh v. State of Rajasthan.*[16] In these two cases the Supreme Court had opined that the power to amend the Constitution including the fundamental rights was contained in Article 368 and the word 'law' enjoined in Article 13 did not include in amendment of the Constitution which is made in the exercise of constituent making power of the Parliament. However, in *Golaknath's* case the Supreme Court while reversing these cases held the power to amend the fundamental rights is not enjoined in Article 368, but in the residuary power of legislation of the Parliament, hence, a law made under Article 368 is subject to judicial scrutiny of Article 13, viz., laws inconsistent with fundamental rights are void.

In *Keshvananda Bharati v. State of Kerala,*[17] the Supreme Court while reconsidering *Golaknath's* case overruled it holding that the *Golaknath's* case was wrongly decided and the word 'law' in Article 13

13. AIR 1955 SC 661.
14. AIR 1967 SC 1643.
15. AIR 1951 SC 455.
16. AIR 1965 SC 845.
17. AIR 1973 SC 1461.

did not include an amendment of the basic feature of the Constitution passed under Article 368. That is, Parliament does not enjoy the constituent power to amend the basic features of the Constitution of India even under the amending power enjoined in Article 368. This means that any previous decisions, which covertly or overtly, permitted amendment of basic features of the Constitution including the fundamental rights, shall not be allowed to be followed subsequently as precedents, because such precedents were wrong and incompatible with the basic features doctrine.

In *Maneka Gandhi v. Union of India*[18] the Supreme Court recognized the due process of law in the Indian context by overruling its previous decision *A.K. Gopalan v. State of Madras*[19] which did not concede due process of law in the constitutional language of 'procedure established by law' enjoined in Article 21. The Supreme Court also established an innovative as well as progressive juridical language of due process of law in the phraseology of 'procedure established by law', viz., 'procedure must be just, fair and reasonable'. Legislative action and State action must be just, fair and reasonable and certainly not fanciful and whimsical. The axiom 'just, fair and reasonable' has become an imperishable rule of precedent or *stare decisis* because it recognizes the importance of fundamental rights in the historic decision of the Supreme Court handed down in the classic language of Justice P.N. Bhagwati: "These fundamental rights represent the basic values cherished by the people of this country (India) since the *Vedic* times and they are calculated to protect the dignity of the individual and create conditions in which every human being can develop his personality to the fullest extent. They weave a pattern of guarantee on the basic structure of human rights, and impose negative obligation on the State not to encroach on individual liberty in its various dimensions".

Bachan Singh v. State of Punjab[20] has in unequivocal terms established a new criminal jurisprudence that death penalty could be awarded under Section 302 of the Indian Penal Code in 'rarest of the rare circumstances'.

Thus, it seems that too rigid adherence to precedent may lead to injustice. Too rigid adherence to precedent may restrict the development of law. Flexibility in rigidity tends to help to depart from the previous decision when it appears right to do so when there is a

---

18. AIR 1978 SC 578.
19. AIR 1950 SC 27.
20. AIR 1980 SC 898.

national crisis of great movement to the life, liberty and safety of the citizenry of the country; rigidity in flexibility also tends to help to adhere to the previous decision if it is advisable not to depart from it when nation's interests are at stake, or the basic direction of the nation itself is in peril.[21]

In the backdrop of the above, it is expedient to analyze the secrets of legal reasoning. The genesis of legal reasoning is The Facts, The Contentious Issues, The Rule or Law—The Statute or the law passed by the legislature and the law declared by the Courts, i.e. the previous decisions or precedent or *stare decisis*, The Analysis, and The Holding, i.e. The Conclusion formulae. It is the process by which lawyers and judges think alike about any legal problem. It is a process of elimination and/or addition. The law students, too, have to think alike, because it allows the law students to make their frame of mind "to think like a lawyer" and to comprehend to reduce the complexities of the law.

Facts: help to understand the circumstances and the situations or cause (causal factors) the disputants or disputant parties or litigants brought to the court.

Issues: help to understand what facts and circumstances brought the disputant parties to the court.

Rule: help to understand what the governing law, i.e. the statute and the previous decisions—precedents—is for the issue in dispute to be resolved.

Analysis: help to analyse whether the governing rule (the statute and the previous decisions or precedents) apply the facts in dispute.

Holding: help to understand how far the court's holding in conclusion interpret the statute and adhere to the precedents or modify the governing law (previous decisions or precedents) and develop the new law by discarding the previous erroneous law.

The above mentioned FIRAH [Facts, Issues, Rules, Analysis and Holding] tends to help the law students to comprehend the legal reasoning or *ratio decidendi* process. This process is interesting, beautiful and fascinating. The law students have to develop fascination for it, which helps to start 'think like a lawyer'. This process is indeed significant as "the facts of a case suggest an issue" or "issue spotting". The facts enable to identify which facts raise which issues. "Issue spotting" process can help which issue to eliminate or which issue to add to a case thereby raising a process of "fact-issue-law" interaction, which helps in developing legal reasoning or *ratio decidendi* process.

---

21. See *Ambika Prasad v. State of U.P.*, AIR 1980 SC 1762.

This way, the law students shall develop "issue spotting skills", and "issue spotting skills" shall make the law students to become effective and efficient lawyers. This indeed is the genesis to the art of lawyering and experiential learning..

What is the law or rule (a statute or a law developed by the courts) is the most ticklish stage that requires skills of issue framing, because "the issue is covered by a rule of law". The basis of "art of lawyering" is the analysis of a case. This again is the most ticklish stage for the law students, because they have to develop the skills "comparing the facts to the rule to form the analysis". Here, the law students have to develop and sharpen their skills by separating irrelevant facts from relevant facts, and which fact shall help to prove or disprove the rule.

Thus, from the analysis, the law students shall come to the conclusion, i.e. holding of a case, as to whether the rule or law applies to the facts.

Chapter XI

DOCTRINAL LEGAL RESEARCH: TECHNIQUES AND TOOLS

I. WHY LEGAL RESEARCH?

The first question that may arise and arouse curiosity in the mind of a law-researcher is: Why Legal Research? The function of a lawyer is not only to know the law for which he is paid, but the task of a lawyer is also to resolve conflict when the law is not clear. Therefore, Legal Research involves two pronged strategic approaches:

1. **Practice:** The practitioner applies law to specific problems.
2. **Theoretical:** The practitioner applies law to a situation that may or may not have appeared as concrete cases.

II. WHAT IS RESEARCH?

The second inquisitive question relates to: What is Research? Research is an act of searching into a matter closely and carefully. Research is about discovery of truth. A researcher must be trained well-equipped with tools of scientific investigation, viz., an investigation of every kind which is based on original sources of knowledge. Professor Eastwood says that he is researching every day of life; he is providing expert solution to immediate problem. In the backdrop of this, research is a quest for knowledge. It requires inquisitive mindset. Research is a fascination; it is a passion. Research is to unfold the correlations of cause and effect. The researcher may love law inasmuch as he loves art, literature, music, which may unfold mystiques of LLL: L = Life (of law); L = Literature (of law); L = Law (Normative science).

Legal research is either doctrinal or non-doctrinal. Doctrinal research is "expositor exploration" through exegetical and exegesis methodology. Its contours are analytical. It is a research study 'law in books'. Its armory is 'law library', which contains a range of equipment and skills available in the form of primary sources and secondary sources, namely, legislative in terms of statutes, reports, rules, regulations, bye-laws; and decisional in terms of law reports, digests, and manuals. Non-doctrinal research is known as 'law in action'. It encompasses the application of 'social sciences research techniques in legal research'. Its contours are socio-legal or empirical or heuristic or behavioural or attitudinal or quantitative and qualitative. How the recipients of law feel about the law is a step forward to know the law functionally or realistically. It involves the application of law, society, and sociology. The tools of legal research methods both doctrinal and non-doctrinal are presented in power point presentation at the end of this chapter and in Chapters XII and XIII.

III. LAW LIBRARIES AND ITS USE FOR LEGAL RESEARCH

A law library is the repository of legal knowledge. It is a treasure house of law—legislative and decisional laws—hidden in the primary sources of law and secondary sources of law. It is of immense use for legal research for 'socio-legal-politico-anthropologic' inquisitives. It helps the lawmen—law students, law researchers, scholars for scholastic quests, law professors, lawyers, judges and jurists in their respective areas of search as well as research explorations and investigations. A law library is different from others in the sense that, by its nature, it is to be a reference library. Mainly it is a research library where one reference leads to another and, therefore, a reader has to consult a number of law reports, digests, journals and periodicals, books, etc. simultaneously to solve one problem. Another peculiar nature of a law library is that it has to keep its collection up-to-date.[1] Besides, legislative material and the law reports, other material for reference is also provided herein like newspaper reports, departmental reports (e.g. reports of various Commissions appointed by the Government of India), magazines (both Indian and foreign), etc.

In India, all categories of law libraries are more or less departmental libraries and hence it is natural that are located at the location of the department which they are supposed to serve. The various categories of law libraries—the university departments' law libraries, the law colleges libraries, the National Law Schools of India

1. H.C. Jain, Law Library Administration and Reference, Metropolitan Book Co. (P) Ltd., Delhi (1972), p. 1.

Universities law libraries, the Supreme Court of India and the State High Courts libraries, the law ministry and the legal remembrance's libraries, the Bar Associations libraries, etc., and the libraries owned by many law firms, solicitors' firms and individual lawyers—are located at places where these departments are placed/situated. Hence, these are not public libraries. Quite apart from these, library of the Indian Law Institute caters the need of persons interested in legal research. It is one of the leading law libraries in India and contains over 63,000 volumes. It receives about 263 current legal periodicals including serial publications. The library remains open from 9.00 a.m. to 8.30 p.m. on all working days and from 10.00 a.m. to 5.30 p.m. on Saturdays and Sundays. The library remains closed on National and Gazetted holidays.

A separate wing of the library issues books to the students of LL.M. and the diploma courses. The library is completely automated and totally computerized and placed on website.

Quite apart the Law Libraries, legal research may also be undertaken (particularly where empirical research studies are undertaken) in the following institutions:

(i) Government Departments
(ii) National Archives
(iii) Social and Welfare Organizations
(iv) Non-Governmental Organizations
(v) Indian Council of Social Sciences Research
(vi) Law Commission of India
(vii) National Human Rights Commission and State Human Rights Commissions
(viii) Scheduled Castes and Scheduled Tribes Commission
(ix) Minority Commission
(x) Regulatory Commissions/Boards under Telecommunication Law, Petroleum and Natural Gas Law, etc.

IV. CITATION OF LEGISLATION

Constitution: The provisions of the Constitution of India are cited by article and clauses. In footnotes the symbol "Art" is generally used and if more Articles are to be mentioned it is cited with a symbol as "Arts." One refers to "Constitution" only if reference is to the Indian Constitution; otherwise the Constitution is specified to which he is referring, i.e., "The U.S. Constitution."[2] However, where it refers to

2. See Miles O. Price & *et. al.*, Effective Legal Research, 4th Ed., 1979, pp. 471-72.

certain amendments made in the Constitution one mentions therein, e.g., Art. 43A of the Constitution (42nd Amendment) Act, 1976. If a reference to be made to the Constituent Debates it is cited by referring to volume and page(s), e.g., *Constituent Assembly Debates* (C.A.D.), Vol. III, 488.

Legislation: In India, we have both Central and State legislations. While referring to Central legislation only the name of the Act followed by the year of passing of such legislation is mentioned. Wherever applicable the section is also referred to. In the footnotes generally for section and sections "S" and "Ss" are used. Wherever a mention has to be made to the amended Act, the reference to the amendment must be mentioned, e.g., Indian Divorce (Amendment) Act, 2001. In case of State Acts the name of the State Acts must be mentioned, e.g., Maharashtra Recognition of Trade Unions and Prevention of Unfair Labour Practices Act, 1971.

There is, however, no uniform system of citation of legislation. However, some authors use abbreviations for various legislations. Some of the instances are given below:

IDA	Industrial Disputes Act, 1947.
IPC	Indian Penal Code, 1860.
CrPC	Code of Criminal Procedure, 1973.
CPC.	Code of Civil Procedure, 1908.
IESOA	Industrial Employment (Standing Orders) Act, 1946.
TUA	Trade Unions Act, 1926.
CLRA Act	Central Labour (Regulation & Abolition) Act, 1970.
IT Act	Income Tax Act, 1961,
CST Act	Central Sales Tax Act, 1956.
PGA	Payment of Gratuity Act, 1972.
PWA	Payment of Wages Act, 1936.
WCA	Workmen's Compensation Act, 1923.

V. HOW TO FIND CASE LAW?—DECISIONAL MATERIAL—(PRECEDENT)

Case Law Material

(a) Official Reports

(i) *Federal Court Reports (11 volumes) (1939-50) (Manager of Publications, Delhi).* This is the official publication of the cases decided by the Federal Court which was abolished with the setting up of the Supreme Court in 1950.

(ii) *Supreme Court Reports, (since 1950) (Manager of Publications, Delhi). This is a monthly publication reporting cases, decided by the Supreme Court.*

(iii) *Computerized Judgments (MS Word)*—The Supreme Court Registry, with the permission of the Chief Justice, also supplies copies of the judgments to a few select libraries.

(iv) *Indian Law Reports*—These are the official publications for the State High Courts, published monthly and cited, e.g., as "I.L.R., Allahabad", "I.L.R. Bombay", after the name of the concerned High Court.

(b) Unofficial Reports

All India Reporter (A.I.R.)—Among the private law reports, the most commonly used and relied upon, even by the courts, is the A.I.R. Apart from the Supreme Court and High Court cases, it contains several useful features such as the table of cases cited and table of cases reversed or affirmed. It is published every month.

Other reports:—There are few law reports exclusively devoted to Supreme Court cases, such as Supreme Court Journal (S.C.J. published since 1950 by Madras Law Journal Ltd., Madras), Supreme Court Cases (SCC published since 1969 by Eastern Book Co., Lucknow), and SCALES (published by National Law Review, New Delhi).

High Court reports: Apart from the A.I.R., almost in each State at least one law report containing cases decided by the High Court of that State, are published as High Court Reports. Some of the reports of long standing are Allahabad Law Journal (ALJ), Bombay Law Reporter (Bom. L. Rep), Calcutta Weekly Notes (CWN), and Madras Law Journal (MLJ).

Specialized law reports: These law reports specialize in cases pertaining to particular branches of law. They report cases decided by the Supreme Court, High Courts and tribunals, regulatory commissions/ boards under petroleum and natural gas laws, telecommunication law, and electricity law, etc. Some of the popular ones are Labour Law Journal (LLJ), Labour and Industrial Cases (LIC), Industrial Court Reporter (ICR), Criminal Law Journal (Cr. LJ), Income Tax Reports (ITR), Company Cases (CC), and Sales Tax Cases (STC).

VI. CITATION OF CASES

Case Citation—The core of a case citation consists of:

→ The parties' names:

— Names are underlined or italicized

— A lower case "v" replaces "versus"
— Names are followed by a comma (,)

→ An address for the case consisting of:
— Reporter volume number
— Reporter name (abbreviated)
— The first page of the case in that volume
— If the reference is to a portion of the opinion, the page or pages of that part will follow the first page, set-off by a comma

→ In most situations only one address is required, in a single preferred reporter.

VII. CITATION OF REPORTS

Citations may sometimes be confusing and, therefore, it may become difficult to know the exact location of the case. For example, the same report may be cited differently or two reports may be cited in the same way. Thus, A.I.R. which is usually cited as A.I.R. 1966 S.C. 1466 may also be cited at times as A 1966 S.C. 1466 or AIR 1966 SC 1466, or I.L.R. may be cited as I.L.R. (1966) All. 141 or (1966) I.L.R. All. 141. Similarly, A.L.J. could be read as Allahabad Law Journal. The names of reports of cases are cited in abbreviated form only. A list of some of the Law Reporters publishing cases are given below:

ACJ	Accident Claims Journal (Monthly): 12, Malka Ganj, Delhi-110007.
AIR	All India Reporter (Monthly): All India Reporter Ltd., Post Box No. 209, Nagpur-440012.
An LT	Andhra Law Times (Weekly): Andhra Law Times, 16.11.418/3, Balaji Sadan, Dilsukhnagar, Hyderabad- 500035.
Arb LR	All India Arbitration Law Reporter (Monthly): 27-28, Gokhale Market, Opp. Tis Hazari Court, Delhi-110054.
CPR	Consumer Protection Reporter C/o Vinod Publications, P.B. No. 1002, Church Road, Kashmiri Gate, Delhi-110006.
Cri LJ	Criminal Law Journal (Monthly): All India. Reporter Ltd., P.B. No. 209, Nagpur-440012.
CLT	Cuttack Law Times (Fortnightly): The Law Times Press, Cuttack-753002.

Exc LT	Excise Law Times (Fortnightly): Central Law Office, 1512-B, Bhishm Pitamah Marg, (Oppt. P.T. College, Defence Colony), New Delhi-110003.
GLT	Gauhati Law Times (Monthly): North Eastern Law House, Gandhi Basti, Gauhati-781003.
Kar LJ	The Karnataka Law Journal (Weekly): No. 5, 2nd Floor, Sujatha Complex, 1st Cross, Gandhi Nagar, Bangalore-560009.
KLT	Kerala Law Times (Fortnightly): Kerala Times Press, Ernakulam, Kerala.
Lab IC	Labour and Industrial Cases (Monthly): All India Reporter, P.B. No. 209, Nagpur-440012.
MLJ	Madras Law Journal (Weekly): MLJ Office, P.B. No. 604, Mylapore, Madras-600004.
SCC	Supreme Court Cases (Fortnightly): Eastern Book Company, 34, Lal Bagh, Lucknow-266001.
SCJ	Supreme Court Journal (Monthly): Orient Law House, B-12, Amar Colony, Lajpat Nagar IV, New Delhi-110024.
SCR	Supreme Court Reports: The Controller of Publications, Delhi-110006.
Tax LR	Taxation Law Reports (Monthly): P.B. No. 209, Nagpur-440012.

VIII. NON-LEGAL MATERIALS

(i) *General Law cannot exist in a vacuum*: It is bound to have intimate connection with other subjects like history, economics, sociology, and politics. For example, if the economic policy of a village is being mapped out the question would arise as to how such taxes should be collected and what would be the machinery to collect them; here the law of taxation comes in and works side by side with the economic policy to make the scheme a success. Similarly, the connection of law with other fields is very apparent. In these circumstances it is natural that many treatises published, articles written and data collected in these subjects, will be of great help in legal research. These materials, referred to here as non-legal materials, are an important source of information to a law student and should not be by-passed. For example, if an article in an "Economic Times" deals with the impact of taxation it will be helpful not only to a student of economics but to a law student who has taken up taxation. Similarly, many treatises and articles treat various topics in a non-legal fashion, but they are, nevertheless, a source of valuable information to a person conducting legal research.

(ii) *Value of Non-Legal Materials*: The value of non-legal materials is undisputable in legal research, especially to those who are writing a legal paper or a thesis or dissertation. However, it is not possible to give any clue as to where the non-legal materials can be found. A law student reading or writing on a specific branch of law like taxation, labour, commercial law, and corporate law could look up publications in the allied fields of Economic and Commerce or a student working in Constitutional law may consult publications in History and Political Science.

(iii) *Authority of Non-Legal Materials*: The authority of non-legal materials, as may be expected is hardly any. Nevertheless, they do occupy an important place in legal research.

IX. LAW DICTIONARY

(i) *General*: The law dictionary defines and illustrates the meaning of words, terms, expressions, and phrases which are legal words and have a legal stand. These words are listed in alphabetical order and the authorities for their definitions are cited or quoted.

(ii) *Authority of Dictionaries*: A law dictionary is not a legal authority. It is not intended to state the law, but to define common meanings of words and terms of legal import. Even when it cites authority, it is not to be relied upon entirely, as the authority cited defines each word or term only in its special context, and the meaning may be modified as conditions change. However, the law dictionary is indispensable because it gives workable definitions which are necessary to the understanding of any legal work. Since most definitions cite their authority, a student may look up the cases himself and find out how and why that particular meaning has been used. A legal dictionary is a must for every law student and he should refer to it frequently so that he may get the correct meaning of the words and phrases he has been reading. For example, Black's Law Dictionary (Indian Reprint); Legal Glossary (Ministry of Law, Justice and Companies Affairs, Department of Legislation); Dictionary of Legal Quotations, etc.

X. LAW JOURNALS: LEGAL PERIODICALS OR REVIEWS

(i) *General:* Legal periodicals or reviews represent one of the important groups of books of secondary source authority. Legal periodicals or law reviews contain scholastic writings by law scholars. These scholastic writings may be analytical or expositor or exegetical or heuristic or empirical or behavioral and attitudinal or socio-legal in content and context. A legal periodical is very useful to students, legal professionals (practitioners), and research scholars in law. It is the most versatile among all the materials available in a law library. It represents diverse points of views, and examines various legal topics on varied legal issues of topical interest comparatively in contemporary framework or structure.

The legal periodicals or law reviews contain discussion, analysis and review of case law and statutes and highlight the emerging trends of legal issues of the day. Many of the articles are written by leading scholars, jurists and prominent members of the Bar in which they offer a thorough critical analysis of the topic, which is not to be found in any other medium. "They frequently present a closer approach to the legal bases and juristic philosophy which underlies the many modern trends towards the changes in our social and economic life, than it is possible for a textbook to express. In such manner they reflect any changed concept of social justice in a way the general law books cannot do."[3] In article of different purposes, the legal periodical discusses the law as it was, as it is, as it is tending and as it ought to be with a thoroughness and thoughtfulness found nowhere else.

(ii) *Tests of legal periodicals or reviews:* The value of a legal periodical literature might well be judged by applying the texts submitted by Professor Morgan, which are:

(a) The standing of the publication.
(b) The learning and ability of the writer.
(c) The authenticity of his data.
(d) The inherent reasonableness of his deductions in the light of legal history, existing social conditions and the known truths of all sciences affecting human conduct.

---

3. Beardslay and Orman, Legal Bibliography and the Use of Law Books.

(iii) *Classification of Periodicals or Reviews:* Legal Periodicals or Law Reviews may be conveniently divided into three groups:

(a) *University/College/Law Schools Reviews and Journals*: The former belong to the academic class. Their function is to express current legal critique or criticism and to interpret or reinterpret trends of modern juristic philosophy which underline the present day court decisions. Often they reflect the scholarly character of attainment of their respective law colleges/university law departments/law schools/national law universities. A list of some of the Journals is given below:

Ban. L.J.	Banaras Law Journal
DLR	Delhi Law Review
Ku. L.J.	Kurukshetra Law Journal
KULR	Kashmir University Law Review
LR	Law Review: Shri Jai Narain Post-Graduate College, Lucknow University
MOL	March of the Law: National Law School of India University, Bangalore
NCLJ	National Capital Law Journal, Law Centre-II, Faculty of Law, University of Delhi
NLSJ	National Law School Journal: National Law School of India University, Bangalore.

(b) *Private Law Reviews*: They contain articles of every branch of law, e.g., the Indian Law Review, or it may deal only with a special field of law as the Indian Year Book of International Affairs. Each legal periodical has its own purpose to fulfil and its own function to perform. A list of some of the Journals are given below:

CMLJ	Civil and Military Law Journal (Quarterly): D-124, Rajouri Garden, New Delhi-110027.
Corp L Ad	Corporate Law Adviser (Monthly): R.B.S. Publishing, 158, Basant Enclave, Palam Road, New Delhi-110057.
ENC	Encounter (Bi-Monthly): Upalabdhi Trust for Developmental Initiatives, C-9, East of Kailash, New Delhi-110065.
EPW	Economic and Political Weekly (Weekly): Skylark, 284, Shahid Bhagat Singh Road, Bombay-400038.
Kali Yug	Kali's Yug: Warlaw Trust, 9-10, Bahadurshah Zafar Marg, New Delhi-110001.

Law Col	The Lawyers Collective (Monthly): 818, Stock Exchange Towers, Delhi-110001.
Mah LJ	The Maharashtra Law Journal: Chandurkar Publishing House, Road No. 12, Dhantolia, Nagpur-440012.
Mains	Mainstream (Weekly): F-24, Bhagat Singh Market, New Delhi-110001.
M & C	Management on Change: 3, Lodhi Institutional Area, Lodhi Road, New Delhi-110003.
JHR	The Journal of Human Rights (Quarterly): No. 101, A-14, Bhandari House, Dr. Mukharjee Nagar, Delhi-110009.
RLR	Religion and Law Review: Institute of Objective Studies (IOS): 162, Jagapal Extesion, Jamia Nagar, New Delhi-110025.

(c) *Law Reviews published by Research Institutes*: Several Research Institutes in India bring out legal periodicals which contain articles, case notes, reviews, book reviews, and other information. A list of some of the Journals are given below:

Adm	The Administrator (Quarterly): Lal Bahadur Shastri National Academy of Administration, Mussorie (UK), 248179.
ASIL	Annual Survey of Indian Law (Annual): The Indian Law Institute, Bhagwan Das Road, New Delhi-110001.
CILQ	Central India Law Quarterly: The Central India Law Institute, 1601, Kasturba Primary School Building, Wright Town, Jabalpur-482002.
CS	Chartered Secretary (Monthly): 22, Institutional Area, Lodhi Road, New Delhi-110022.
FTR	Foreign Trade Review (Quarterly): Indian Institute of Foreign Trade, B-21, Institutional Area, South of IIT, New Delhi-110016.
Guj LH	Gujarat Law Herald: City and District Law Library, Bhadra, Ahmedabad-380001.
RDJ	Helpage India: Research and Development Helpage India, C-14, Qutab Institutional Area, New Delhi-110016.

IA	The Indian Advocate (Quarterly): The Bar Association of India, Room No. 20, Supreme Court Building, New Delhi-110001.
Ind Bar Rev	Indian Bar Review (Monthly): The Bar Council of India Trust, New Delhi.
IASSIQ	IASSI: (Quarterly): Indian Association of Social Science Institutions (IASSI) Institute of Applied Manpower Research, Indraprastha Estate, New Delhi-110001.
IICQ	India International Centre Quarterly (Quarterly): 40, Max Muller Marg, New Delhi-110003.
IJCC	Indian Journal of Criminology & Criminalistics (Quarterly): The Controller, Department of Publications, Civil Lines, Delhi-110054.
IJIL	Indian Journal of International Law (Quarterly): Indian Society of International Law, Bhagwan Das Road, New Delhi-110001.
IJIR	India Journal of Industrial Relations (Quarterly): Sri Ram Centre for Industrial Relations and Human Resources, 4E/16, Jhandewala Extension, New Delhi-110055.
IJPA	Indian Journal of Public Administration (Quarterly): Indian Institute of Public Administration, Indraprastha Estate, Ring Road (East), New Delhi-110002.
IJSW	Indian Journal of Social Work (Monthly): Department of Publications, Tata Institute of Social Science, Deonar, Bombay-400008.
IQ	India Quarterly (Quarterly): Indian Council of World Affairs, Sapru House, New Delhi-110001.
ISLJ	Indian Socio-Legal Journal (Annually): Indian Institute of Comparative Law, Bhardwaj Bhawan, Rani Bazar, Bikaner-334001.
JCPS	Journal of the Institute of Human Rights: Institute of Human Rights, Jarikatha, Nagpur-440014.

JILI	Journal of the Indian Law Institute (Quarterly): The Indian Law Institute, Bhagwan Das Road, New Delhi-110001.
JPI	Journal of Parliamentary Information (Quarterly): Lok Sabha Secretariat, Parliament House, New Delhi-110001.
PCIR	The Press Council of India Review (Quarterly): Faridkot House, New Delhi-110001.
SA	Social Action (Quarterly): Indian Social Institute, Lodhi Road, New Delhi-110003.

(iv) *Authority of Periodicals*: Legal periodicals are only persuasive. No court ever cites a law review as mandatory authority, but they are frequently referred to in opinions and footnotes in such a manner as to leave no doubt as to their persuasiveness.

XI. INTERNET, CD-ROMS, ETC.

Besides dictionaries and legal periodicals, Internet can be an extremely useful means of legal research these days. It can be extremely helpful to a legal practitioner as well. Internet is used to help one to find particular sites on any given topic. Advocates and legal professionals, i.e., other people involved in legal field are increasingly discovering how useful the Websites can be for legal research. Faculties, institutions, departments concerned with law have realized the importance of internet revolution and, therefore, in all these places, in-house training is also provided to staff to be able to cope with new revolution. On the internet, there are valuable search engines. One widely known example of a research engine is Yahoo, which has made a huge splash with its stock and is still regarded as one of the best resources available. Another very useful example is being Google engine. On the spot information provided by these sites and search engines can be extremely helpful in preparation for trial and/or mediation as well as during negotiations where one can go on-line and immediately get answers.

Now-a-days, computers/laptops are also being considered as valuable aids in the law teaching, for instance, use of power points with varied signs as well as insignias/symbols. As a matter of fact, there are so many ways in which computers can be of a great help and utility in the modern legal education.[4] And, therefore, many law schools, law colleges, law institutes and law faculties have launched their own websites and provide their useful links and search engines. For instance, the use of Information Technology has been inducted in the Dr. Ambedkar Law University, Chennai. Computer is used for creation of data base for books and journals. Supreme Court Case Finder (CD-ROM) with updated versions is available for use by lawyers, law faculty members and research scholars. A Web-page has been designed and created for the University and published from the Institute of Mathematical Sciences Server, Taramani, Chennai URL Address is "http;//www.imsc.ernet in/`~tandalau". It finds a place in the global law website.[5]

Computers have an equally significant role to play in legal research For instance, every researcher working for a post-graduate essay, or an LL.M. dissertation, or for a Ph.D. thesis has to prepare a working bibliography. Many authors put their latest articles/papers on the website. Important information for research could be collected from the websites of international institutions and inter-governmental bodies. Most of the premier institutes engaged in legal research, for instance, the Indian Law Institute, New Delhi, have all the computer-related facilities for its researchers.

As a matter of fact, a computer offers direct benefits to a legal practitioner. The data base that a lawyer must research in order to determine the answers to his client's problem is expanding rapidly. Not only are the legislatures enacting new laws, but new fields of law are coming into prominence. In India, a Lucknow-based law publishing company—Messrs Eastern Book Company Ltd.—has now successfully ventured in this field. They have introduced, what they call an "Extremely user friendly and a revolutionary research tool for the legal community—a computerized law information database". The said company has come out with a unique Case Finder—SCC Online. This software package is in the form of a Compact Disc-Read Only Memory (CD-ROM) that contains the case law on all topics right from the year 1950 with a regular update service. It can be installed on one's personal desktop or portable computer. According to the publishers, the installation procedure for the Case Finder Software Programme is extremely useful and simple. This package is not only useful for lawyers but for scholars, jurists, teachers, researchers, students, social

4. For further details see, Thomas Burris, Teaching Law with Computers: A Collection of Essays, New York, West Views Press, 1979.
5. http://www.tn.gov.in/plicy/judis-e.htm

scientists as well. Most of the law libraries in the country have acquired this package or are in the process of acquiring it[6]. Similarly, All India Reporter, Nagpur, Manupatra and Westlaw have developed their software and which are being used by legal professionals and law libraries extensively.

XII. WEBSITE

Besides, there are many useful websites designed by the Government as well as private organizations, institutes, lawyers' firms and textbook publishers that are good source for a legal research. So, by going first to www.nic.in, one will find that one is probably just a mouse click or two away from the information, thanks to the far-reaching resources of the World Wide Web. This site is the product of National Information Centre, Department of Information Technology under the Ministry of Communication and Information Technology. On "search" option provided by this site, one may have access to number of useful informations in the field of law, in html format as well as in pdf.format. Then after clicking: *Parliament and Apex Institutions* one may find listed, along with other apex organizations of the country, *Supreme Court of India*, i.e., *http://supremecourt of india.nic.in*

On this site various links could be found.

The link of *constitution* gives information as to the constitution of the court and its various departments, officers, types of advocates entitled to practice before it, etc.

On opening the link of *jurisdiction* one would be able to find very useful and detailed information about jurisdiction of the court. It does not limit there but proceeds to give full write-up on the aspects of *Public Interest Litigation, Legal Aid, Amicus Curiae, Lok Adalats, High Courts*, etc. The write up is simple and could be understood even by layman. It is very informative, precise and lucid. Similarly, there are other useful links provided by this site which are very useful to legal luminaries as well as scholars, practitioners, clients, editors, etc. These are: "Golden Jubilee", "Rules", "Former CJIs", "CJI and Judges", "Calendar", "Indian Courts", "JUDIS", "Daily Orders", "Case Status", "Cause List", "Courts Websites", "Indian Code".

"Golden Jubilee" link contains articles and speeches made by former Judges and Chief Justices and other legal jurists of the country

6. The Indian Law Institute, New Delhi and Judges Library of the Supreme Court of India already possess these.

on the occasion of golden jubilee celebrated by the Court on completion of its 50 years on 26th November, 1999.

Link of "Rules contains The Supreme Court Rules, 1966 along with (i) Regulations regarding Advocate-on-Record examination, (ii) Rules to regulate proceedings for contempt of the Supreme Court, 1975, and (iii) the Supreme Court (Enlargement of Criminal Appellate Jurisdiction) Act, 1970.

Every provision is listed and could be copied in any word file.

Apart from the above, the following links provide useful resource material and information regarding regulations, rules, case law, and many other topics related to the field of law.

Laws passed by the Parliament are easily accessible at "Indian Code" which is a subscription site. www.judis.nic.in is a subscription site. www.supremecourtonline.com and www.mahalibrary.com are free sites. The AIR (All India Reporter) Manual of Central Laws is an exhaustive collection of laws enacted by the Parliament together with decisions of the Supreme Court and the High Courts on these laws. The AIR Manual can be a good starting point for research of the laws enacted by the Union. This site, however, is not easily accessible. Laws passed by the States are more difficult to access. The States are slowly attempting to launch websites and may take a couple of years to complete. For the present, State laws are accessible through book sellers in India.

Judgments of the Supreme Court and the High Courts are available at www.judis.nic.in and www.mahalibrary.com which are subscription sites. www.supremecourtonline.com is a free site[7].

XIII. OTHER LEGAL SITES

Other Indian legal sites are http://lawinindia.com and vakilno1.com (free sites), lexsite.com and indianlaw.com (subscription sites).[8]

Then there are private law firms that have come together and opened up firms which run pay sites or subscription sites as they are commonly referred to with the objectives:

1. To collect, analyze, process, store, generate, retrieve and transmit full and updated information related to Law and other connected fields;
2. To disseminate and/or make available the aforesaid

---

7. *Op. cit.*
8. http://www.indiaconnect.comdialn.htm

information to all concerned, in India and overseas, by:

— Software development, exchange and sale.

— Establishment and maintenance of information services.

— Issuance of suitable publications.

All these service providers charge fee for queries. Examples of such service providers are:

DIAL-N—from ignorance to knowledge.

Daily Indian Abridged Legal News—Date and subject-wise legal news as available from the judgments of the Supreme Court, Bar and leading Newspapers.[9]

SPOTLAW—from the ocean of chaos—a pearl of wisdom.

This is the largest reservoir of databases in India of Case Law. Not merely a text search software but interlinked data relating to Cause Title, Corresponding Citations, Notes/Follow-up, Statute Index, Subject Index, Books and Periodicals, Maxis, Words and Phrases and Random Search with respect to the judgments of the Supreme Court and High Courts of India and of the Courts of Australia, Canada, United Kingdom, U.S.A. and others considered therein.

A unique software relating to Acts, Rules, Circulars, Orders, Regulations, Directions, Memorandums and their amendments with text.

DHRUVA—from blank pages to ready matter.

Drafts, Help, Research Utilities and Vital Assistance—An extremely useful database of articles published in various journals, textbooks and other information like court fees, practice and procedure followed in different courts, formats of petitions, deeds and other documents. Also contains ASLI (Genuine)—Accessible Sites of Law on Internet and MASALA—More Allied sites Available for Law Access.

PLEA—from disorder to efficient order.

Professional Lawyer's Electronic Assistant—Perhaps the only software to cater to the specific needs of advocates practicing in various courts in India to help them organize their files, daily appearances and billing system.

VAKALAT—from rookie to tough cookie.

Various Anecdotes and Knowledge around Law for Advocates and Trainees designed to assist the novice advocate in becoming a professional.

COLA—from minutes to days.

---

9. *Ibid.*

Calendar of Lawmen Activities provide information on seminars, group discussions, etc. being organized by legal organizations in India.

XIV. TEXT BOOKS OR TREATISES

Text books have long been accorded an important place in the literature of law. When treatises are mentioned in opinions and briefs it is because the judge or attorney citing them adopts their reasoning or statements, with accompanying citations to authority, as their own. But it is the cases which are the authority, not the authors' analysis. Books are important but least important.

XV. ENCYCLOPEDIAS

General: While a text book deals with one subject or one branch of a subject of law, an encyclopedia treats all subjects. It is like a comprehensive treatise on the entire field of law.

Authority: Legal encyclopedias are not primary authority or primary source of law, but only guides to it and they are at the most persuasive.

XVI. DIGESTS

A digest is a subject index to the rules of law raised or discussed in reported cases. The common form of a legal digest presents a collection of paragraphs containing concise statements of legal principles arranged under a heading of classified headings. These principles may be gathered from careful study of the decisions to form a digest of case law.

Authority of Digests: The digest is not an authority but only a guide to it. Its purpose is to serve as a topical index of the decisions or as a "handle to be used in picking up the law".

XVII. PRESS REPORTS

The important cases decided by the Supreme Court or High Courts are published and also commented upon in Standard English and some Hindi Daily Newspapers as soon as the judgment is delivered by the court concerned. These cases are not exhaustively reported. However, editorial comments or letters to the editor or articles or write ups help to generate public opinion, and as such they are persuasive in nature.

XVIII. ORGANIZATION OF DOCTRINAL RESEARCH

1. Title of the legal research topic.
2. Explanation of the legal research topic.
3. Selection and formulation of the legal research problem and its explanation.
4. Collection of materials and contemporary research literature and review of the legal literature showing the scope and imperatives of legal research on the legal research problem conceived with innovative points/issues/research inquisitives/ questions to show the new approach different from the earlier research otherwise it would be replica.
5. Card maintenance: Primary sources > Statutory and cases [Article 141]; secondary sources.
6. Research questions formulations.
7. Objectives of the research.
8. Plan of research work, i.e., division of the materials collected into chapters, viz., chapterization.
9. Interpretation and analysis of materials, i.e., definitions, concepts and doctrines.
10. Thesis/Dissertation writing.
11. Citation of foot notes: at the bottom of the text or at the end of the chapter: Case law, articles, books, reports, Section(s) Repetition: *Ibid.*, *Id.*, *Supra*, *Infra*, *op. cit.*, *et. al.*, *cf.*, *i.e.*, *e.g.*
12. Conclusion and suggestions.

XIX. MODE OF CITATION: A GUIDELINE

A. Books

1. For an Authored Book

(a) By a single author

Name of the author, *Title of the book* p.no. (if referring to specific page or pages) (Publisher, Place of publication, edition/year of publication).

E.g. S.C Srivastava, Industrial Relations & Labour Law, 7th edn., 2007 (Vikas Pulishing House).

(b) *By two authors*

Name of the authors, Title of the book p.no. (if referring to specific page or pages) (Publisher, Place of publication, edition/year of publication).

E.g. M.P. Jain and S.N. Jain, Principles of Administrative Law, 38 (Wadhawa, Nagpur, 2001).

(c) *By multiple authors (more than two)*

Name of the first two authors, *et. al.*, Title of the book p.no. (if referring to specific page or pages) (Publisher, Place of publication, edition/year of publication).

E.g. Jerry L. Mashaw, Richard A. Merrill, The American Public Law System, West Group, St. Paul, Mn [Cases and Materials, 50 (1992)].

2. For Edited Books

(a) By a single editor

Name of the editor (ed.), Title of the book p.no. (if referring to specific page or pages) (Publisher, Place of publication, edition / year).

E.g. Nilendra Kumar (ed.), Nana Palkhivala: A Tribute (Universal Publisher, Delhi, 2004).

(b) By two editors

Name of the editors (eds.), Title of the book p.no. (if referring to specific page or pages) (Publisher, Place of publication, edition / year).

E.g. S.K. Verma and S.C Srivastava (eds.), *Rights of Person with Disabilities*, 38-42 (ILI, Delhi, 2002).

(c) By more than two editors

Name of the editors, the first two only, *et. al.* (eds.), Title of the book p.no. (if referring to specific page or pages) (Publisher, Place of publication, edition / year).

E.g. Chatrapati Singh, P.K. Coudhary (eds.), *Towards Energy Conservation Law, 78* (ILI, Delhi, 1989).

(d) By, or an auspices of, an organization / institution

Indian Law Institute, *Index to Indian Legal Periodicals* (ILI, Delhi, 2002).

B. Mode of Citation for Articles/Essays

(a) Citation of a paper published in a journal/periodical

Name of author of the article, title of the essay within inverted commas, volume number of journal, *Name of the journal in abbreviation* & page number (year).

E.g. K. Madhusudhana Rao, "Authority to Recommend President's Rule under Article 356 of the Constitution", 46 JILI 125 (2004).

(b) Citation of a paper published in a case reporter

P.K. Thakur, "Permissibility of Probation in Offences Punishable with Minimum Imprisonment," 2 SCJ, 26-38 (2002).

(c) Citation of an essay published in a book edited

Name of author of the essay, title of the essay within inverted commas, in Name of the editor(s), *title of the edited book* page number (publisher, edition/year).

E.g. R.K. Nayak, "Evolving Global Drugs Law for the 21st Century" in D.C. Jayasuriya, R.K. Nayak *et. al.* (eds.), *Global Drugs Law*, 70 (1997).

(d) Citation of an essay published as a part of a Survey of Law (e.g. Annual Survey of Indian Law,—[an annual publication of the Indian Law Institute, New Delhi].

Name of author of the essay, title of the essay within inverted commas, volume number, *name of the survey*, page number (year).

E.g.: P.S. Jaswal, "Constitutional Law-I," XXXVIII ASIL 115-150 (2002).

(e) Citation of a write-up published in a news paper/periodical

Name of the writer, Title of the write-up within inverted commas, *Name of the newspaper*, date.

Robert I. Freidman, "India's Shame: Sexual Slavery and Political Corruption are Leading to an AIDS Catastrophe", *The Nation*, April 8, 1996.

(f) Citation of an editorial from a newspaper

Editorial, Title of the Editorial within inverted commas, Name of the newspaper, date.

Editorial, "Short-circuited," *The Times of India*, August 2, 2004.

(g) Citing a reference from Encyclopedia

Edwin R.A. Seligman (ed.), XV Encyclopedia of the Social Sciences (1957), The Macmillan Co., NY.

C. Websites

If the websites gives information as to when it was last modified, must be cited, if not one must cite the date of visiting the website.

(a) Information Technology Act, 2000, India, *available* at: http://www.mit.gov.in/it-bill. Asp (Last Modified July 29, 2003).

(b) Information Technology Act, 2000, India, *available* at: http:// www.mit.gov.in / it-bill. Asp (Visited July 29, 2003).

D. Unpublished Works

(a) Unpublished Research Work (E.g., Dissertation /Thesis)

Name of the Researcher, *Title of the dissertation / thesis* (Year) (Unpublished Ph.D. thesis, Name of the University/organization).

Raman Mittal, xyz (2004) (Unpublished Ph.D. dissertation, Punjab University).

(b) Interviews

Interview with M. Veerappa Moily, Law Minister, *The Hindu*, July 25, 2004.

(c) Forthcoming publication of a book

G. Gann Xu, *Information for Corporate IP Management* (In Press, 2004).

(d) Forthcoming publication of an article

Shabistam Aquil, "Classification of Human Rights", in S.K. Verma, Shabistan Aquill, *et. al.* (eds.), *Human Rights: Cases and Material* (In Press, 2004).

E. Mode of Citation of Case Law

(a) All India Reporter (AIR)

If the case name and citation together are to be written in the text of the article itself [Note: This format is not allowed in JILI):

Kesavanada Bharathi v. State of Kerala, AIR 1973 SC 1461.

If the name and citation are to be written in the footnote itself:

Kesavanada Bharathi v. State of Kerala, AIR 1973 SC 1461.

Where the case title is written in the body of the text, only the name of the case shall be in the text, e.g. *Kesavananda Bharathi v. State of Kerala* and the citation is written in the footnote as AIR 1973 SC 1461.

(b) Supreme Court Cases (SCC)

(i) If the case name and citation together are to be written in the text of the article itself [Note: This format is not allowed in JILI]

Jassa Singh v. State of Haryana [(2002) 2 SCC 481]

(ii) If the name and citation are to be written in the footnote itself:

(iii) *Jassa Singh v. State of Haryana* (2002) 2 SCC 481.

(iv) If the case title is to be written in the body of the research paper, only the name of the case shall be written, e.g., *Jassa Singh v. State of Haryana* then the citation would be written in the footnote as (2002) 2 SCC 481.

(c) Criminal Law Journal (Cr. L.J)

Lakhwinder Singh & Ors. v. State of Punjab, 2003 Cri. L.J. 3058 (SC).

Ujjagar Singh v. State of Haryana, 2003 Cri.L.J. 1691 (P&H).

(d) All England Reports (All ER)

Wilcox v. Jeffery [1951] 1 All ER 464.

(e) If parties to a case are numerous, for e.g.

State of Punjab and others v. Union of India and others

This case is to be cited as:

State of Punjab and others v. Union of India (1977) 3 SCC 592.

F. Acts

The Information Technology Act, 2005 (Act 21 of 2005).

G. Reports

(i) Law Commission of India, 144th Report on Conflicting Judicial Decisions Pertaining to the Code of Civil Procedure, 1908 (April 1992).

(ii) Government of India, Report: Committee on Reforms of Criminal Justice System (Ministry of Home Affairs, 2003).

Chapter XII

EMPIRICAL METHOD: TECHNIQUES, IDEAS AND TOOLS OF LEGAL RESEARCH

I. WHAT IS RESEARCH?

- Quest for knowledge
  - Inquisitive mindset
    - Cause and effect
      - Researcher
        - » The researcher may love law inasmuch as he may love art, music, literature, which may unfold LLL:
        - » L Life (of law)
        - » L Literature (of law)
        - » L Law (as such: *Normative science*)
- A science which lays down norms and standards for human behaviour in a specified situation or situations enforceable through the sanction of the State. Law is a social science on account of the simple fact that it regulates human conduct and relationship is its normative character.
- E.g. Drift; Deviant; Criminality.

II. RESEARCH IN LAW

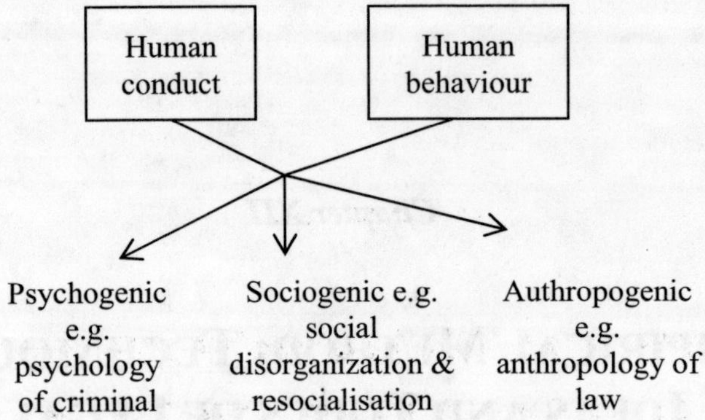

III. WHAT MAKES RESEARCH WORK SATISFYING AND INTERESTING?

- The only answer in one word is 'fascination'.
- Research is fundamental to learning; learning is intrinsic to positive growth; and positive growth is mankind's innate drive *to find all truths.*
- It discerns that if we stop researching, we die intellectually; we become intellectually deaf and dumb.
- Quality research demands innovative and creative thinking than merely textbook knowledge.
- In research, we strive to create a synergistic mix of objective and subjective elements to attain maximum decision power.
- Research means *development of idea.*
- "As a rule there are in everyone all sorts of good ideas, ready like tinder. But much of this tinder catches fire, or catches it successfully, only when it meets some flame or spark from outside". (Dr. Albert Schweitzer)
- " Don't despair of a student if he has one or some clear idea". —(Nathaniel Emmons)
- There are four ways to develop an idea about research:
    1. *Replication*: to replicate, i.e., to repeat, the study to verify, reinforce or attempt to contradict the earlier findings. Replication involves conducting an identical study to that done previously, using a different, but similar, method/mode/sample.
    2. *Quasi-replication*: This method does allow for greater flexibility and creativity for the researcher. The researcher

may wish to study a topic previously researched but find the want or need to alter parts of the design. The alterations may be substantial, but are commonly minor. This approach is very popular and, as in the case of replication studies, will also aid substantially toward finding truths.

3. *Original idea*: Through a review of literature or from a simple "brainstorm", the researcher may develop a truly original research idea. Knowledge of previous research by earlier scholars through their scholastic writings would help immensely the researcher to develop new insights of original research ideas, which indeed is imperative to develop good research work.
4. *Recommendations from superior/advisor*: These help to select research topic; research problem; new inquisitives; new quest. They work as mentors.

Which method of approach from the above the researcher should apply? The researcher may adopt none or adopt any one. It depends upon the researcher to evaluate entirely according to his interests and situations. It is a research axiom: "After hundreds of hours of investment, the researcher deserves to have a satisfying final product. Take great care in selecting a final research topic that means something to the researcher".

IV. FUNDAMENTALS OF LITERATURE REVIEWS AND SEARCHES FOR GOOD LITERATURE

- There is a good axiom:
  — "The information in books is … constantly changed, amended by events, adapted to the world. I will only read a few thousand books in my lifetime, about a tenth of one percent of the contents of the richest libraries … The trick is to know which books to read". (Dr. Carl Sagan)
    » *The purpose of literature review:*
      1. After finalizing and formulating the research topic, the next chain link involves an in-depth review of literature by references. The literature review will greatly assist in topic focusing.
      2. A literature review is meant primarily to set the foundation for the research questions. The

literature review is profiteering to the researcher to better understand the research problem conceived in terms of historical background, theoretical framework, and current research developments or trends or currents.

- Research is a quest for truth and to find truth there is a chain of truth:
  1. Develop idea of research and channels for developing idea of research are:
     (a) Research, (b) Quality Research, (c) Ordinary Research, (d) Applied Research, (e) Or Mix of (a), (b), (c), and (d).
  2. Literature Review Techniques: (a) computer, (b) by hand, or (c) Mix of (a) and (b).
  3. Develop Specific Research Questions: (a) Quantitative, (b) Qualitative, or (c) Mix of (a) and (b).
  4. Hypotheses: (a) Null, (b) Research.
  5. Research Design: (a) Descriptive, (b) Experimental, or (c) Mix of (a) and (b), (d) Quantitative, (e) Qualitative, or (f) Mix of (d) and (e).
  6. Sample: (a) Random, (b) Stratified, (c) Cluster: Return to literature review and return to develop idea for further creative and innovative ideas generation.
  7. Data Collection:
     (i) Questionnaire: Mail
     (ii) Interview Schedule: Personal—One on one/telephone/computer voice/video-conferencing.
  8. Interview diary.
  9. Observations.
  10. Tabulation: Coding, Editing.
  11. Statistical Analysis: Quantitative to qualitative:
      — Interpretation of data: descriptive; difference: differential scale: Interpretation of statistical data with the help of theory and observation and presenting some innovative and creative finding for the development of future theory.
  12. Formal writing: research report: thesis/dissertation.

Quality Research Depends on Quality Research Design for Quality Results

- "Scientific research can reduce superstition by encouraging people to think and view thing in terms of cause and effect". —(Dr. Albert Einstein)

- "No one type of research study is inherently superior to any other type. Strong methodology within the chosen study type is the only path to a quality study".
- "It is a shameful thing to be weary of inquiry when what we search for is excellent".—(Cicero)

V. LEGAL RESEARCH WHY AND WHAT?

- Quest for legal knowledge
  - — Inquisitive mindset:
    - » Aptitude;
    - » Attitude;
    - » Dedication;
    - » Devotion;
    - » Comprehension;
    - » Assimilation; and
    - » Dissemination
- The sum total of the above expression is Thoughtronicking, which is essentially imperative to understand *cause [causal] and effect relationship.*
- *Depends on the understanding and comprehension of:* "Who says what to whom, when, where, how, and why for what purpose and under what circumstances."
- Who: Researcher
- Whom: Recipient; reader; public; policy-maker; judge; lawman
- When, Where, How and Why: Research problem; research questions; hypothesis
- For What Purpose: Aims and objectives of legal research
- Under What Circumstances: Cause and effect [causal factors]
- Legal Research, therefore, is a process of Legal Method. In Legal Method the emphasis is on the *techniques of legal thinking.* If a *law student [law researcher]* can become familiar with that, his acquisition of a store of legal knowledge will be greatly facilitated.
- However, legal research like legal method, is the *Cinderella* of legal science. Why?

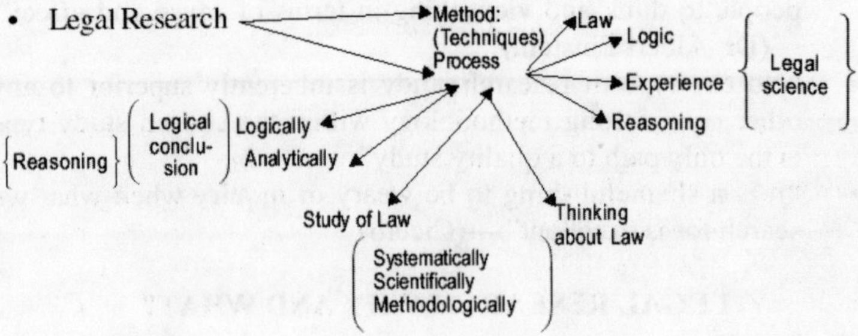

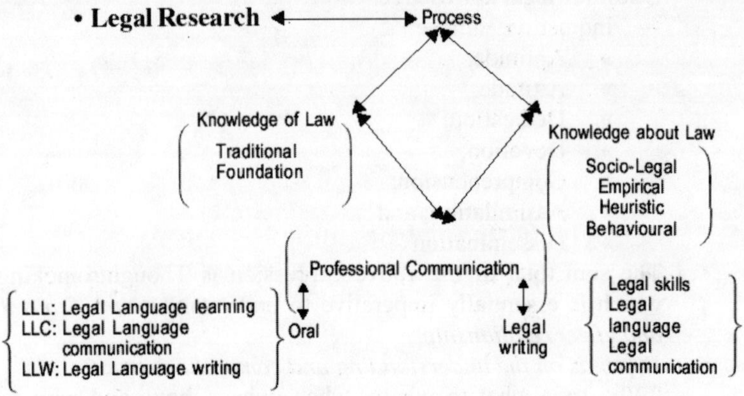

- Legal research, thus, is an approach to finding law through scientific methods relevant to the legal research problem. It is to find out the truth *with* the and *within* the hidden treasures of knowledge.
- For example: Article 142 of the Constitution of India has been described as "Flashing the flaming sword of its inspiration"--- Justice Shri Vivian Bose in *Ramjawaya v. State of Punjab, 1954.*
- Justice Shri V.R. Krishna Iyer always regarded *language as a vehicle for ideas.*
  » *Language and legal language important/potential/ significant instruments for effective legal research.*

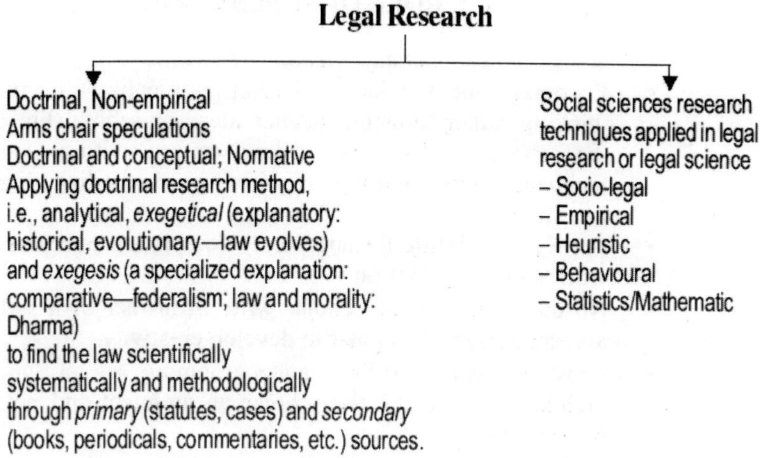

VI.

- **Finding through Scientific Methods**

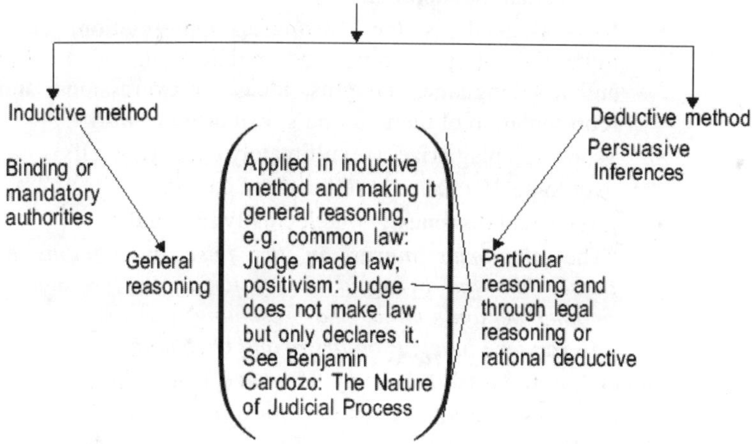

- Assignment:
- What is inductive and deductive method in doctrinal legal research?
- Inductive theories reason from specific observations to general patterns. Deductive theories start from general statements and predict specific observations.

VII. ROLE OF SUPERVISOR

- Guide, philosopher and friend.
- Encourage the scholar to develop originality: original thinking rather thrusting his/her ideas or scholarship on the scholar: Reading; making notes; writing—legal language—good writing requires good reading legal literature.
- From research title formulation to completion of research work/thesis/dissertation.
- No dictation—let the scholar write in his/her own style, and encourage the scholar to develop creativity.
- Brushing with grilling and grooming as a good architecture to make the scholar an architect and not a mere mason.

Plagiarism and Copy Right:

- Derived from the Latin word *plagiarius* means "kidnapper", viz., a kind of intellectual theft and intellectual kidnapping.
- It is defined as the "wrongful appropriation, close imitation, or purloining and publication, of another author's language, thoughts, ideas, or expressions, and representation of them as one's own original work".
- When you plagiarize, you ultimately cheat yourself.
- Not to be *plagiarius* is self code of conduct.
- Intellectual dishonesty; Intellectually immoral.

  "The *plagiarius moves on the false assumptions of authorship, the wrongful act of taking the product of another person's mind, and presenting it as one's own". [Alexander Lindey, Plagiarism and Originality]*

- **According to Gordon Harvey, Harvard University:**

  "In academic writing (unlike everyday speech), all language, information, and ideas not the writer's own are scrupulously attributed to their original sources. Knowledge never stands alone. It builds upon and plays against the previous knowledge of previous knower and reports, whom scholars call "sources". These are not, in a scholarly paper, the source of your particular argument (you are), but rather persons or documents that help you arrive at your argument. They are sources of information that you interpret; of ideas you support, criticize, or develop; of vivid language that you quote and analyze."

- When a researcher starts research he ought to take the under-mentioned essentially imperative steps:
    1. Go back and read what everyone else has said about your research topic; research problem; research questions.
    2. You as a conscientious researcher draw some conclusions, make some new points that advances the field of knowledge otherwise it shall be replica.
    3. Then as a conscientious researcher you should mention who said what and when and why, as a way of history.
    4. Then move forward, attributing to those who went before you or make a statement and use data from writers and researchers to back it up. Namely, refer findings, terms and phrases of others in quotation forms and citing the authorities in the foot notes.
    5. The purpose of collecting information is to create your own thoughts and ideas around the information you have read and taken notes. If you copy someone else's words, you are not forming your own thoughts and creative style."
- Is plagiarism against copyright law?
- Copyright violation is against the law.
- Plagiarism is moral outrage. (Shook)
- Plagiarism is academic dishonesty and a breach of ethics, subject to sanctions like expulsion and other severe career damages. Not so in the arts, i.e., praising of plagiarism in art. [give examples of LL.M. and Ph.D. works: where even genetic engineering shall fail to produce the replica].
- A plagiarist can commit copyright infringement.
- Plagiarism is not a crime but is disapproved on the grounds of moral offence. It may be a case for civil law if it substantially constitutes copyright infringement.
- But what happens when, for example, you or I as a scholar lift whole information that is either in the public domain or which has had the copyright lapse? You or I are plagiarizing but not infringing on copyright. In such cases, the objection is moral or ethical rather than legal.
- The sole safeguard: If you as a scholar are saying what someone else said, quote them. This shall help to develop your intuition, ability to know things, and creativity for academic writing.
- Thus, plagiarism is using someone else's creative work

without giving proper credit, which may include a song, a video, a movie clip, a piece of visual art, a photograph, and other creative works without authorization or compensation.

- The courts enforce copyright infringement.
- Plagiarism does not have to include copyright infringement if not copyrighted. E.g. Shakespeare's plays, Kalidas's scholastic writings, etc.
- These days scholars use internet and use cut, copy paste without quoting.
- Safeguards.
- Put those words in quotation marks or indent them to indicate clearly that they are not your own words.
- Add a footnote to give credit to the original author.
- Keep the length of your quotation down to a few sentences so you won't be guilty of copyright infringement.

VIII. SOCIAL SCIENCES RESEARCH TECHNIQUES APPLIED IN LEGAL RESEARCH

- What is a social science research? What is its utility and relevance in legal research?
  - Social science research techniques applied in legal research mean study of law in society or law in relation to society or law and society relationship.
  - How do the recipients of law feel about the law? How does the law benefit the recipients? What is the behaviour pattern of the recipients about the law?
  - Society: Human beings perception; their behavioural attitude; their motivational pattern; their background characteristics and treatment in the society; their socio-economic-politico backgrounds.

Expressions used for Social Sciences Research

- Socio-legal
- Empirical, Mathematical or statistical
- Heuristic
- Interdisciplinary
- Behavioural science or attitudinal study or beliefs or motivations:
  - Of human beings in the society.
  - E.g. behaviour of legislators in enacting the statute.
  - E.g. behaviour of administrators in framing/implementing

rules, regulations, bye-laws/actions.

- Behaviour of Judges: majority/minority/dissenting opinion; voting pattern; background characteristics (e.g. George H. Gadbois); Trial courts trial and Trial courts management; Judicial good governance.
- Behaviour of lawyers, para-professionals: Munshis, touts, clients, Social Action Groups (SAG).

- Social science research in law means applying social sciences research techniques in legal science.
- A law researcher who is not a master in legal science, i.e., his own home or area, can't understand and apply the social science research techniques adequately, effectively and efficiently.
- Mastery over legal research techniques is prerequisite and imperative for the successful application of social science research techniques in legal science and legal research.
- What, in practice, we specially need to know at any particular moment in which people or groups influence what kind of legal action, in what manner and through what means.
- Similarly, we need to know how different types of legal actions influence which people or groups, in what manner and through what means.
- The above two parameters, thus, expound the genesis of:
- *"Who says what to whom, when, where, how and why under what circumstances for what effects."*
- Social sciences research technique is the systematic, methodological and scientific way of study of prior as well as subsequent stimuli—society and human beings.
- In order to appreciate this approach the law researcher has to know and understand/comprehend legal research techniques thoroughly. This may be taken as a warning as well as caution for/by the law researcher.

  » *"A fundamental need therefore in relation to modern researches is to caution our researchers that while much will be expected of them within their specialty, it will be 'insufficient' for them to become one-eyed workers in their narrow field. The danger of falling into this trap is generally today than ever before."*

IX. INTERACTION: LEGAL ORDER AND SOCIAL ORDER

- In the field of law, since nineteenth century, analytical positivism has obsessed the thinkers of the Bar, the Bench and the academia to such an extent that no other approach to the understanding of the nature and purpose of law could really have thrived.
- The main concept of or concern of or thrust of analytical jurisprudence has been to facilitate our vision of the logical coherence of the several propositions and parts of a legal order, and to formulate definitions of the terms used and the presuppositions, which will maximize such coherence.
- This kind of coherence tends to identify "law" and "a legal order" only with those elements which are stable in the form of legal propositions.
- The analytical positivist concentrates merely on the "form of law" as emanating from its source, i.e., as turned out by the legislature or any State authority, whose power he does not question.
- He works on this material by means of a system of rules of legal logic, conceived as complete and self-contained.
- The legal system is made water-tight compartment against all ideological intrusions and all problems are coached in terms of legal logic.
- It was only in the first half of the twentieth century that the relations of the legal order with the wider social order became established beyond question as a central juristic and jurisprudential concern.
- Thus, emerged the "Sociology of Law"; "Sociological Jurisprudence"; "Law as Social Engineering"; "Law and Society"; "Empiricism"; "Realist School of thought"; "What the courts say, there is nothing pretentious about it, is the law in the real sense." (Holmes); "Judicial Activism as the brandishing sword of inspiration."

X. SOCIAL SCIENCE RESEARCH TECHNIQUES APPLIED IN LEGAL SCIENCE: NON-DOCTRINAL OR EMPIRICAL

Concept

- It is a pragmatic approach or realistic approach or heuristic approach or empirical approach or socio-legal approach to understanding the Indian legal system or Indian law in practicality or functional in society or application in society or experiential.

- It has come to Indian legal science recently; it is a new born baby; it has now progressively moved from cradle to crawl to walk; it has to be nourished properly.
- To understand law in action rather than law in books.
- It helps to remove the inadequacies of legal research through a sociological and legal-anthropological approach.
- It is not to replace legal research, but it is to supplement/supplant and compliment legal research. Both have to be mutually cooperative, responsive and have to be strengthened.
- It is a scientific, systematic and methodological method of research.
- It pertains to society and sociology:
  (i) Inductive method: General to particular.
  (ii) Deductive method: Particular to general—becomes empirical generalization.
- Social science research enables us to find out the deficiencies/lacunae in law/enactment/policy frame-work and the problems of its implementation what the arms chair speculations fail to achieve.
- Law is an instrument of social change. It must keep pace with a progressive modern society—free economic market; economic liberalization and globalization.
- Law is never static; it is dynamic; it changes according to the socio-economic-politico moves of the society.
- Change is the law of nature. So, law changes progressively inasmuch as the progressive societies move from status to contract or from legalese/legal archaism to meaningful audibility.
- The problems of the economic market of today—economic liberalization and globalization—cannot be solved by the methods or tools known to legal science research.
- These will have to be altered from time to time to suit the changing social-economic-political circumstances.
- Strong public opinion and awareness against age-old prejudices alone can help to bring lasting—long-term and short-term—results in the legislation, e.g., Delay in disposal of cases problem, trial court management lest it is purloined by outside

influences, contract labour, economic market and contractual appointees are contract labour or bonded labour problems as there seems visible shift from welfare State to *laissez faire* State.

- Empirical research is a behavioural perspective towards law, and refers to a specific conceptual and methodological orientation.
- The conceptual orientation views law not as a set of rules and decisions to be read by law students, applied by lawyers and evaluated by law professors. Instead, law is viewed mainly as the responses of law-makers to prior stimuli, and as stimuli to subsequent responses of law appliers/enforcers and law recipients.
- This orientation thus involves viewing legal policies and decisions in their total context as both effects and causes.
- With regard to methodology, a behavioural orientation towards law tends to emphasize the quantitative testing of empirical generalizations about the relations between various legal phenomena and other phenomena.
- The quantitative testing generally involves determining (i) some hypotheses to test; (ii) a sample of persons, place or things on which to make the tests; (iii) measurements for the relevant characteristics of the entities; and (iv) tabulation of the relations between the measured characteristics.
- Legal policies represent the heart of the legal process. Legal policies deal with human beings as *policy-makers* (e.g., legislators or judges), *policy appliers/enforcers* (e.g., administrators, policemen), *policy recipients* (e.g., persons or contractors, automobile drivers, workers, citizens, etc.).
- Such process involves substance or procedure and any field of public law (government-to-citizens and government-to-government relations) or private law (citizen-to-citizen relations).

XI. RESEARCH DESIGN: MAJOR STEPS IN RESEARCH DESIGN

- There are six major steps in making a research design:

I. Statement of purpose made in the form of formulation of the research problem:

(a) Selection of research problem empirically.

(b) Formulation of research problem empirically.

It is an old and wise saying that "a problem well put is half solved."

II. A description of the study design. It involves the following major steps:

1. Identification and selection the research problem.
2. Choice of a theoretical framework (conceptual model) for the research problem and its relationship with the research.
3. Specification of objectives of the research problem conceived, and the scope.
4. Formulation of hypotheses to be tested quantitatively to arrive at qualitative results to reaching to empirical generalizations.
5. Design of the experiment or inquiry.
6. Definition and measurement of variables: Independent and Dependent.
7. Sampling procedure.
8. Tools and techniques for gathering data: Interview schedule; Questionnaire; Observation—Participant and non-participant.
9. Coding, editing and processing data.
10. Analysis of data—selection and use of appropriate statistical procedures for summarizing data and for statistical inferences (deductions).
11. Reporting—description of the research process; presentation, discussion and interpretation of data; generalization of research findings and their limitations; and suggestions for futurology or further research.

- These major steps can be succinctly grouped into four major stages of research design:
  (a) The planning stage [Problem].
  (b) The design stage [research design, hypotheses, variables, sampling, tools of data collection: interview schedule, questionnaire].
  (c) The operational stage [data collection].
  (d) The completion stage [tabulation and interpretation of data, presenting data in statistical forms, inferences, empirical generalization, chapterization, citation].

XII. HYPOTHESIS

- Hypothesis is an assumption/hunch/speculation formulated not in the air, but on the genesis of literature.
- Hypothesis should be in the positive and never in the negative.
- Hypothesis should have variables to be tested for attribution. Variables are independent or dependent, e.g., Independent variables gender; Sex: Male/female; Area: Urban/rural; Occupation; income group; religion; caste, etc. Response process is dependent variable dependent on the independent variable.
- Hypothesis should be related to the research problem.
- Hypothesis is a wheel of social sciences research applied in legal research, i.e., socio-legal or empirical research or behavioural research.
- It is qualitative and quantitative data collection and data analysis method to arrive at empirical generalization. Hypothesis should not be based on lies of assumptions or fictions, but should be on the basis of factual and actual factors of literature or statute and case law.
- Rightly observed by Benjamin Disraeli: "There are three kinds of lies: lies, damned lies, and statistics".
- The theory and social science or socio-legal or empirical research: Source: Walter Wallace, The Logic of Science in Sociology, 1971:

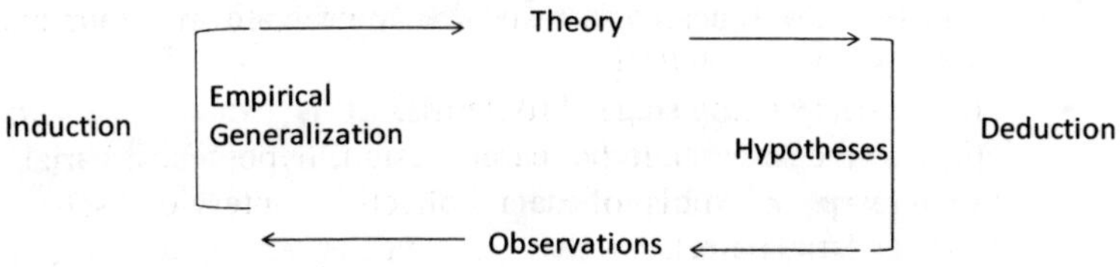

- Qualitative and Quantitative Research: The Genesis of Hypotheses: Quantitative data are numerical; qualitative data are not.
- "Why is it that our modern world insists upon drawing such a very sharp line of demarcation between the arts and the science? … Today, the artist lives on one side of the street and the scientist lives on the other side and the two hardly speak to each other". —(Hendrik Willem van Loon)
- Research questions and hypotheses are Conjunction between qualitative and qualitative research. They emanate from final formulation of research topic, research problem, research objectives, and research design.
- In the qualitative mode, there will be no statistical testable/ investigated hypotheses, rather the conjectural research questions.
- In the quantitative mode, there will be statistical testable/ investigated hypotheses, termed as "null" (H(O)) hypotheses and/or research hypotheses.
- *There is a research axiom:* "In all studies, research questions are derived from final topic(s), but only in a quantitative study, will formal null hypotheses be subsequently developed and statistically tested".
- *Null hypothesis:* The null hypothesis is simply the hypothesis of *no difference* or *no relationship*. E.g., "There will be no statistically significant difference in career awareness mean across between the career education classroom students and the traditional classroom students". This hypothesis shows that there is no difference between the groups, unless statistically demonstrated otherwise.
- The null hypothesis is simply the scientifically stated phrase that can be statistically tested.
- *Research hypothesis:* What does the researcher think the study will find? E.g., "The classroom students receiving career education training will score significantly higher on the career

education awareness test than will the traditional classroom students."

- *Alternative or alternate hypothesis:* It is exactly the same entity as the research hypothesis.
- Some examples of hypotheses:
    - "The Marxist assert that religion is an opiate for the masses".
    - "In a youth-oriented society, old people and senior citizens would be more deprived of secular gratification than would the young".
    - "Those with low social status were more involved in the church than were those with high social status".
    - "The family that prays together stays together".
    - "Men enjoy more status than do women in our generally male dominated society".
    - "Women are more likely to support women's liberation than are men".
- Thus, a hypothesis is the basic statement that is tested in research. Typically a hypothesis states a relationship between two variables. Hypothesis makes a prediction about the relationship between the two variables, it must be testable so you can determine if the prediction is right or wrong when you examine the results obtained in your study.
- A hypothesis must be stated in an unambiguous manner to be clearly testable.
- E.g., attitudes towards women's liberation. Such attitudes can be measured from opposed to women's liberation, neutral, supportive of women's liberation.
- The most technical step is the *Research Design.* Research design involves:
    1. decide on a general topic;
    2. formulate the research problem empirically;
    3. review the relevant prior literature;
    4. decide which hypotheses to test;
    5. decide on the research design to make the tests;
    6. compile the data in accordance with the research design;
    7. draw conclusions from the data in accordance with the research design;
    8. offer explanations for one's findings;
    9. draw (deduce) inferences; and
    10. make summations on the basis of empirical generalizations arrived at.

XIII. STEPS INVOLVED IN EMPIRICAL TESTING GENERALIZATION

- The most technical step is the *Research Design.* Research design involves:
  1. decide on a general topic;
  2. formulate the research problem empirically;
  3. review the relevant prior literature;
  4. decide which hypotheses to test;
  5. decide on the research design to make the tests;
  6. compile the data in accordance with the research design;
  7. draw conclusions from the data in accordance with the research design;
  8. offer explanations for one's findings;
  9. draw (deduce) inferences; and
  10. make summations on the basis of empirical generalizetions arrived at.
- This is not the final step. However, the researcher is free to reconsult the relevant literature or reformulate the hypotheses or research design out of the sequence presented.
- The research design would alone involve to determining the sample of entities on which to test the hypotheses; to indicate whether the hypotheses have been confirmed/proved or refuted.

XIV. DESIGN OF SAMPLE

(a) Design of sample

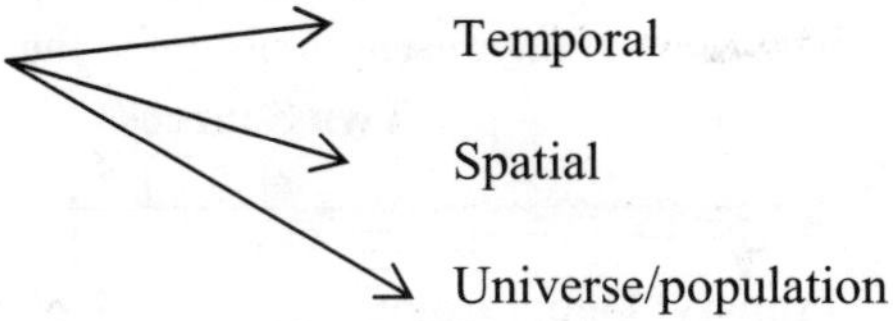

(b) Types of sampling

(i) *Simple random sampling*: It is the form applied when the method of selection assures each element or individual in the universe an equal chance of being chosen. It can be drawn either by lottery method or by using odd or even numbers (known as Tippet's number) or by grid system or by selecting from sequential list.

(ii) *Purposive sample*: When the researcher deliberately or purposively selects certain units for study from the universe it is known as purposive selection. In this type of sample selection, the choice of the selector is supreme and nothing is left to chance.

(iii) *Stratified sampling*: It is the combination of both random and purposive samples. Under this system the universe is first divided into a number of *strata or group*. Then from each strata, certain number of items are taken on random basis. In selection of strata purposive method is used, and in selecting actual units from each stratum, random method is used.

(iv) *Quota sampling*: This is a special form of stratified sampling. According to this method, the universe is divided into different strata. Then the number to be selected from each stratum is decided. This number is known as quota. The field worker is asked to select the quota from the stratum according to his will.

(v) *Multistage sampling*: This method in fact is a combination of random sampling and stratified sampling, and if conducted judiciously, it possesses the advantages of both the types.

(vi) *Convenience sampling*: A sample is selected according to the convenience of the field worker or researcher. It is used when universe is not clearly defined, sampling unit is not clear or a complete source list is not available.

(vii) *Self-selected people*: Sometimes a sample is not actually selected but people themselves opt to be included in a sample.

XV. SOURCES OF DATA COLLECION EMPIRICALLY

- The heart of any research design is the collection of data from:

Two Sources

Primary: Direct from Respondents
Interview schedule
Questionnaire
Observation
Largely depend on aim, nature, scope and contour of the research study

Secondary
Published and unpublished material: Library research

- Interview schedule and Questionnaire

(a) Questionnaire is mailed and source of data collection is similar/identical as through interview schedule. Interview schedule is used in direct interaction/contact with the respondent or direct observation and is filled up by the researcher himself after eliciting proper views from the respondent.

(b) Questionnaire and interview schedule are designed to collect data from a group of people coming under the purview of the research study. These are designed to collect data from large, diverse and widely scattered groups of people. Thus, it is a device for securing answers to questions by using a form which the respondents or the field worker or the researcher himself fills in. This is mailed or personally administered to the respondents or a group of people.

(c) Contents of questionnaire or interview schedule:
   (i) Socio-economic background of the respondent
   (ii) Awareness about law
   (iii) Opinions/attitudes about multifarious aspects of law
   (iv) General impressions about the function of law
   (v) Content aimed mainly at ascertaining facts about law
   (vi) Contents aimed mainly at ascertaining beliefs about what the facts (law) are

(d) Essentials of a good questionnaire or interview schedule:
   1. Clarity
   2. Brevity
   3. Unambiguity
   4. Reliability
   5. Communicability
   6. Direct questions should be avoided
   7. The language should be simple and easy to grasp—free from legalese and legal archaism—audible
   8. The annoying questions must be avoided at all costs

(e) Process of construction of questionnaire or interview schedule:
   1. Decide what information should be sought
   2. Decide what type of questionnaire should be used—structured or unstructured

3. Write the fresh draft
4. Re-examining and revising questions
5. Pretesting
6. Editing the questionnaire and specifying procedure for its use
7. The questions should be few, short, clearly worded, simple and easy to reply—without jargons
8. Long, complex personal, suspicious and leading questions should be avoided

(f) Interviewing respondents: Art and Skill:

1. Not to move with pre-conceived notions, or pre-judgment issues. The researcher should move with open mind to get/elicit the right information.
2. An increasing amount of interest is being generated for understanding the behavioural dimensions of the role that actors like judges, lawyers, citizens play in shaping the legal and judicial system in a country.
3. There are several ways of collecting data about what is happening to individuals or organizations. One way is to *observe* an event and then describe and understand the behaviour of people participating in the event. Another way is *to ask* the actors what and why is happening.
4. Do not allow the respondents to feel that the researcher is a stranger. Rather, researcher should appear to be one among the respondents.

(a) Interview schedule: Self-contact
  (i) open-ended or unstructured
  (ii) Structured
(b) Questionnaire: Mailed
  (i) Open-ended or unstructured
  (ii) Structured
(c) Observation: Participant and non-participant
(d) Case method/study
(e) Scaling: Attitudinal
(f) Interview diary

Classification and Tabulation of Data

- Tools of data interpretation
- Law and statistics:

(a) Classification of data:

1. Quantitative (according to variables);
2. Qualitative (according to attitude);
3. To express the complex, scattered, haphazard facts into concise, logical and intelligent form;
4. To make the point of similarity and dissimilarity clear;
5. To afford comparative study;
6. To avoid strain on mind in understanding the significance; and
7. To display underlying units of time.

(b) Tabulation of data:

1. Put the data in statistical tables;
2. Classification of Tabulation are interdependent, i.e., responses as per gender, or area, or income group, or occupation, or religion, or caste;
3. To make the purpose of inquiry clear;
4. To make its significance clear;
5. To express the data in least space as for as possible;
6. To make comparison easy;
7. To present data frequency and percentage-wise;
8. To present data average-wise;
9. To present data in Scalogram form;
10. To present data in graphs; and
11. To present data from quantity to quality to arrive at empirical generalizations.

(c) *Content analysis:* It is a research technique for the objective, systematic and quantitative description of the manifest content of communication. In content analysis one has to start with certain questions. Let us take the example from judicial process:

1. What is the length of the judgment?
2. What different types of symbols or terms have been used in them? How has the trend in use of symbols changed? What are the similarities and differences in the use of symbols by various judges?

3. How has the trend in judgment changed with the change in legislation?
4. How many judges participated in the judgment? How many in majority side and how many in minority side or how many in minority or dissenting side?
5. What is the ratio and what is the obiter dicta and the jurisprudential value?
6. Socio-economic-politico background of the judge and its impact on the judgment?
   — The content analysis though a very useful technique, however, is time consuming and requires a trained researcher for it.

XVI. LEGAL RESEARCH AND LAW REFORMS

- Role of Judges; Jurists; Law Commission of India; Law Schools; Law Research Institutes (ILI, ISIL, BCI, ICSSR, IIPA)
  — Assignments:
    - ➢ Make a list of ILI publications
    - ➢ Make a list of IIPA publications
    - ➢ Make a list of ISIL publications
    - ➢ Make a list of LCI publications
      - And state what major law reforms were proposed, accepted, adopted and implemented.
- The method of legal research:
    - ➢ Analysis of facts: Exegetical; exegesis; descriptive
    - ➢ Objectives
    - ➢ Historical: Evolution, growth, development
    - ➢ Interdisciplinary
- Order of legal research:

  1. Search of authorities
  2. The statute approach
  3. The fact approach
  4. Conceptual and/or analytical approach
  5. Words, phrases and expressions approach

- The mechanism of legal research

1. Identification of research problem and title
2. Formulation of research title
3. Formulation of the legal research problem
4. Analysis of the legal research problem
5. Critical Review of the legal literature: as a tool for the preliminary review of the subject matter of legal research problem
6. Search of primary sources: statutes, rules, regulations, bye-laws
7. Search of primary sources: cases in point
8. Search of secondary sources: Books, periodicals, commentaries, reports, etc.
9. Search of loose leaf services
10. Search of miscellaneous materials
11. Completing the research
12. Appraising the authorities found
13. Mode of foot notes citation
14. Bibliography

XVII. STEPS TO FIND OUT LEGAL MATERIALS

Law Reports :
Primary Source
Eyes and ears of Law Library
(a) Law: Statutes:
Law reporting generally done on statutes
Including rules, regulations, bye-laws, viz., delegated legislation

Journals; Periodicals :
Secondary Source
It is a compilation of scholastic works: Articles/ Research papers/ Notes and comments/case analysis; book review/editorial

- Indian:
  JILI; Bar Review; AIR; SCC
- Foreign:
  USA; UK;
  Other:
  Columbia Law Rev.; Yale Law Rev.; Harvard Law Rev.

Secondary sources:
Books; reports; commentaries; encyclopedias;
Important; least important but not most important

Law: Statute Contd.
Official: Parliament; State Legislature: Government Publication
Non-official:
Centre/State/Municipal:
Non-Governmental/Private publishing houses
(b) Cases/Decisional material: Indian and foreign
S.C.; H.Cs.; P.C.; F.C.;
USA; UK; Canada; Australia; Civil Law Apex Courts.

Indian
SCJ; MLJ; Universities; other research institutes, e.g. Journal of IIPA; ICSSR; Criminology; etc.

Foreign
American Journal of International Law; Journal of Legal Education; Modern Law Rev.; International and Comparative Law Rev.; Cambridge Law Rev.; etc.

Official: Centre and State
S.C.R.
Non-official:
Moors Digest; A.I.R.; SCC;
MLJ; SCJ; Bom. L. Rep.;
CWN; ILR; P.C.; F.C.;
Digest of Cases: Yearly; 15
years; AIR Millennia; SCC
Manual AIR
UK: Empire Digest
USA

Chapter XIII

LEGAL WRITING, CASE ANALYSIS, ANALYSIS OF STATUTE AND BOOK REVIEW

I. LEGAL WRITING

- Why do researchers/law students come to law schools? Do they come for learning law or acquiring legal knowledge or like to develop writing skills?
- Seldom they respond that they come to law schools because they like to learn writing skills.
- Law learning and acquiring knowledge about and of law primarily and predominantly require writing skills, writing habits, writing aptitude and writing attitude.
- To be a good researcher or a good lawyer, you must be a good writer. To be a good writer, you must have both a good understanding of law and a good grasp of principles of writing.
- Good legal writing requires, as a prerequisite, reading good and not rotten legal literature.
- In law, the quality of writing matters.
- As a researcher or a law student or a lawyer, you should not be a mere pen pusher.
- Good writing can win cases, and bad writing can lose them. A good case is lost because of bad advocacy/pleading, and a bad case is won because of good advocacy/pleading.

- Language moulds every human thought. Language is embedded in the very way we perceive the world. So it is impossible for a researcher or a law student or a lawyer or a judge to focus exclusively on "the merits" of a case without being affected by the language used to express those merits.
- Bad briefs can lose strong cases.
- "The written word is irrevocable. If it fails to convince or persuade the reader, there is no opportunity to switch to other ground. You make your play and you cannot renege." (Edward N. Teall, Putting Words to Work, 1940, 146)
- "The persuasive style (of writing) requires two qualities: clearness and simplicity. If it is lacking in either of these it fails to persuade." (Demetrius Phalereus, On Style, ca. 300 B.C.; T.A. Moxon Translation, 1943)
- The most significant form of communication in the practice of law is the written word.
- Law is not amorphous (vague, inchoate, indeterminate), but rather consists of words and phrases prescribing or proscribing social conduct, which are constantly being reinterpreted by courts and rewritten by legislatures.
- As a legal researcher/scholar/lawman, you must develop and refine your writing skills.
- Legal writing must be simple and plain, legal English writing free from the jargons of legalese and legal archaism.
- Presentation of legal writing:

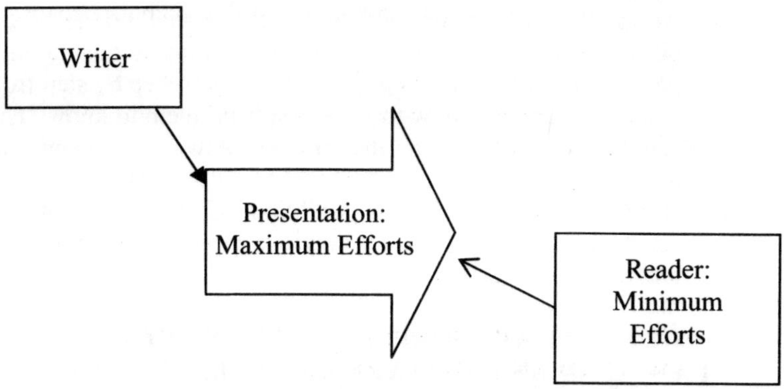

- Legal writing builds on principles acquired in the study of English language composition. A good foundation in the basics of English language composition is an absolute prerequisite to legal writing in the legal setting. Writing requires tremendous efforts.
- William Zinsser, in his *On Writing Well*, 1990, writes:
  - *"Writing is a hard work. A clear sentence is no accident.*

Very few sentences come out right the first time, or even the third time. Remember this as a consolation in moments of despair. If you find that writing is hard, it's because it is hard. It's one of the hardest things that people do."

- Legal writing builds on principles acquired in the study of English language composition. A good foundation in the basics of English language composition is an absolute prerequisite to legal writing in the legal setting. Writing requires tremendous efforts.
- The concept of presentation is relevant to legal writing.
- Legal writing must be logical in its presentation.
- Legal writing has various applications and forms: notices, correspondence, instruments, office memoranda, litigation memoranda pleadings, trial briefs, motions, discovery documents, appellate briefs, writ petitions; legal research reports, thesis, dissertations.
- Your role in drafting each will depend on such factors as the complexity of the legal matter and document, attorney ethics.

II. EXPOSITOR LEGAL WRITING

- The goal of legal writing is to discuss principles and explain how they affect or relate to particular factual situations.
- The style of writing can be referred to as exposition. Expository legal writing describes factual information and legal principles in a detailed and impersonal style.
- All in all, legal writing must be logical, factually detailed and objective. This can be done by communicating an idea to other persons (readers). That is guiding the readers step by step from what they already know to what you want them to know. This can be done by developing bridges between concepts—an application of logic.
- Readers expect an honest rendition of the facts and the relevant legal principles. This style is expected that maintains and assures writer's credibility.

III. LEGAL AUTHORITY: ANALYSIS OF CASE LAW-READ AND ANALYZE A JUDICIAL OPINION

- Case analysis means "Briefing" (summarizing) each case.
- Brief is a written synopsis of the important points of the case, i.e., to understand the case.
- Besides, briefing also includes the impact of the previous case as a precedent on the present case under analysis. This is called analyzing the relationship between the present case and

the past case and identifying the significant parts of a judicial decision.

- Researchers or lawyers or lawmen compare cases by drawing analogies and making distinctions between them. By comparing their problem to decided cases, lawmen decide how the decisions of the previous cases apply to the new problem. One should be careful not to distinguish cases too easily, because each case has some differences from other cases. The distinguishing facts you select must be significant. By comparing and contrasting your case brief with the precedents, you will be able to show how the rules of those cases fit your case brief. This in turn enables to offer your probable for your conclusion. This process is called reasoning by analogy.
- Briefing a Case Law: Typical components of a case brief:
  1. *Facts:* The facts component describes the events between the parties to the litigation. It speaks how the case came before the court that is now deciding it. It includes those are relevant facts to the contentious issue, not irrelevant fact, that the court must decide and to the reasons for its decision. It also includes the relevant background information for the case.
  2. *Contentious issues*: The contentious issue is the question that the court must decide to resolve the dispute between the litigant parties in the case before it. To find the issue, we have to identify the rule of law that governs the dispute, i.e., a question that combines the rule of law with the material facts of the case, *viz.*, those facts that raise the dispute.
  3. *Holding*: The holding is the court's decision or legal statement on the question that is actually before the court for decision. The holding provides the answer to the question in the contentious issue. If the legal statement does not relate to the question, it is *obiter dicta*. If there is more than one issue, there may be more than one holding.
  4. *Reasoning*: The court's reasoning explains and supports court's decision. It is *ratio decidendi* of a case. It is essentially imperative or important to isolate the court's reasoning from the facts and the holding of the case.
  5. *Policy*: Underlying legal decisions are the social policies or objectives or goals or aims that the decision-maker wishes to further. The court may refer to such social policies in a case, such information must be included in a case brief. E.g., social policy of sexual harassment or girl child as a domestic servant, another form of bonded

labour or contractual employment is not only another form of bonded labour, but a regressive movement of society from social welfare to *laissez faire*. If the court does not explain the social policy on which it bases its decision, then the researcher should identify it for himself in case brief.

IV. OUTLINE FOR A CASE REPORT

- Name/Title of Case or Writ:
- Court or Tribunal or Regulatory Authority/Commission or Human Rights Commission or Consumer Forum:
- Date of Decision:
- Citation:
- Judges:
- Judgment or Judgments—Majority View and/or Minority/ Dissenting View:
- Procedure by which case came before Court or Tribunal or Regulatory Authority/Commission or Human Rights Commission or Consumer Forum:
- Facts (found or assumed) before Court for decision:
- Issue or Issues or Contentious Issue(s):
- Arguments of Counsel(s):
- Decision:
- Reasons for decision:
  1. Ratio decidendi:
  2. Obiter dicta:

V. BOOK REVIEW

- Title of the book:
- Publisher's name and address, pages, price:
- Name of the author of the book:
- General introductory remarks about the book and the author:
- Critique analysis of each chapter of the book stating whether the book contains anything worth of the challenges or does the book contribute anything worth to the legal knowledge and legal literature:
- Critique analysis of the cases—whether the book contains the ratio of the cases analyzed by the author in proper perspectives:
- Whether the price of the book is within the reach of the reader:
- General impression(s) about the book:
- Exercises:
  1. Write a book review on Fali S. Nariman, Before Memory

Fades …, 2010.

2. Make analysis of …………………. [title of the case(s)]
3. Make a research plan:
   - Formulate a title of legal research problem of your interest,
   - Formulate a legal research problem on the conceived research title,
   - Formulate research questions on the conceived research problem, and
   - Formulate the objectives of your research problem.
4. Collect material on the conceived research problem and make a bibliography: Primary and secondary sources.

VI. LEGAL AUTHORITY: ANALYSIS OF A STATUTE— READ AND ANALYZE A STATUTE

1. To read the text of the statute/Act carefully to know what it says and to whom it is addressed, the exact conduct it prohibits, requires or permits, and how the parts of the statute relate to each other. To isolate the issue in your problem by determining what question is raised by the statutory language in terms of the facts of the case. The case may involve one Section or more than one Sections of the statute.
2. To find the statutory provisions or issues related to the problem of the case.
3. To know the techniques of statutory interpretation. Once you identify the disputant fact and statute relationship, your next step is to analyze how the statutory language applies to the facts of the disputant case. A statute applies to future conduct of happening which is unforeseen at the time of enactment, and as such statutory language is more general than is the language in a judicial opinion. A judge is called upon to interpret what the statutory language of the enactment means:
   A. *Legislative intent:* Courts employ a variety of approaches to determine what the legislature intended the statute to mean:
      (i) Plain meaning.
      (ii) Extrinsic evidence: If the court cannot determine the statutory language by plain meaning because the language is ambiguous, it may permit the parties to introduce other evidence to show what did the legislature intend to mean. This is creative or innovative or activist or realistic way of interpretation by filling the gaps.

B. *Canons of construction:*
   (i) *Ejusdem generis*: means of the same genus or class. It is applied to mean that whenever a statute contains specific enumeration followed by a general catchall phrase, the general words should be construed to mean only things of the same kind or same characteristics as the specific words.
   (ii) *Expressio unius, exclusio alterius:* means expression of one thing excludes another. If a statute expressly mentions what is intended to be within its coverage, then the statute excludes that which is not mentioned.
   (iii) *Statute in pari materia*: mean on the same subject matter. Statutes in *pari materia* should be read together, i.e., they should be interpreted consistently with each other.

C. *Stare Decisis and statutes:* Once a court interprets a statute, the principle of *stare decisis* applies and the court will then follow the interpretation it has previously adopted unless it overrules it.
   — *Mimansa* rules of interpretation.

VII. REPORT/THESIS/DISSERTATION WRITING

- Introduction,
- Problem,
- Objectives,
- Hypothesis,
- Other chapters—Law, literature and statistical data and interpretation and deducing inferences,
- Conclusion and summation for future course of action, and
- Citation of footnotes either at the bottom of the text of the chapter or at the end of the chapter or in between the running text within brackets.